MW00856064

# EARLY CHILDHOOD EDUCATION SERIES

Sharon Ryan, *Editor*

(continued)

To look for other titles in this series, visit www.tcpress.com

# Eight Essential Techniques for Teaching with Intention

WHAT MAKES
REGGIO and OTHER
INSPIRED APPROACHES
EFFECTIVE

## Ann Lewin-Benham

*Foreword by Howard Gardner*

**TEACHERS COLLEGE PRESS**

**TEACHERS COLLEGE** | COLUMBIA UNIVERSITY
NEW YORK AND LONDON

Redleaf Press®
www.redleafpress.org
800-423-8309

Saint Paul
Minnesota

Published simultaneously by Teachers College Press, 1234 Amsterdam Avenue, New York, NY 10027 and Redleaf Press, 10 Yorkton Court, Saint Paul, MN 55117

Figure 1.2 is reproduced courtesy of Reggio Emilia and Redleaf Press. © Preschools and Infant-toddler Centers—Istituzione of the Municipality of Reggio Emilia (Italy), from Edwards, C., & Rinaldi, C. (Eds.), *The Diary of Laura. Perspectives on a Reggio Emilia Diary*, St. Paul, MN, Redleaf Press, 2009.

The Norman Rockwell Museum Digital Image Collection provided the image of Tom Sawyer whitewashing the fence (Figure 2.4). The original appeared in the 1936 edition of Mark Twain's *The Adventures of Tom Sawyer* published by The Heritage Press, Inc. The image is © MBI, Inc.

Figure 4.2 is copyright Torstar Syndication Services. Reprinted with permission.

*Library of Congress Cataloging-in-Publication Data*

Lewin-Benham, Ann.
    Eight essential techniques for teaching with intention : what makes Reggio and other inspired
        approaches effective / Ann Lewin-Benham ; foreword by Howard Gardner.
            pages cm
    Includes bibliographical references and index.
    ISBN 978-0-8077-5657-7 (pbk. : alk. paper)
    ISBN 978-0-8077-7380-2 (e-book : alk. paper)
        1. Reflective teaching. 2. Reggio Emilia approach (Early childhood education)  I. Title.
    LB1025.3.L49 2015
    371.102—dc23                                                        2015003324

ISBN 978-0-8077-5657-7 (paper)
ISBN 978-0-8077-7380-2 (ebook)

Printed on acid-free paper
Manufactured in the United States of America

22   21   20   19   18   17   16   15              8   7   6   5   4   3   2   1

For all early childhood teachers
Sheppy Lewin
and
The Moo

# Contents

# Foreword

As my bookshelf testifies, there is no shortage of books about teaching. One can read about how teachers are the major problems in education today, and about how teachers are the optimal—indeed, the only—solution to our educational problems. One can learn the philosophy of teaching, from Plato to Dewey; the psychology of teaching, according to Bruner, Piaget, Skinner, or Vygotsky. Also abundant are manuals on how to teach specific subjects, from dance to geometry; how to teach specific ages, from preschoolers to senior citizens; how to teach special populations, from the learning disabled to the gifted and talented.

I know of no book like the one that you are now reading. Ann Lewin-Benham has been a teacher, a social case worker, the head of a school, the founding director of a major children's museum, and the creator of two unique schools located within that museum. She is deeply versed in theoretical and scientific studies of teaching and learning. She is perhaps the leading expositor in English of the pedagogical approach of Reuven Feuerstein, as well as one of the most effective describers and analysts of the Reggio Emilia approach to children and community. To top it off, she is a gifted author, having written several well-received books in the field.

In this unique volume, drawing on a lifetime of practice and reflection, Lewin-Benham sets forth the essential techniques of teaching. In eight carefully wrought chapters, she provides a description of the technique, a vivid set of detailed examples drawn from a wide range of teaching situations, and clear procedures for determining when a particular technique has been properly implemented.

The techniques are not ones that could readily have been anticipated. They range from attention to voice and hand (and their interplay), to messages communicated by the eyes, to the choice of words, to more macroscopic techniques that span cognitive and emotional terrains. And thanks to a splendid final chapter, readers have an opportunity to step back and assess their overall capacity to teach effectively.

But what sets this book apart are the overarching concepts of intention and reflection. The recommended practices may work well in isolation or in concert, but they are most effective when they are conceived within the overall capacity of the educator to know what she believes and is trying to accomplish, to observe herself in action, and then to step back and evaluate the effectiveness of her actions and, as appropriate, to correct course, either slightly or more dramatically.

Lewin-Benham's special gifts of observation, understanding, and exposition are on full display. Permit me an analogy. It is as if at once the reader can zoom in on the finest details of teaching practice, while at the same time beholding a wide landscape of the class and monitoring her own stances and goals within that class. And while Lewin-Benham insists that her book is practical, rather than academic, she expertly weaves into the narrative timely conceptual material from many authors, as well as relevant findings from the research literature on teaching and learning.

Whether you have never stepped into a classroom as a teacher, or whether (like me) you have taught various subjects at various ages for decades, you cannot fail to learn from this book. Indeed, I suspect that the teaching of many readers will be changed qualitatively, as will the learning experiences of their fortunate students.

—Howard Gardner, Cambridge, MA, professor of cognition
and education at the Harvard Graduate School of Education,
author of *The Unschooled Mind* and *The Disciplined Mind*

# Acknowledgments

I gratefully acknowledge the administrators and teachers who welcomed me into their schools and talked to me about their visions and struggles. I likewise appreciate audience members who have asked thoughtful questions, related their perspective, and told their stories. The Dedication and last page of Chapter 9 express the depth of my admiration for early educators.

In this book I turned to longtime influences: psychologists Howard Gardner and Reuven Feuerstein (deceased April, 2014), neurologist Frank R. Wilson, and psycholinguist Steven Pinker. All are scholars, practitioners, and authors; their books, some of which I have referenced, are my constant companions. I acknowledge these mentors' stellar scholarship and breakthrough thinking; my quotes summarize the tiniest bit of their deep knowledge. A new influence is Professor Kelly G. Wilson; I hope teachers can bring his exercises on mindfulness to their children.

Publisher expertise makes books possible. I am fortunate to work with Teachers College Press, a venerable 100-year-old institution. This book was born because of the belief of my longtime editor, Marie Ellen Larcada, retired October, 2014. Working with an editor is an intense process of, above all, mutual trust. I am ever grateful for Marie Ellen's wisdom, on which I relied through four earlier books and the initial stages of this sixth book. My new editor, Sarah Biondello, has grasped the reins quickly. I look forward to her partnership through whatever books come next.

Teachers College Press has first-rate professionals. Foremost among them is Senior Production Editor Karl Nyberg, who is responsible for turning manuscripts into books, for every aspect of a book's appearance and thus its readability. Readers who tell me how easy it is to navigate my books have Karl to thank. This is our sixth book together.

Others at TCP involved in making a book are the Press' executives: Carole Saltz, Press Director; Brian Ellerbeck, Executive Acquisitions Editor; Nancy Power, Marketing Manager; Christina Brianik, Rights and Permissions Manager. Readers do not know these people, but there would be no books without them. Other hard work on this book was done by Publicist Emily Renwick, Copyeditor Myra Cleary, and the team in Production.

A challenge in this book was images, many far removed from classrooms. I am ever grateful to Thomas Mesquita, Registrar at the Norman Rockwell Museum, who led me to MBI, Inc., the rights holder of the classic Tom Sawyer painting, and who furnished a copy of the image, and to Michael Hendricks of MBI, Inc. who provided the rights to use the image. I appreciate Joanne MacDonald, Rights

Licensing, Torstar Syndication Service, for the rights to use a 1938 Tom Callan cartoon. I thank the educators of Reggio Emilia for permitting us to reprint their classic images known as "Laura and the Watches." Without Jennifer Azzariti, the first *atelierista* in the United States who appears on the cover with "Tofu," and teacher Yolanda Jones who shot the photo, there would not be a classroom image on the cover. When the web failed to provide names of photographers for flowers, my nephew Michael Cruickshank, professional film maker, took the necessary photos. Above all I thank my grandson, Sheppy Lewin, who, despite a demanding school load, made 18 original drawings when we could not find images in the public domain.

And I thank my family: my husband Robert, whose forbearance through deadlines is heroic; my son Dr. Daniel Lewin, whose professional counsel and friendship are potent forces in my work; and my niece Alexandra Cruickshank, a 21st-century educator whose work assures that children's early experiences are worthy of their competence.

# Introduction

I was 23 when I took my first job in education as administrator of a parent-run Montessori school. The school was housed in the social hall of a fire station. Parents had designed large cabinets on heavy castors that served as shelving, room dividers, and movable walls so that the school could be rolled away for firefighters' frequent events. The cabinets divided the space into four classrooms; each had 35 students, one teacher, and one aide.

My office was in the coatroom, with a large window facing the classrooms. Two of the classrooms were settled, the children engrossed in using the Montessori materials. The other two were chaotic; children flew around using their smocks as capes, crying "B-a-a-a-t Man"! How, I wondered, could one method produce such different results? Perhaps, I thought, I should become trained as a Montessori teacher in order to understand why the classes were so different. My motivation was the strong curiosity generated by scenes from the coatroom.

The differences in the teachers were pronounced. Miss Johnston, a former grade school teacher, knew how to control children's behavior: A mere look and no child would step out of line. She was genuinely affectionate, enjoyed the children's remarks, and shared her enjoyment with them. But under the love and laughter was an iron will that children knew not to test. (*Note:* Throughout the book, names of all persons have been changed.)

Miss Nuñez was Mexican, with flashing eyes and intensity in carriage and tone of voice. Her vivacity mesmerized children; her enthusiasm enticed them. She conveyed authority in a manner that said, "No nonsense, please, we have important things to do." Her children would never fly around in their smocks. Parents considered her the "best" teacher.

Except for those parents who adored Miss Lindsey: young, attractive, and with abiding faith in the Montessori method. She talked in a zealot's mystical terms. She loved the children; they were wonderful and could do no wrong. Parents reveled in her love for their children. They were unconcerned about children flying around—or perhaps did not notice. There was no parent observation.

The fourth teacher was older. Miss Neal spoke in vague terms as her face glowed at the wonder of being a Montessori teacher. Miss Neal did not know how to manage a class and the children knew it. The Board dismissed her in June. In September I headed to the Montessori Institute to learn what I had watched that year.

Today I know: Miss Johnston and Miss Nuñez were intentional teachers, centered in their beliefs about children, themselves, their teaching, and expectations for what children would achieve. They used their adult authority to keep children's behavior in bounds.

## THE EIGHT ESSENTIAL TECHNIQUES

In this book I present eight essential techniques for being an intentional/reflective teacher. Each technique is the subject of its own chapter. The eight techniques are:

1. *Observe yourself teaching:* Differentiate these behaviors—interrupt, interfere, intervene, intend, reflect, mean, transcend.
2. *Communicate precisely:* Master nuances in using the body, eyes, face, hands, and voice.
3. *Use language exuberantly:* Build on children's love of language by playing with words and hands to express meaning.
4. *Examine your beliefs honestly:* Search for mindless habits and replace them with determined actions.
5. *Choose words strategically:* Understand the impact of words on children.
6. *Manipulate materials purposefully:* Provide diverse materials to stimulate increasingly skillful eye/hand coordination from birth on.
7. *Engage children's cognition:* Use cognition to mediate disruptive or distracting emotions.
8. *Structure motivating lessons:* Cause children to strengthen both cognitive and socio-emotional skills.

I provide research that affirms the techniques, show each technique in practice in many scenarios, and give readers exercises with which to try the techniques themselves. Throughout there are tips, key points, and summaries. The emphasis is on practice, not theory. This is a how-to book with a focus on the distinction between intentional/reflective and other teaching. You will see nuanced uses of eyes, voice, hands, body, word choices, and the sounds and expressions in language—what I call "micro-actions," minute glances, slight inflections, subtle gestures, or exact words that express intention precisely. Intention and reflection are shown in many scenarios; those with ineffective teaching are immediately followed by the same lesson taught *with* intention and reflection so that you can make comparisons. Scenarios are all based on my decades-long work in early education—with names changed. Numerous exercises offer techniques to deepen your understanding and, through practice, expand your skill at intentional/reflective teaching.

The last chapter is an assessment to benchmark your degree of intention/reflection prior to reading the book. I suggest that you read the assessment first: You may want to use it as you read each chapter to determine whether your teaching is becoming more intentional and reflective.

## THE ESSENCE OF INTENTIONAL/REFLECTIVE TEACHING

Intention refers to *how* we teach, reflection to how we *think about* how we teach. Teaching is *intentional* when your actions (1) are consistent with a belief in children's competence and (2) convey a sense of purpose and authority. Teaching is *reflective* when you (1) consider what you do before, during, and after doing it and (2) base future actions on your reflection.

Intentional/reflective teaching has enormous impact on children because it is:

- Deliberate and purposeful
- Consistent across all of a teacher's behaviors
- Focused on observing and listening to children
- A model of
  - ➤ Thinking that is both analytic and emotional
  - ➤ Interactions that recognize children's rights
  - ➤ Empathetic values

Intention and reflection are two sides of a coin, intention the what/how and reflection the when/why of teaching. Reflection without intention is empty; intention without reflection is mindless. Only through the union of intention and reflection can thoughtful teaching arise. My examples of *what* and *how* are inspired by educators in the Municipal Preschools of Reggio Emilia, Italy; Montessori principles; great teachers I have observed; and select philosophers, educators, psychologists, scientists, and neuroscientists. My examples of *when* and *why* are drawn from my reflections on a lifetime of classroom observation. The *what, how, when,* and *why* provide structure for the book: Scenarios show *how* teachers behave, *when* they intervene in children's work, *what* they do, and *why* it works.

Intention involves intervening in children's activity with deliberateness, to offer meaning and to build relationships between current experience and what children already know or can imagine in the future. Reflection involves analyzing how intervention can build children's cognitive and socio-emotional capacities. I do not often see this combination of techniques outside Reggio schools in Italy. Reggio-inspired schools in the United States are young by comparison and could benefit from deepening the intentional/reflective aspects of their practice.

Intention and reflection are *the* forces that make teachers compassionate and cause them to modify their beliefs and actions, as the following story illustrates: In 2007, the renowned Israeli professor and psychologist Reuven Feuerstein (1920–2014) gave a short address to a group of 200 teachers and education leaders in Memphis, Tennessee. He spoke about his life's work improving the functioning of children who were cognitively challenged, and about reconstituting meaningful lives for children and youth who were Holocaust survivors, for others who faced genocide in different countries, for youth who had suffered bullet wounds through the brain, for others with congenital brain defects or other seriously debilitating problems. Audience attention was riveted on this man, who spoke from such diverse and compelling firsthand experiences as escapee, visionary, theorist, practitioner, clinician, and founder/president of a major international center for enhancing learning potential.

Feuerstein related a heart-wrenching story of young Holocaust survivors who had witnessed the extermination of their families, destruction of their homes and countries, and starvation, and who by some miracle repeatedly escaped from imminent threats of death. He described how these youth were rehabilitated in Israel only to face death again as the new state went to war to fight for its right to exist.

A teacher in the audience asked how Feuerstein had the fortitude to persevere in this emotionally draining work and how he knew what to do with youth whose only skills were animalistic behaviors: kill or be killed, steal or starve. "You see," replied Feuerstein, "I had no choice." He continued:

We [the Jewish people] were almost wiped out. So many millions were murdered that every survivor was precious. We had to make sure the youth did more than survive; they had to thrive. Because we *believed* that we could change these children, we made ways to do so. When you believe, you do.

In this book, I draw on Feuerstein's theories and practices—in Chapter 1 to describe effective teacher/child interactions and in Chapter 7 for techniques to help children self-regulate their emotions.

If you believe that competence, curiosity, concentration, empathy, and joy are young children's natural state, you will make sure to teach so that children's apathy, boredom, and misbehavior cease. To teach with intention is to take charge, to be in command of your teaching so that you:

- Modify children's perspective if they are not joyful
- Spur their curiosity if they are apathetic
- Build cognitive function if they lack thinking skills

To teach with reflection is to make yourself aware of precisely what you have done to elicit competence, curiosity, concentration, empathy, and joy. Belief in children's innate and diverse competencies drives teachers' intention and impels them to be reflective.

## WHY IS THIS BOOK IMPORTANT?

The current standardization of young children's education hampers development from age 0 to 8; moreover, requiring children to master specific content at predetermined times ultimately may kill motivation. I believe that to keep alive faith in the human spirit, outlier approaches such as Reggio, Montessori, Waldorf, and other "progressive" schools must flourish. I believe that philosophies espoused by Tolstoy, Montessori, Dewey, Vygotsky, Hawkins, Feuerstein, Papert, Postman, Malaguzzi, Gardner, and other progressive educators of their ilk are important to nourish and motivate teachers.

While a majority of schools depend on standardized curricula, there must be alternatives. Reggio practices show the heights that children can achieve in schools that use open-ended time, richly equipped space, and an "emergent curriculum." Reggio schools show sophisticated, aesthetic, competent work, and young children's capacity for complex thinking, collaborative endeavor, and skilled performance beyond what most believe possible. From the field of neuroscience we can draw a mantra for Reggio-type work: "brain-worthy education." But to translate words into practice, the structure and systems of brain-worthy schools must be shown in text and in classrooms. The practices I define as intentional and reflective are most compatible with schools and teachers who want alternatives to standardized education. These teachers prefer to work in schools where schedules do not dominate, the curriculum is not test-driven, and lessons are not formulaic. Some of these teachers have embraced Reggio practices and, in struggling to use the Reggio philosophy, seek guidance in how to put the philosophy into practice. This book is a resource for such teachers. But there is a wider audience because, regardless of one's philosophy, any teacher can use this book's techniques, scenarios, and exercises to become more effective.

Throughout our culture uncertainty permeates our lives: What is the appropriate role for government? Should the United States intervene in other nations' affairs? Should private citizens bear arms? How can we support the values of Muslims, Jews, Christians, and nonbelievers equally? Should persons of different sexual orientations be permitted to teach young children? How will climate change affect my grandchildren?

Uncertainty raises parents' and teachers' questions about education: What should I expect from an infant/toddler program? How do I know if my school is "good"? What is the optimum amount of time for a 3-year-old to spend in school? When should children learn letters? At what age should children move on from infant/toddler care to a 3/4-year-old program? How do I reconcile the need for play with the pressure for "readiness"? How can one classroom accommodate different languages, diverse cultures, and wide-ranging congenital inheritances?

A strong relationship exists between intentional/reflective teaching, value-laden questions, and one's beliefs about childrearing and schooling. This book shows how teachers' beliefs impact children's attitudes, and how teachers' actions shape children's behavior. Teachers mold children's:

- Self-confidence
- Belief in their own competence
- Capacity for empathy
- Respect shown (or not shown) for others
- Ability to regulate behavior
- Disposition to persevere
- Skill in collaboration
- Propensity to remain curious

Teachers drive children's passion for finding out about living creatures, natural objects, the earth in their schoolyard, the stars in the heavens. Teachers influence the beliefs young children espouse, the interests they pursue, and the values they live.

I believe that the inner peace we want children to feel and their ability, ultimately, to fulfill their potential are shaped minute by minute, year by year, by behaviors that children observe—and ultimately adopt and emulate. In other words, teachers *are* what children will become. The forces of intention and reflection underpin humanistic values and cause them to thrive. Through their every act and word, intentional/reflective teachers instill in children a penchant toward purposeful action and a tendency toward thoughtfulness and collaboration, capabilities with which children will address whatever challenges they meet in the future. We become what we behold (2 Corinthians 3:18). Because we live in an era when the most pervasive form of education is authoritarian and standardized, I hope this book empowers teachers to form their own judgments and trust their own beliefs about children's innate drive to learn.

## OVERVIEW OF CHAPTERS

Brief descriptions of the chapters follow.

*Chapter 1: "What IS Intentional Teaching?"* I begin by explaining words that define intentional/reflective teaching. I analyze whether teaching in the scenarios I show is or is not intentional/reflective. And I provide exercises teachers can use to practice intentional/reflective techniques.

By chapter's end readers should be familiar with the nature of intentional/ reflective teaching and able to recognize whether their own teaching is intentional and reflective.

*Chapter 2: Micro-Actions of Intentional/Reflective Teaching.* I show intention and reflection in the micro-actions of body, eyes, and face, and how to:

1. Convey purpose and feelings with slight movements
2. *Look* in numerous ways—scan, study, glare
3. Express meaning and emotion with subtle facial expressions
4. Use numerous micro-actions

By chapter's end readers should be able to:

1. Observe themselves teaching
2. Identify intentional/reflective techniques of body, eyes, and face
3. Use techniques with increasing intention and reflection

*Chapter 3: The Voice and Hand in Intentional/Reflective Teaching.* The chapter begins by exploring two aspects of speech—vocalization and word meanings—in overviews of (1) the vocal system and (2) English as a "combinatorial" system of phonemes and morphemes. Many exercises include games to encourage children to speak articulately, to use sound to emphasize meaning, and to choose words that best express thoughts.

I present micro-actions of the hands by studying their use in American Sign Language. And I recap an H. G. Wells story as a parable about how deprivation of one sense—vision—impacts both human capacities and an entire culture.

By chapter's end readers should be able to (1) reflect critically on their teaching to exploit the vocal system's capacities and (2) assess their use of voice and hand as intentional teaching tools.

*Chapter 4: The Influence of Belief on Teachers.* I describe specific forces that influence beliefs—families' culture, where we live, the zeitgeist, marketers, politicians, educators, current research, the news. The chapter contains scenarios, case histories, research, historic incidents, and summaries of investigative reporting, and shows how these forces influence beliefs.

By chapter's end teachers should be more reflective in:

1. Determining what they believe about children
2. Knowing whether what they do is based on habit
3. Identifying relationships among beliefs, actions, and intentions

***Chapter 5: Choosing Words That Speak with Intention.*** This chapter is about intention and reflection in word choice and about listening mindfully—that is, with focus and presence. I dissect word choices, show scenarios where word choices influence children's responses, and suggest techniques for intentional/reflective use of words. I portray techniques in mindfulness through useful exercises with children age 2 and older.

By chapter's end, readers should intentionally:

1. Choose statements, phrase questions, and form responses
2. Use specific mindful techniques with children
3. Help children themselves use mindful techniques

***Chapter 6: Intentionally and Reflectively Connecting Hand/Eye.*** The hand/eye connection, vital to developing higher-level thinking, may be relegated to workbook exercises and dried-out markers. Contrasting scarce materials with a rich array, I show how intentional use of materials impacts brain development.

By chapter's end readers should be able to:

1. Equip classrooms with rich materials
2. Be intentional in introducing materials
3. Involve children with increasingly complex materials
4. Explain these activities' importance to parents

***Chapter 7: Behavior, Intention, and Reflection.*** I explore teachers' vital role in children's learning social and emotional intelligence, drawing on work by:

1. Jerome Kagan on temperament
2. Stanley Greenspan on challenging children
3. Reuven Feuerstein on guiding children from emotional to cognitive responses

In five scenarios I contrast ineffective and effective ways to handle common classroom occurrences. Each negative scenario is immediately contrasted with an intentional/reflective alternative.

By chapter's end readers should:

1. Understand some dynamics of personality
2. See the relation between cognitive and emotional behavior
3. Have examples of techniques to help children reflect on and alter their behavior

*Chapter 8: Structuring an Intentional/Reflective Classroom.* I show the role of intention and reflection in structuring classroom time and space. Techniques from earlier chapters are integrated into scenarios of daily classroom life that pinpoint precisely those lessons that help individual children acquire cognitive and/or emotional skills.

By chapter's end readers should (1) understand the relationship between one-on-one and small-group work and intentional/reflective teaching and (2) see how to structure practices in order to work with children for long time periods one-on-one and in small groups.

*Chapter 9: Am I Teaching Intentionally and Reflectively?* This chapter is a self-assessment to determine whether your teaching is intentional and reflective. It can be used diagnostically—to see "where I am" in adopting intentional/reflective teaching practices—and/or prescriptively—to glean "to do's" that will foster increasingly intentional and reflective teaching. For each technique, questions assist readers in listing behaviors they observe in themselves and their children. If answers are not as positive as you would like, I suggest rereading the scenarios and using the self-assessment along with exercises and scenarios to pinpoint actions that will increase intentional/reflective teaching.

In summary, Chapter 1 is about subtlety in teacher/child interaction, and Chapter 2 about nuanced ways of observing and using micro-actions in human facial expression. Chapter 3 explains the precise meanings in different sequences of sound, and Chapter 4 how beliefs affect teaching behaviors. Chapter 5 shows the impact of words on children and the power of embedding mindfulness in teaching. Chapter 6 describes the hand's role in learning and implications for classroom activities. Chapter 7 illustrates using cognition to quell out-of-bounds emotions. Chapter 8 shows intention and reflection as organizing forces in teaching practices. And Chapter 9, the self-analysis tool, embeds the book's ideas in practice.

## AUTHOR'S MOTIVATION

I am writing this book because intentional/reflective teaching is the exception, not the norm. I hope the book will help you understand what is involved and inspire you to try what might be new techniques. Intentional and reflective teaching can incline children not to develop the self-absorbed, materialistic values of what is called "the Me generation." Intentional/reflective teaching can help

- Children change so that temperaments Jerome Kagan calls "inhibited" and "uninhibited" are ameliorated
- Teachers learn techniques they can use themselves and teach to parents so that what Stanley Greenspan calls "challenging" children become calmer, more flexible, less prone to tantrums, and in other ways more emotionally secure
- Instill values that reflect a belief in the effectiveness of collaboration and of placing the common good over individual desires

Perhaps most important, intentional/reflective teaching can moderate children's innate dispositions so that they persevere in the face of adversity and maintain a joyous outlook.

These outcomes are not Pollyanna, pie-in-the-sky wishes. They are possibilities documented by psychologists and educators and witnessed in Italy's 50 Reggio schools. The outcomes are backed by findings in neuroscience on the brain's plasticity, on the human tendency to imitate, and on the new field of positive psychology. Outcomes reflect recent research showing that cognition depends on movement and on the emotions, both of which are integral to and inseparable from all thinking.

Early childhood experiences set each child's emotional and cognitive compasses for the rest of the child's life. I hope this book helps readers set children's compasses so that they are prepared, psychologically and cognitively, to take on the problems of an economically driven, technology-saturated, and ecologically challenged planet.

# CHAPTER 1

# "What IS Intentional Teaching?"

The little things are infinitely the most important.

—Arthur Conan Doyle

---

**TECHNIQUE 1**

Observe yourself teaching: Differentiate these behaviors—
interrupt, interfere, intervene, intend, reflect, mean, transcend.

---

The words *intentional teaching* mean different things to different teachers. Often the words are used to define a choice between a range of behaviors: How authoritarian should I be? Or, how easy? Some use the words *intention* and *reflection* interchangeably and make little distinction between the two processes; others use only one word or the other. I define intention and reflection as two distinct parts of the same process: *Intention* refers to any behavior that can be seen or heard or to your determination to do or say something; *reflection* refers to the many varied ways to analyze what you have done or said. I define intention and reflection broadly as *every* action and thought teachers have with regard to their children, their environment, and their own second-by-second behaviors.

Throughout the book I use many words with different shades of meaning to define behaviors that convey intention and reflection. For example, I describe the difference between *deliberating* and *weighing* one's reactions, two reflective processes, or the difference between *glancing* and *scanning*, two different ways of taking in information. These fine shades of meaning offer new ways for teachers to analyze their behavior. Like designers saying "the devil is in the detail," so the art of teaching is defined by the choices teachers make in what I call their *micro-actions*—a fleeting glance, a turned head, pursed lips, raised eyebrows, vocal shadings—the innumerable ways humans use body, face, and voice to communicate.

Children read actions long before they understand words. Thus, children will not follow the admonition, "Do as I say, not as I do." Because no action escapes children's notice, we must say: "Do as I *do*, not as I *say*." Because children are watching, I encourage teachers to (1) "color" their behaviors by consciously selecting them from a full palette of human behavioral response, (2) pay attention to the nuanced meaning in every behavior, and (3) understand the following ideas from the book *Changing Minds* by renowned psychologist Howard Gardner (2004):

- The mind contains ideas that are more precisely defined as content, stories, theories, and skills.

- Content, stories, theories, and skills can be expressed in any one of several ways that constitute the multiple intelligences first proposed by Gardner in 1983.
- The mind changes very easily, and particularly so during youth . . . however . . . theories, concepts, stories, and skills are formed early, and many resist change (p. 61).

Because early educators work with such young children, teachers' thoughtful listening, careful reflection, and intentional responses carry special weight.

Only rarely do I see classrooms where intention and reflection are practiced as I define them. Notable exceptions are: teachers in Reggio schools, teachers who excel as practitioners of Mediated Learning (ML), some Montessori teachers, and a few others. For these teachers, intention and reflection are the norm, not add-on techniques but a deep-seated way of being with children.

In America we tend to adopt words very quickly; think, for example, how we frequently use words from Reggio practice such as *documentation, provoke, negotiated curriculum, studio teacher*. Think how we make much of these words in books, articles, and discourse. Yet robust practices in Reggio schools, ML, or elsewhere lose their strength as they become absorbed in American early childhood education (ECE). As ideas trickle down following a visit to Reggio or reading a book about Reggio or ML, powerful practices become diluted. We may feel inspired, but we are inhibited both by established patterns of behavior that make change difficult and by the constraints of formulaic American curricula and prevalent testing.

Using examples from Reggio, ML practitioners, Montessori, and a few isolated classrooms, I show what intentional teaching is and how intentional and reflective teaching are interdependent. For example, consider the following scenario in which intentional/reflective teachers start their day with a morning meeting.

Susan and Catherine teach a mixed-age group of 25 children ages 3 to 6. Each morning they sit on a circular line. That is a signal for children to join them and within minutes, the class gathers as a group and children sit on the line, chat with friends, or look expectantly at the teachers, ready for the meeting to begin. The children's behavior reflects the teachers' intention about how morning meeting should work. The gathering may seem automatic but is a result of the teachers' long and consistent effort to make sure children understand and follow procedures. If children forget or become sloppy in using the procedures, the teachers practice them—with the full class, a small group, or a single child.

After a short greeting, Susan says, "Remember yesterday? Robbie asked: 'Can we go to the library and see if they got books on hurricanes?'"

Immediately recalling the incident, Phillip responds: "They gots to. Books on hurricanes."

Robbie, emphatically: "We need to go *now*."

Phillip, knowingly: "We got questions."

Carlie, seriously: "It'll take a lotta time."

A conversation ensues. The class hears many children's ideas, comments of all who raise their hand. There are no side conversations, no squirming, no poking. No one butts in while another speaks. Responses flow easily in logical questions or statements. A plan emerges and, with a plan agreed on, Catherine says, "Let's go!" The five children who expressed most interest in hurricanes leave for the library with Catherine. The conversation, like the meeting itself, results from the teachers' intentions about how conversation works, a topic I return to in Chapter 8. The next procedures are:

- Children announcing what they intend to do
- Dismissal from the line
- Teachers working with undecided children

These procedures are also smooth because they are intentional and practiced.

Susan begins, "Sit down and close your eyes" (and demonstrates). Then in a slow, hypnotic voice with low tone and deliberate pacing: "Now, imagine what you want to do this morning." She pauses again. "When you know, open your eyes." The children respond gradually. One by one 15 state a clear purpose and leave the circle to begin. Five remain. Knowing that Joanne has set herself the task of tracing the names of all 25 children, Susan asks Joanne if she would like to continue name tracing. Clarissa says she wants to make name tracings too. Three young 3-year-olds (ages 2.11–3.2) are left. Susan addresses them with an enticing smile and a positive, "Come! I have something special to show you." She takes the small group to a table and introduces three sandpaper letters that are new to these children. So the class settles in for the long morning period that generally lasts 2 or more hours. It is a typical day's beginning. Later that day Susan and Catherine confer about the meeting and all else that happened that morning; their discussion considers children's behavior and learning, and whether today held ideas worth following up on tomorrow. This daily procedure is a reflective process.

The scenario shows a class where intentional/reflective teaching has been the norm for several years. It includes:

- Lengthy, focused conversation
- Teachers' reflective responses
- A small group of children's out-of-school expedition
- Children's choice of what they will do at the start of a morning's long open-ended work time
- Teachers' trust in the children's maintaining their focus as they settle into their work
- Teachers' self-confidence that they can help children who wander from their stated choice to select an activity with the power to sustain their attention
- The short lesson a teacher will give to three children, in this instance the youngest, before they too settle into an activity of interest either with other children or on their own
- The intentional procedures are a vital factor in determining whether open flow works smoothly, a topic I explore in Chapter 8

These are a few characteristics of intentional/reflective classrooms. In successive chapters, I show how teachers' intention and reflection are the factors that enable children to achieve the focus and self-direction that typify Susan and Catherine's children.

In this chapter, I explain teaching with intention and reflection by pulling apart words that define teaching behaviors, analyzing teachers' "micro-actions," and illustrating explanations with scenarios. Throughout are exercises to test your understanding. I conclude by showing a scenario with 2-year-olds in which teachers are *un*intentional and *un*reflective. Then I analyze the scenario by describing what changes would make the teaching intentional and reflective. No matter how intentionally they act, without reflection teachers are not likely to understand what has occurred or to change their behavior.

## UNDERSTANDING INTENTION AND REFLECTION

To understand intention and reflection, you must understand these words: intervene, interrupt, interfere, intention, meaning, transcendence, and reflection. Moreover, you must recognize whether these behaviors are present in your own and others' teaching. The following explanations and examples show what each word means in practice.

### Intervene

The word *intervene* has two roots: "Inter" comes from the Latin word *inter*, which means between, and "vene" from the Latin verb *venire*, which means to come. So, intervene literally means to come between. A commonly understood meaning is to involve yourself deliberately. That is precisely what intentional teaching is: deliberate involvement by a teacher in children's activity.

*Tip:* Word hounds will enjoy getting lost in the Online Etymology Dictionary (www.etymonline.com) and browsing the byways of words and their parts.

*Example:* Featured on the cover are Tofu (age 3) and *atelierista* Jennifer Azzariti, who is helping Tofu learn to use a scissors. The more techniques a child "owns," the more creative the child can be. For evidence, examine publications from the Reggio schools and reflect on both what children produce and the many intentional ways that Reggio and other effective teachers intervene to facilitate children's acquisition of techniques.

**Interrupt: A Contrast.** To understand the word *intervene* more fully, contrast it with the word *interrupt*. Both words have the same beginning: between. "Rupt" comes from the Latin noun *ruptura*, which means break. So, interrupt literally means to *break* between. A commonly understood meaning is breaking in or stopping something that is ongoing. When teachers interrupt, they disturb a child's focus because they break the flow of an activity.

*Example:* Noah, a student teacher in a 5-year-old class, observed Jennie, age 5 years, 2 months, intently watching Carol and Renee, both age 5 years, 7 months, who were deeply absorbed in completing a complicated puzzle: "Will you let Jennie help you?" he asked Carol and Renee, interrupting the concentration of all three children. The three spoke at once: Jennie: "I don't want to!" Carol: "We don't need any help." Renee: "No! *We* want to do it ourselves."

Noah's involvement was spontaneous and unintentional. His question interrupted the girls' concentration. Interrupting, as the root "break" implies, is a negative act. As this scenario shows, by age 5 some children are capable of fending off interruptions.

***Interfere: Another Contrast.*** For an even fuller understanding of the word *intervene*, consider the word *interfere*. It has the same beginning: between. "Fere" comes from the Latin verb *ferire,* which means hit, strike, or kill. So, interfere literally means to get between and injure. A common meaning is to offer unwanted advice. Teacher interference can kill children's self-initiated activity. Frequent interference can kill children's motivation to do things on their own.

*Example:* Jessica, assistant teacher in a 4-year-old room, saw a group of four boys in the block area making a complex structure. She sat down with them and said to the group at large, "Would you like to get the basket of people to add to your construction?" Two of the boys, their focus broken, went off and wandered at random; a third began to knock down the construction; the fourth began to hit the child who was knocking down the construction.

Jessica's question was spontaneous and unintentional. It killed the boys' focus. As the root "ferire" implies, interfering is a negative act. The less focused children are, the more likely that interference will prevent focus from deepening.

Had Noah or Jessica been intentional, they could have:

- Watched silently and/or
- Listened to the children's conversation and/or
- Withdrawn without saying anything when they noticed the children's total concentration, animated conversation, complex work, and seamless collaboration

---

**KEY POINTS:**

- It is common to see teachers interfere because they do not understand either that children learn to focus by focusing, or that breaking in on a focused child can destroy the child's concentration.
- It is common to see teachers interrupt because they do not understand that interruption stifles children's motivation to continue working on a self-initiated activity.
- Intentional teachers anticipate what effect their intervention will be likely to have. Note: It helps to know your children well.

---

More than once when I was a new Montessori teacher, from across the room I would watch a child struggling to perform some action such as opening a jar or carrying a large item. I would start toward the child to assist, but halfway there realize that the child had managed on her (or his) own; seeing this, I would stifle my impulse to help. I learned that children are far more competent than I had realized at overcoming difficult challenges, that in fact many children crave challenge, that a sad fact is we offer children far less challenge than is required to spark or sustain their interest. Another sad fact is that inexperienced teachers may interrupt focused children instead of working with those who are unfocused. While this is understandable because it may be difficult to engage unfocused children, they are the ones who most need teachers' attention.

## Intervention at Work in Classrooms

Several exercises in observation, focused on intention and reflection, can help teachers hone the capacity to be intentional and reflective. Try these exercises. In the first, observe another teacher; in the second, observe yourself as you teach; in the third, reflect on your reasons for intervening.

### ✦ Exercise 1: Observing in Another Teacher's Classroom

Observe a classroom, but not your own, during free-choice time (that is, not at group or circle time). Choose a classroom where the free-choice period extends for, at minimum, 30 minutes. If no class in your school has that long a period, try to visit a Montessori or a Reggio-inspired class (two approaches characterized by children having long, uninterrupted time in which to pursue activities based on their own interests). When you make arrangements, confirm that your visit will be on a day when "special" activities are not scheduled that would interrupt children's flow during the period of self-directed work.

Explain to the teacher that you are looking at the nature of adult/child interaction and specifically children's responses to an adult. Use the following guidelines for any observation.

1. Make sure all adults in the classroom will be comfortable being observed.
2. Ask if the teacher and other adults will be available and willing to talk with you after class about what you observed. If the teacher is not open to discussing your observations, find a class with a willing teacher.
3. Be a noninvolved, invisible observer. That is:
   • Avoid eye contact with the children by dropping your eyes.
   • Do not talk with the children.
   • Do not respond to anything going on in the class.
   • Try to fade into the wall (!) so that your presence has as little effect as possible on adults and children.
4. Observe with these intents:
   • Note every instance when an adult (teacher, aide, volunteer, other) intervenes in a child's (or children's) activity. Consider:
      ➤ Precisely what the children were doing when the adult intervened
      ➤ What you think motivated the adult to intervene and why you think that
      ➤ How each child responded to the intervention. Look for irritation, loss of interest, change of focus, irrelevant responses . . . whatever behavior/emotion/movement the child displayed or what the child said
      ➤ What each child did immediately after the intervention
      ➤ A few minutes later, what (if anything) changed in each child's behavior

5. After class, remind each adult with whom you speak of the interaction you are recounting. For each intervention an adult made, ask:
   - Do you recall why you intervened in this situation?
   - Specifically, what was your intent?
   - Did the intervention accomplish what you intended?
   - Why do you think you fulfilled your intent? (Or, depending on the answer, why do you think you did not fulfill your intent?)
   - What do you recall about each child's response?
   - Was the response typical for that child?
6. Later, on your own, read your notes and, considering only your own opinion, reflect:
   - Did the adult have a clear intent for intervening? Why, or why not?
   - Did the intervention *interfere* with the children's activity? The answer may differ for each child. Explain.
   - Did the intervention *interrupt* the children's activity? The answer may differ for each child. Explain.
   - Did the adult who intervened fulfill his or her objective in intervening?
   - Considering each child individually, did the children benefit enough to justify the intervention? (In other words, was the intervention worthwhile?)
   - Explain how each child benefited from the intervention.

Reflection means to consider the results of your actions.

### ✦ Exercise 2: Reflecting on Your Own Classroom

Stop teaching and observe your own classroom. Try to do so once a week for 20 to 30 minutes at a time. Follow the guidelines with your own class that are listed above for observing in another teacher's class. Observe yourself and other adults, one adult each time you observe.

- Recall what you said as you entered into an activity with a child or children.
- Note in writing precisely what you said.
- Recall what the children did immediately after you intervened.
- Note in writing the children's responses.
- Read your notes in order to determine what impact your intervention had on the children. Did one or more children:
  - ➤ Become more deeply focused?
  - ➤ Learn and use a new technique?
  - ➤ Get on with their work more readily?
  - ➤ Make a remark that related in some way to what they were doing?
  - ➤ Make a remark that responded to what you did or said?
  - ➤ Repeat what you said to another child?
  - ➤ Incorporate into future activity something that (may have) occurred?

If you answer "yes" to the above questions, the intervention was intentional. If you answer "no," the intervention may have interfered or interrupted. Learning to analyze the effect of an intervention is the essence of reflective teaching.

---

**KEY POINTS:**

- You can train yourself to be intentional by reflecting on the results of your interactions.
- You can become intentional by repeating the above "Three R's"—recall/write/reflect—until you have habituated these reflective behaviors.

---

✦ Exercise 3: Why Intervene?

Here are a few good reasons to intervene. To:

- Listen to children
- Observe children
- Demonstrate a technique
- Ask a question
- Provide an answer
- Offer a relevant book
- Present a material
- Amplify a meaning

Think of as many additional reasons as you can. Do this exercise with a colleague or a group and brainstorm reasons to intervene. Good reasons to intervene are virtually unlimited and arise from careful observation of what children are doing.

When your list is developed, use it to reflect on your observations. Did you do anything on your list? What did you do? What was the result?

The four key issues are:

- *Why* are you intervening?
- *When* should you intervene?
- *How* should you intervene?
- *What* should the content of your intervention be?

> **KEY POINT:**
> Intervention is an ultimately intentional act; the more teachers reflect on their interventions, the more likely they will become better at teaching so that children learn.

If you judge the above examples inconsequential, reflect: Children are shaped by the myriad of micro-actions that occur over the years they spend in ECE environments. It is the accumulation of "micro-actions" over time—like water wearing away rock over geologic time—that shapes or reshapes children's tendencies. Therefore, especially in the years from 0 to 8, teachers' every micro-action matters. Little effects have big consequences. But in the matter of shaping children's temperament, cognition, or motivation, it is as difficult to relate cause to effect as it is to imagine a specific noncataclysmic moment when a geologic force shaped the mountain or formed the beach. In this book, I am arguing for the importance of minuscule actions that may seem inconsequential. Call them cascading effects and reflect with care on their cumulative effect. They all matter. Consider Howard Gardner's (2004) explanation of young children's process of *identification*. Because young children want to become like adults whom they find desirable, "skilled or manipulative adults are able to exploit the phenomenon of identification in order to bring about changes of mind and behavior that they deem important" (p. 169).

## Intention

The renowned psychologist Reuven Feuerstein (1920–2014) considers intention *the* most important teaching behavior. First I define intention, then I describe characteristics of intentional teachers. Finally I discuss how to choose words that express intention.

**Definition.** For Feuerstein, the driving force behind every teacher/child interaction is the teacher's intention. Intention has two equally important roles: When a teacher intervenes in a child's activity, (1) the teacher approaches the child with a deliberate purpose in mind and (2) the teacher communicates that purpose to the child.

*Example: Arousing a Child's Interest.* Peter, an intern in the infant/toddler center, was curious about whether a 10-month-old would focus on the activity of rolling a ball back and forth with an adult. Before he chooses a baby to work with, Peter chooses a ball:

- In a color bright enough to catch a baby's attention
- In a texture that will roll easily on the carpet but not slip out of a baby's hands
- In a size that will fit a baby's hands
- In a weight light enough for a baby to lift

In advance, Peter also browses the classroom to find a place:

- Away from foot traffic
- With adequate space for a ball to roll freely
- As free as possible from distraction
- With seating for himself and a baby that allows freedom of movement

Then Peter thinks about which baby to choose. He recalls that recently Andy crawled to a large, lightweight beach ball, an occasional object in the classroom, and became involved for almost 5 minutes attempting to move it. Therefore, Peter believes that Andy might be interested in ball rolling. Before beginning the activity, Peter communicates his intention by:

- Putting the ball where Andy can easily see it
- Catching Andy's gaze with his own
- Directing Andy's gaze by making eye contact and holding Andy's gaze as he (Peter) moves his own eyes toward the ball
- Testing to see whether bouncing, dropping, or rolling the ball keeps Andy's gaze focused

• Watching for the moment when Andy might be ready to sit and roll the ball back and forth

Peter judges Andy's "readiness" as the child's state at this moment, not as an indication of Andy's developmental level. Peter judges Andy's state by observing:

1. How long ago Andy was changed and fed
2. How recently Andy napped
3. How attentively Andy looks at the ball
4. Whether Andy makes any attempts to reach for the ball
5. Whether Andy makes any noises, gestures, or other movements that indicate he might want to play with the ball

Peter intended to choose a baby who would be interested. Because Peter knew that Andy had a good nap, and was changed and fed, and because Andy was looking at, reaching for, and "talking" animatedly to the ball, Peter determined that Andy was not only ready to play ball, but was eager and excited by the thought.

Choosing a child, a material, and a place for an activity, arousing a child's interest, and communicating your purpose are intentional acts, preliminary to the interaction itself. With great intention Peter chose the activity, specific stimulus, location, time, and particular child, and aroused the baby's interest before starting the game. Because of Peter's intentionality, when he sat Andy on the floor, the baby was all smiles and leaned forward eagerly as Peter rolled him the ball.

In contrast, consider what the reaction might be of a baby who is hungry, tired, and has a wet diaper; who has never shown any interest in a ball; and who is not drawn toward any attempt the adult makes to engage him with a ball.

✦ Exercise 4: Engaging an Unresponsive Child

You have a lesson in mind for Tommy and bring him and the material to a table, but Tommy is not responsive. Describe what you would do to engage Tommy. Would you:

• Choose another time?
• Go ahead with the lesson anyway?
• Select a different stimulus?
• Bring another child to work with you and Tommy?
• Choose a different child to work with?
• Other (describe).

Explain why you made the choice. If you are describing an actual classroom experience, describe what happened. Did the child:

• Become engaged at once?
• Become engaged gradually?
• Not pay attention at all?

- Wander off?
- Resist? Describe how.

*Characteristics of Intentional Actions.* Behaviors that are the essence of intentional teaching look like this:

1. An engaged attitude that conveys: This will be fun! This is important! You will like what we are going to do!
2. Salient, so that the stimulus the teacher uses is conspicuous and will arrest a child's attention, as with Peter and the ball.
3. Multimodal, with the teacher using many different ways to amplify the effect of a stimulus—gesture; vocal tone, rhythm, pitch, inflection; singing the presentation; humor; rhyme; large body movement. Gardner would say we are appealing to different children's different intelligences.
4. Nuanced, as described in Chapters 2 and 3.
5. Mind-full, in that the teacher adjusts his/her second-by-second interactions to bring them in tune with the child.
6. Resonating, meaning that the teacher's perspective feels right to a child. Gardner (2004) considers resonance one of seven "levers" with which to change someone's mind.

When they experience these kinds of teaching behaviors, children become more focused, ultimately "get" the meaning, change their minds, and thereby learn.

✦ Exercise 5: Explain attitude, saliency, multimodality, nuance, mindfullness, and resonance by describing occasions when you have observed yourself or other teachers using these behaviors.

## Meaning

The word *meaning* refers to any content, material, exercise, lesson, technique—*anything*—that a teacher wants to convey to a child. Intentional teachers make decisions every minute about what to convey. Minds express meaning as (1) concepts (the ideas a mind contains), (2) stories (recounting of events over time with a main character and actions toward an outcome), (3) theories (explanations about how the world works, whether accurate or not), and/or (4) skills ("procedures that individuals know how to carry out" whether through words, actions, or movements) (Gardner, 2004, p. 20). The purpose of this book is not to lay out content but to offer intentional/reflective techniques that can be used with any content.

First, consider the process of *choosing* content. There is a world of content in children's environments (home, school, neighborhood, community). Assuming that classroom content is not constrained by a curriculum, the first act in conveying meaning is for a teacher to *choose* what content to present from the vast amount in the world. Philosopher, educator, computer scientist, and MIT professor Seymour Papert created the computer language Logo and later united Logo and Lego, thus opening new avenues for creative inventions by children around the world. Papert once said that because paper and pencils became the "tools" of school, curricula were limited by what you could do with paper and pencils. Jerome Bruner, pioneer in developmental psychology, believed you could give children *any* content depending on how you presented it. Montessori materials contain science and math content that children often meet only in middle school. A key feature of the Reggio schools is the vast range of materials and tools, all content-laden, and the intention with which teachers use them as building blocks of children's competence. Loris Malaguzzi, founder of the Reggio schools, referred to children expressing themselves facilely with tools and materials as "speaking 100 languages." Montessori and Malaguzzi, for whom content differed markedly, would have agreed that all experience must be embedded in movement. For Montessori, movement meant an apparatus that only "worked" if children moved it. For Malaguzzi, movement meant the manipulation of an enormous variety of materials and tools. For both, children were free to move at will and the hand was a major force in all learning.

### Four Examples: Choice of Contrast to Teach Content

1. Emily is teaching 2-year-olds to associate the words *green, orange,* and *purple* with objects in those colors. Emily has chosen green/orange/ purple, not yellow/gold/orange, because the colors in the first trio are far more distinct. A consideration in choosing content is the impact of contrast on learning.

*Note:* Teaching color to 2-year-olds is tricky because if you choose objects such as a car, a crayon, and a book to learn color names, you cannot determine whether children are focusing on the object or its color. Instead choose a color tablet (if you have this material) or color chips (free at paint stores). *Tip:* Use the larger chips. Color is *the* defining attribute of color tablets and paint chips; these materials have few identifying characteristics *other than* their color.

2. Henry is teaching 2½-year-olds the names of farm animals. To ensure ample contrast, he uses cow, chicken, and cat, not cow, calf, and horse.
3. Angela is teaching 4-year-olds the names of plants; she uses plants with distinct features (Polka Dot Plant, Cyclamen, Kalanchoe), not plants with similar flowers (Carnation, African Violet, Begonia), as in Figure 1.1.
4. Roland, a Montessori teacher, is teaching the shapes and sounds of letters to 2½-year-olds by introducing three letters at a time that contrast in sound and shape. He does not introduce *m, n,* and *u* together; *m* and *n* are too close in sound and appearance, and *u* looks like *n* upside-down. Roland uses trios such as *m, a,* and *p; s, i,* and *t; b, o,* and *x,* because the letters in each trio are distinct from one another in both sound and shape.

*Tip:* Children may find beginning reading easier if they have been taught the sounds that letters make rather than the names of the letters. For examples: mmmmm, not "em;" sssss, not "ess;" aaa (as in hat), not "ay."

Figure 1.1. Young children learn new content more readily from examples that are distinct and have high contrast, like the second row shown here.

| Carnation | African Violet | Begonia |
|---|---|---|

| Polka Dot Plant | Cyclamen | Kalanchoe |
|---|---|---|

Photographs by Michael Cruickshank

I have described sandpaper letters in other books, and there are books on the Montessori method, notably *The Discovery of the Child* by Montessori (1948) herself, in which she describes the process of teaching letters. Outside Montessori schools, I rarely see her method used to teach beginning reading. I find this frustrating. In my opinion, for the vast majority of children who do not learn to read intuitively, the sequence of Montessori sound game, sandpaper letters, and movable alphabet is a highly effective approach. Why, I wonder, do we reinvent the wheel when a time-proven method is readily at hand?

✦ Exercise 6: For every child in your class, list three specific things you can present to extend content the child already knows or to provide new content.

Listing content gives you a tool to spark children's interest. Your list is a guide for children who have difficulty making their own choices. As you use your list, observe and take note of children's responses. Later reflect on your observation:

- Why did the children respond as they did?
- If you repeat the activity, would you do it differently?
- For those children who became involved, list three more ways to extend the children's content knowledge.

If, for example, you want to use content to help children learn attributes, focus your lesson on the defining aspects of the stimulus:

- Noticing animals' size and body parts (toddlers)
- Hearing and feeling the sound and shape of letters (2½- to 3½-year-olds)
- Identifying rocks by their color, texture, cleavage, hardness, gleam (4- to 6-year-olds)

*Note:* A website with clear explanations of the hardness of rocks and how to test for hardness is geology.com/minerals/mohs-hardness-scale.shtml.

Most natural materials provide opportunities for hands-on exploration. Whereas 2- to 3-year-olds are noun-hungry, wanting names for everything (as we'll see later in the toddler featured in Figure 5.2), by age 4 children are eager to expand their knowledge. Learning the attributes of man-made or natural materials opens doors to knowledge.

✦ Exercise 7: Look critically at your nature table to determine whether there are objects to take apart, examine with lenses, or, as with the rocks, test properties in numerous ways.

The web offers excellent information as well as cutesy junk! Select with care. *Tip:* "Sets" offered by made-for-school companies often contain inferior specimens and are more expensive than what you can collect yourself on a walk, find at a rock show, or purchase individually from a scientific supply company.

Or, for example, if you want to design multimodal lessons, consider how the sandpaper letters, described above, lend themselves to a multimodal approach by simultaneously using visual, tactile/kinesthetic, and auditory senses to observe, feel, and hear letters' sound and shape. In Chapters 2 and 3, I offer numerous techniques for using different parts of the body in varied ways; all are examples of multimodal teaching and engaging children's multiple intelligences.

✦ Exercise 8: In the next lesson you give, use two different modes to engage children's attention.

Choose modes with intention: Use your observations of the children to help you select. Does Kathy require extra stimulation? Consider a tactile experience. Will Todd be distracted by complexity? Select objects with high visual contrast, not objects with features that are similar to one another, indistinct, or cluttered. In planning your lesson, make notes of why you are choosing particular modes for a given child. Observe the result. Did the child respond by becoming engaged? Did the child withdraw? Reflect on what the children's responses mean and what you will do the same or differently next time.

---

**KEY POINTS:**

- In conveying new meaning to children of any age:
  - ➤ Choose stimuli with high contrast
  - ➤ Focus on salient attributes
  - ➤ Involve more than one of the children's senses
  - ➤ Use a multimodal/multiple intelligence approach
- Selecting for contrast, focusing on one attribute, and using varied modalities to convey meaning are intentional teaching acts.

---

### Transcendence

Transcendence is a simple concept and a highly intentional act. It means that once meaning has been chosen and conveyed and children have grasped the meaning, the teacher challenges the children to think of something that the meaning relates to in the past or present, or something the child can imagine in the future. Gardner (2004) would say that children can do this using the mind's content, storytelling, theory-making, or skills. Some questions that stimulate the process of transcendence are:

- What does this remind you of?
- What else works like this?
- Where would you be most likely to find one of these?
- Can you act out what you mean?

Transcendent acts require the brain to establish a relation between two or more different things. To establish relationships requires a multitude of cognitive acts, for example: comparison, analysis, synthesis, the retrieval of memories from different memory centers, or finding specific words in the brain's mental dictionary—to name just five. In turn, each act requires different networks of neurons.

Intentional teachers help children build cognitive functions when they encourage children to recap meaning by building relationships. The brain naturally seeks patterns and relationships. Transcendence raises the brain's relationship-building function to a conscious level. The goals are for children to want to seek relationships and to do so spontaneously. When used consistently, when lessons are stimulating, and when children are made aware that they are using transcendence, the act of transcending becomes a habitual part of acquiring meaning. *Tip:* Make sure children are very familiar with content before asking them to transcend.

✦ Exercise 9: Put transcendence to work in your lessons.

- For 1 week, use transcendence every time you teach content.
- Keep track of the questions you use to encourage children to build relationships.
- Save the questions to become the basis for a collection of Questions That Lead to Relationship-Building.

## Reflection

Reflection is *the* act that gives meaning to intention. To reflect means to think carefully and unhurriedly about something that you have observed or done. If, as an intentional teacher, you have a purpose in mind when you interact with a child, then when you reflect, you will determine whether you have realized your purpose. You will weigh what you intended against your observation of what happened.

The word *reflect* has a range of meanings:

> **KEY POINT:** Intentionally focusing on transcendence helps children acquire strong and flexible thinking habits.

- Recall, bringing something to conscious attention, as when Susan quoted Robbie's statement to him
- Muse, making your memory abstract, as in a daydream
- Ruminate, as when you rethink a memory over and over
- Consider or ponder, as when you carefully search for details of what happened
- Weigh, debating with yourself or another about what happened in order to reach a conclusion or make a decision
- Deliberate, engaging in slow and mindful thought to relate a sequence of actions to their consequences

Reflection may take place alone or, as is generally the case in Reggio schools, with one or more others—colleagues and/or children. As we see in the following scenario, when you reflect, you may learn something entirely new about what has happened. Observation without reflection may result in missing so many points that the action may as well not have happened.

Consider the well-known Reggio six-photograph episode of Laura, age 10 months, shown in Figure 1.2.

1. In the first photo, we meet Laura turning the pages of a magazine while her teacher sits beside and observes.
2. In the second, Laura comes to a two-page spread, each page covered with life-size images of four similar watches that are all displayed similarly, with watch face and about 2 inches of wristband.
3. In the third, Laura points to a picture of a watch and simultaneously engages the teacher's eyes.
4. In the fourth, Laura fingers the teacher's watch, which is similar to those in the magazine.

Figure 1.2. The interaction between Laura and the teacher is reciprocal, intentional, and full of surprises for both teacher and baby.

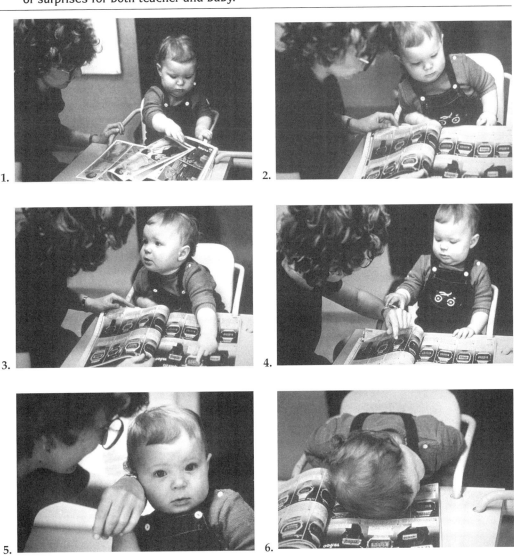

5. In the fifth, Laura listens wide-eyed as the teacher holds her watch next to Laura's ear.
6. In the final photo, Laura has placed her ear on one of the watches in the magazine spread.

The photo series reflects many intentional acts of the teacher, who:

- Has equipped the classroom with furniture that enables a baby to sit upright and work on a tabletop with a chair for a teacher that fits nearby—evident in all photos
- Has provisioned the infant school with magazines not intended for children, but with content the teacher suspects might fascinate children—evident in all photos
- Records the sequence in six photos
- Synchronizes her movements to Laura's, moving in sync with the baby—evident in photos 2, 3, 4, and 5
- Engages responsively so that when Laura looks at her beseechingly, the teacher holds her head close to Laura's head and makes eye contact—evident in photo 3
- Scaffolds Laura's interest by holding out her wrist so the baby cannot help but notice the similarity between the teacher's watch and the watches in the magazine—evident in photo 4
- Holds her wristwatch to Laura's ear so the baby can hear the ticking sound—evident in photo 5

The photo sequence is captivating because of the unusual subject matter—a baby carefully handling a magazine and becoming deeply engrossed in the high-quality photos and the action of turning pages. But only through reflection is the significance clear—the baby is engaged in high-level cognitive activity. In:

- Photo 1, the 10-month-old turns large-format magazine pages casually but with interest and care, an activity not usually offered to 10-month-olds. Because of Laura's eye/hand coordination and finger/hand skill, we guess that this is not Laura's first use of a magazine.
- Photo 2, the pages with the watches grab Laura's attention so that her gaze changes from casual to concentrated and her actions become more focused and highly intentional.
- Photo 3, Laura *intentionally* "tells" the teacher—by pointing and with eye contact—that she is interested in the watches.
- Photo 4, Laura switches her attention from the symbolic object (the picture of the watch in the magazine) to the real object (the watch the teacher wears).
- Photo 5, Laura's face registers utter surprise, her eyes widening, as she hears the teacher's watch tick. Here we watch a baby's reaction to a first-time auditory sensation and witness the power of sensory experience.
- Photo 6, as Laura presses her ear to the picture of watches, we intuit what Laura is thinking: "If this watch (yours, the teacher's) ticks, maybe these (the magazine pictures) do too." Laura has created a hypothesis—all watches tick. She is testing her hypothesis by listening to the magazine photo.

✦ Exercise 10: Recall books you have read that describe episodes between teacher and child. Choose three. Analyze the interactions in terms of the teacher's intentions/reflections and child's responses.

Do you agree with what the teacher did? What would you do the same or differently? Wherever you see teacher/child interaction, train yourself to reflect on the outcome of teachers' intention by "reading" the children's responses.

---

**KEY POINTS:**

- In studying the "Laura" photos, the teacher's intentionality is obvious; the meaning of the baby's actions becomes clear on reflection.
- Without reflecting, you are not likely to grasp the nuances of a teacher's micro-actions or the meaning of a child's behavior.

---

## CASE STUDY:
## MAKING AN UNINTENTIONAL LESSON INTENTIONAL

Consider the following scenario as an example of teaching that lacks intention. Then reflect on what could change to make the teaching intentional.

### Scenario

The setting: A class for children around age 2½ in a pleasant school—big windows, no commercial materials, many natural materials, and two teachers per class.

*The players:* A classroom teacher and two boys.

*The action and stimulus:* The teacher is videotaping. One boy, Tom, is using a rug, just large enough for a 2½-year-old to lie on. The rug is pale blue, pleasingly soft, and a weight that will allow it to roll and unroll easily.

*What happens:* Tom unrolls the rug on the floor, struggles to smooth it out, in speech that is just barely intelligible calls it a "night-night," and lies down on it.

The teacher, in a pleasant voice, invites another child, Stephon, to join. We do not see, nor are we told, what evoked the teacher's invitation.

At once, Stephon comes running and squats beside Tom's rug. (*Note:* Stephon imitates many other children's actions.) The teacher utters, "Mmmmmm." Her tone conveys approval but not a clear meaning.

The camera now focuses on Stephon. He has run to the teacher's side, insistently and rapidly points several times toward Tom, and with increasing urgency says something to the teacher. Stephon's speech is also unclear; he seems to be asking what the rug is or perhaps to use it. For emphasis, Stephon jabs his pointing finger toward Tom or the rug; it is unclear which. The teacher does not reply to Stephon. Tom gets off the rug.

Stephon runs toward Tom and stretches out on the rug. We cannot tell whether Stephon:

- Does not perceive Tom's intention toward the rug
- Is drawn by the rug's attributes—pale blue color, soft texture, size
- Is imitating with no other specific intent

Instantly Tom screams, "No!" and simultaneously looks at the teacher. Then Tom screams more raucously, "No! No!"

Over Tom's scream, we hear the teacher: "Tom?"

Stephon, agitated by Tom's screams, flails at Tom, but does not actually touch him.

Tom screams even louder.

Teacher, coaxingly: "Stephon, hitting hurts. If you hit Tom, you can hurt him. Please. Don't hit Tom."

Tom, approaching a tantrum, continues to scream.

Teacher, commanding: "Stephon, get off the rug." Then sternly: "GET . . . UP . . . FROM . . . THE . . . RUG." Addressing Stephon insistently: "Can you find something else to play with?" Then emphatically, edging toward desperation: "FIND SOMETHING ELSE TO PLAY WITH!"

Stephon makes no move to get off the rug.

The teacher demands of Tom: "Tell Stephon what else he can play with."

Tom, face petulant but with glints of triumph, points (the camera does not show what Tom points at): "That." His mouth forms a small grin suggesting satisfaction.

The video stops. We do not see Stephon's next action.

## Reflection

What is intentional? The use of video to document the experience and the presence of an appealing rug. We have not been told a context for the rug, its function in the classroom, whether there are more, or how children typically use rugs when playing alone or together. Nor are we told of teachers' prior discussions with the children about rugs.

What *might* have been intentional? Consider. Intentional teachers:

- Have serious debates on what material to put in the classroom
- Brainstorm all aspects of a material's potential
- Consider many different activities that might occur when children use the material
- Determine whether possible activities have the potential to branch in different ways that are meaningful

These conversations may have been held. We are not privy to them.

Intentional teachers also have lively debates and long deliberations about which children to choose for a small-group experience. They consider:

- Mix of personalities
- Ages
- Skills each child possesses
- Possible influences of each child on the others
- Possible interactions the material might stimulate between or among children

These debates may have occurred; we do not know.
What was unintentional?

- Making the extraneous sound "Mmmmmm"
- Inviting a child to join another's play without asking if it is all right with the other child
- Disrespecting a child's right to play alone if the child so chooses
- Failing to answer Stephon's query
- Becoming rattled by Tom's screams
- Not diverting Stephon
- Not videotaping the conclusion of the boys' interaction

✦ Exercise 11: What could have been intentional?

Before reading on, list what could have made the experience intentional. When your list is finished, compare it with the following list.
If intentional, the teacher would have:

- Added meaning by conversing with the children before and after
- Asked any one of these questions: "What is this?" "Have you ever seen a rug before?" "What do you do with rugs?" "What would you like to do with this rug?" (*Note:* One question is enough; conversation stimulated by a single question may continue for several days.)
- Taught skills to handle rugs:
  - ➤ Demonstrated techniques
  - ➤ Practiced techniques so children develop precise movement skills; for example with a rug:
    - Rolling neatly
    - Carrying so it does not unroll
    - Placing on the floor to lie smoothly
    - Unrolling with a gentle pushing motion
    - Rerolling if it goes askew
    - Straightening if it does not lie squarely
  - ➤ Challenged children to remember; for example: "Do you remember how to *carry* a rolled rug?" "Can you show me how to unroll a rug?" "Can you make the run lie *smoothly*?"
  - ➤ Answered a child's question
  - ➤ Asked a question that stimulates children to think, for example, "Tom, do you want Stephon to join you?" or, "Stephon, what do you intend to do with the rug Tom is using?"
  - ➤ Videotaped Stephon's final response
  - ➤ Reflected on the experience together with colleagues
  - ➤ Deliberated how to handle an altercation like Tom and Stephon's
  - ➤ Used images and the children's own words to spur the children's memory

> ➤ Studied images with the children who were involved by asking questions such as, "What happened here?"
> ➤ Kept interest in the rug kindled by asking, for example, "Do you remember when you said you wanted to use the rug to [quote from child's comment]?"
> ➤ Asked children to think transcendently, for examples, "What does a rolled rug remind you of?" "Have you ever had feelings like Tom's?"

> KEY POINT: Children's displays of temper are rich opportunities for reflection

Intentional teachers reflect on their teaching by:

1. Anticipating and hypothesizing about situations in advance
2. Observing themselves while they are in the moment of their teaching
3. Reflecting on experiences after they are over, alone or with colleagues

If the scenario was anticipated, revisited, or reflected on, we are not told of the conversations.

What was evident in the scenario? The teacher acted as observer and recorder. Observing and recording are two important aspects of the role of researcher, one of several roles that intentional teachers play.

## CONCLUSION

Here is a summary of what you may have learned from reading this chapter.

1. What intentional teaching looks like in practice
2. The difference between intervening, interrupting, and interfering
3. How to choose a stimulus and select a particular meaning to convey about it
4. Ways the brain can convey meaning—relating content, telling stories, inventing theories, using skills (Gardner, 2004)
5. That teaching children to think transcendently can develop the brain's higher-level thinking capacities
6. What it means to reflect on an experience, and examples of teacher reflection
7. How much the process of reflection enhances a teacher's understanding of what happened
8. How to analyze why a typical classroom situation is or is not intentional, and some of the ways it was or could have been intentional

In the next two chapters, I examine micro-actions, the nuanced, second-by-second behaviors that occur in all aspects of teachers' work.

# CHAPTER 2

# Micro-Actions of Intentional/Reflective Teaching

From an early age, children learn to use and read signals that are expressed, not through words, but through behavior.

—Stanley Greenspan, 1995, p. 17

> **TECHNIQUE 2**
> Communicate precisely:
> Master nuances in using the body, eyes, face, hands, and voice.

Many parts of the body express intention and reflection. Think of the iconic sculpture *"Discobolus"* ("Discus Thrower," 5th century B.C., Figure 2.1) by an unknown Greek sculptor. Every muscle in the young man's body declares his intention to win the Olympic championship. And think of the renowned work by French sculptor Pierre Rodin, which he presented in 1902, *"The Thinker"* (Figure 2.2). It has become a world icon of how someone looks who is absorbed in deep reflection.

In this chapter, I explain how to teach by using body movements, eyes, and face to communicate intention to children before, during, and after intervening in any activity or giving a lesson. Throughout I suggest exercises to:

- Reflect on the use of body, eyes, and face
- Consider whether using the exercises helps to communicate intention
- Determine *how* or *why* an exercise helped
- Reflect on how it feels to act with intention
- Consider where there is room for improvement

By the end of the chapter, teachers should be able to:

- Observe themselves teaching
- Identify how they use intention and reflection
- Increase their intentional use of body, eyes, and face
- Reflect on how they can use techniques of intention and reflection with more precision

Figure 2.1. "*Discobulus*"—You can read the young man's intention in every muscle.

Figure 2.2. "*The Thinker*"—Many nuances in expression and posture convey total absorption.

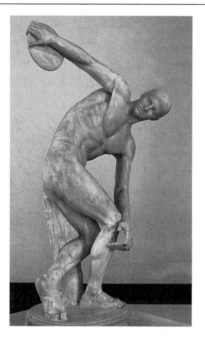

*How* do you teach with intention and reflection? There are two essential aspects—teachers' actions and the reflective techniques teachers use to critique their actions. The results, in terms of impact on children, will be different for every child depending on the child's temperament (discussed in detail in Chapter 7).

In this chapter, I first describe two highly intentional groups: mothers of infants, and actors. Then I describe techniques for using body, eyes, and face intentionally. In Chapter 3, I continue by describing techniques for using hands and voice intentionally. As you learn these techniques, they become powerful tools to communicate your intention and to teach more reflectively.

Being an intentional/reflective teacher is complex, which is good: Complexity is the antithesis of boredom; it keeps one alert and makes every minute different. Intentional/reflective teaching also changes the paradigm—from teachers as conveyors of information to teachers as researchers who study the effects of their actions on children. The issue is getting from your starting place to your emergence as an intentional, reflective teacher.

## DEMEANOR AND THE INTENTION OF MOTHERS AND ACTORS

What is demeanor? What is its relation to mothers and actors? And why is this important for intentional and reflective teaching?

## The Meaning of Demeanor

Demeanor refers to how we act. Our demeanor conveys who we are—serious? shifty? reliable? dishonest? We convey these impressions subconsciously. Attempts to project who we are often appear disingenuous to someone trying to size us up. Our demeanor conveys more than anything we say about what we believe about ourselves and what we expect of others. Demeanor is, in Howard Gardner's definition of human intelligences, kinesthetic; that is, demeanor is expressed through movement and is the sum of little movements:

- Sounds we coax from our vocal system that shape tongue and lips
- Intentional and unintentional movements of the face
- Posture
- Slight shifts of torso, arms, shoulders, feet, and eyes
- Hand positions
- Finger extensions
- Head turns, tilts, and carriage

*Every* part of the body contributes to demeanor and thus tells others about us.

Gestures reflect demeanor: We summon by beckoning that can be commanding, seductive, or insistent; that can implore help urgently, or mark us as supplicants. Shrugs reflect demeanor: If we draw together arms, back, head, and neck, like a turtle pulling into its shell, we communicate discomfort, fear, or resignation. If we shrug with eyes partially closed, we express disdain. A quick, simple shrug says, "I don't know"; a simple shrug and turn of the head, "I don't care."

Dr. Stanley Greenspan (1995), child psychiatrist, infant advocate, founder of Zero to Three, and author, says that even in infancy (by 6 weeks if not before) babies

> can carry on a rich dialogue with smiles, frowns, pointing fingers, squirming, wiggling, gurgling, and crying. . . . They understand most of life's basic emotional themes—approval, praise, love, danger, anger—through gestures, facial expression, body language. (pp. 17–18)

We are born with the potential to make the actions I analyze in this and the next chapter. Here I describe how to make the most of this potential in order to engage children to the utmost. Demeanor, which is the essence of intention, is readily apparent in the actions of mothers of infants and in actors.

## Mother—The First Intentional Teacher

Mothers are instinctively intentional when they engage their infants' attention. Mothers are the first intentional teacher for each of us. The skills mothers intuitively use with their infants provide a model for intentionality in the classroom. Here I describe what teachers can learn by watching mothers with infants.

Most mothers communicate naturally with infants in a language called Infant Directed Speech (IDS). IDS is a high-pitched, slow, and heavily articulated manner of talking that emphasizes individual words in phrases or sentences, exaggerates syllables, and isolates individual sounds (called phonemes) in words. Mothers also engage infants in many reciprocal behaviors—smiling, laughing, reaching for each other, playing games, holding conversations in a language that is marked by sound, gesture, and movement and that is full of emotion. These acts that take place in infancy set the stage for a child's trust, self-regulation, social engagement, empathy, and disposition toward life. It is impossible to overestimate the importance in infancy of the mother/infant relationship and the ramifications for a person's emotional health later in life. Nor can we find a better or more natural example of intentionality than mothers.

✦ Exercise 1: Learn intentional behaviors by watching a mother with her infant.

Observe a mother and infant as they interact. Write down every aspect of intentionality that you see in the behaviors of both mother and infant. Repeat this exercise with different mother/infant pairs until you have a long list of interactions. Then practice them with your infant/toddlers and preschoolers.

✦ Exercise 2: Determine the impact of your Intention on your children.

Reflect on your children's responses to your interactions:

- Which of your behaviors keep children focused?
- How long do they stay focused?
- Which behaviors cause them to laugh?
- What movements do your children make in response? What sounds do they make?
- If your children are at an age where they talk, ask them about each behavior; for example:
    ➤ What does it tell you about me when I _____? What is the meaning of this (noise, face, gesture) _____?
    ➤ What do I mean when I speak like this (adopt different qualities of voice—low, high, growly, loud, whisper, raspy, etc.) _____?
    ➤ What do I mean when I speak like this (speak with different intentions—command, request, urgent order, invitation, greeting, praise, etc.) _____?

✦ Exercise 3: Reflect on your communication with infants.

Find an infant and engage in a dialogue. As you do so, prepare to reflect on the experience by:

- Noting how you use your face and body
- Attending to your tone of voice, emphasis, and parsing
- Noticing the intensity with which you focus on the infant

- Observing the care with which you sync your words or movements to the infant's movements and vocalizations
- Thinking about your facial expressions
- Being aware of your movements
- Paying attention to any other ways you are acting with intention

Your reflection will sharpen your awareness of what it means to act with intention.

*Tips:*

1. Analyze your engagement with the infant in order to become conscious of your instinctive responses.
2. Transfer the intentionality of how you act with an infant to your classroom as soon as possible after being with the infant.

Mothers instinctively establish reciprocity with their babies. Their faces are alive; they smile easily, make eye contact, establish a rhythm to the call and response of mother/infant communication, and are present in every moment. The mother/infant relationship is as clear a picture of true love as can be portrayed, and watching mother/infant interchanges provides teachers with an ideal model of intention to reflect on and to emulate.

## Actors—*The* Model of Demeanor

Actors learn and master the skills to be intentional. Some actors are naturals; others study and practice endlessly to acquire the ability to portray a character. Actors' intentionality in playing their roles provides a model for how teachers can use their voices and bodies in the classroom. A fine actor can communicate virtually any idea with the subtlest movements and shifts in tone of voice. Subtleties actually involve highly nuanced use of body, face, eyes, and voice. Actors practice continually to perfect the connections between:

- What they want to convey (anger, delight, suspicion, sarcasm, irony, and hundreds of other feelings); and
- The method they use to convey it—eyes, lips, forehead or other facial expression; movement of fingers, hands, or other parts of the body; slight gesture, sweeping gesture, and the many other ways in which to portray feelings

Actors reflect on whether they realized their intentions by:

- Watching themselves in a mirror
- Judging audience response
- Hearing directors' feedback
- Practicing with and receiving feedback from other actors
- Studying with a drama coach who specializes in helping actors reflect on their performance

Teachers can try some of these techniques by working with their colleagues.

✦ Exercise 1: Learn to recognize intentional behaviors.

Choose a dramatic movie. View the entire film with the volume off. See how much you can understand merely by watching the actors' bodies, faces, eyes, and hands. Test your understanding by briefly summarizing the plot and the role of each character.

✦ Exercise 2: Analyze your ability to spot intentional behavior.

Reflect on your film viewing by writing notes on the intentions, feelings, and motivation of two or three of the main characters. Explain what each actor did that you used as the basis for your notes. Concentrate on movements in which actors use their bodies to convey intention, feelings, and motivation.

✦ Exercise 3: Learn to recognize reflective behaviors.

Watch the film again but now look for examples of actors' *reflecting* on what they or another character has done. Notice how many different ways actors show us that they are being reflective. Adapt these modes of reflection for yourself.

Actors are readily available models of intentionality and reflection because film is woven so deeply into our culture and movies are so easily accessible.

---

**KEY POINTS:**

- Mothers and actors provide readily available models of intention.
- For your demeanor to communicate what you want others to know about you, you must exercise conscious control over your actions.
- Practice will make your conscious efforts automatic.

---

## INTENTIONAL BODY AND EYE MOVEMENTS

Here I elaborate on the use of body movements, eyes, and face. Using these parts of the body intentionally and reflecting on how you use each are important skills. Practice, as suggested below, to enlarge your repertoire of intentional, reflective techniques.

### Using Body Movement Intentionally

One's movements communicate in many ways. How we carry ourselves and how we move tell children who we are. Are we available? Do we have authority? Do we have in mind an activity that will spur a child's interest? Are we empathetic? Do we concentrate on our interactions with children, or are we distracted?

Consider the teacher in Figure 2.3. Descriptive words that come to mind are irresolute, undetermined, depressed, out-of-touch. Clearly, the teacher is not commanding the children's attention. Here I first explain intentional use of your body by describing presence and movement. Then I describe how to reflect on the way you use your body and on what your body communicates.

**Presence.** Presence refers to how one carries oneself. The word *carry* connotes power, as in carry a load, like Atlas with the world on his shoulders. As an aspect of presence, carry can mean to carry a crowd, an audience, or a full class of children. Intentional teachers' presence can encompass these meanings and many more. When we move our body with intention, we make an immediate impression on children. Presence reflects our internal state—the way we are feeling at any given moment, what we expect, what we ask children to follow, whether we mean what we say, whether we care.

Presence does not mean how we are dressed, coiffed, or made up, but rather refers to what we think of ourselves, whether we are:

- Secure
- Confident
- At ease
- In control
- Open and available to listen
- Aware of what is taking place around us
- Prepared to observe, act, laugh, engage

**Figure 2.3. The teacher's demeanor says that his focus is elsewhere—and the children respond accordingly.**

Presence is reflected in every aspect of our bearing.

✦ **Exercise 1: Use words to describe people's demeanor.**

Consider these sentences: She had the appearance of a hippie but the air of a noblewoman. His eyes said he was shifty because they looked downward and moved slightly from side to side. Now complete the following sentences:

- He had the appearance of a _____ but the air of a _____.
- He had the movements of a _____ even though he _____.
- You could tell from her _____ that she felt _____.
- His body conveyed an air of _____ because _____.
- You could see in her eyes that she felt _____ because _____.

✦ **Exercise 2: Observe people's demeanor, then describe it.**

Using syntax like the sentences in Exercise 1, create statements that show a person's inner state conveyed by something the body does. If you are working with a group, read one clause of your sentence and have others fill in the blank.

✦ **Exercise 3: Analyze precisely what different persons' demeanor tells you about their intention.**

Sit in a public place and observe passersby. When you spot someone whose presence communicates intention, write down everything about the person's bearing that makes you think she or he is intentional. Reflect on whether your own bearing makes you look intentional and why it does or does not.

✦ **Exercise 4: Analyze what children's demeanor tells you about their state.**

Observe a child and use the child's demeanor as the subject of a sentence. For examples, I know Jane [child's name] feels tired [state] because she is squirming and keeps rubbing her eyes [describe the behavior and body parts]. I know Phillipe feels sad because his mouth is drooping and he has folded his arms around his body. I know Alicia is amused because her eyes are twinkling and her head is cocked back.

Reading the meaning in a child's face, eyes, or other movements is an intentional act; determining what the movements mean is a reflective act. Practice in "reading" and interpreting meaning in others' movements sharpens teachers' skills as intentional/reflective practitioners.

*Movement.* Look again at Figure 2.3. The teacher's shoulders are slumped, his arms hang limply, his head is not upright, his eyes have a glum expression, he shows no determination. Every aspect of posture, head position, and body provides insight about how a person is feeling. The teacher's posture suggests defeat, exhaustion, or disengagement. If he has an intention, we cannot read it in his demeanor.

In contrast, intentional movement conveys an air of accomplishment. It suggests that one *can* effect what one intends and connotes an act of will. Intentional acts exhibit one's skill, power, and mental or physical determination. These acts are the opposite of the passivity and inertia we see in Figure 2.3.

Movement is concrete and implies an end goal, like a move in checkers or the strategic move of a political campaign. Movement suggests a definite aim or objective. Example: "I move that the proposal be adopted." The word *movement* implies changes, transitions, and processes. Teachers who move with intention have in mind specifically what they are going to do, what they want to accomplish, and what their first steps will be toward their goal.

✦ Exercise 1: Hone your ability to recognize intention in others.

Photograph several people who are moving intentionally. Show them their photos and ask what they had in mind. If you have captured an intentional movement, the person probably will have a clear memory of what his or her goal was at that moment.

✦ Exercise 2: Sharpen your capacity to analyze intentional acts reflectively.

Using the photos you have taken, reflect on what about the movement caught your eye, and whether you could have predicted what the person's memory would be. Consider: Were your prediction and the person's reflection the same?

When my son was a baby, his father was in the Marine Corps. The identical uniforms made it difficult to distinguish individuals until they were at close range. Whenever we went to the base to pick up Daddy, Danny, at age 6 months, would start to quiver. Following his gaze, I would spot his father. The baby had spotted him first. Trying to figure out how, I realized that my husband had a distinctive gait, something the baby knew but I had never noticed. Movement identifies people definitively.

✦ Exercise 3: "Read" your children's movements and reflect on what they mean.

---

**KEY POINTS:**

- One's movement is as distinct as one's thumbprint and signature.
- Movements reflect a person's intention.

## Using the Eyes Intentionally

Cicero (106–43 B.C.), Roman philosopher and statesman, said: "The face is a picture of the mind with the eyes as its interpreter." Intentional teachers use their eyes to command, give or withhold praise, empathize, and point. In these and dozens of other ways teachers let children know what they intend without speaking a word. Here I explain a bit about the brain's visual system and explore two different ways to use the eyes: interpreting what we see and conveying intent.

*The Brain's Visual System.* Seeing is a biological function that is possible because human vision comprises 30 or more brain systems, each of which has increasingly microscopic and complex subsystems. Comparing humans and other animals shows that in response to different environments, about 40 types of visual systems have evolved across all species. These systems became differentiated and each ultimately became highly specialized so that in any environment living things could perceive threats, food, shelter, and mates. The goal for most species has been: "Eat! Don't *be* eaten!" (Parker, 2003).

Among the varied visual systems, the human eye perceives a limited range of optical wavelengths, can neither detect polarization nor function in low light, and becomes confused by what we call "illusions" (responses to visual stimuli that cause the eye to "stutter"—think of two common illusions: beautiful young girl/ugly hag, or face/vase). We have only two eyes, spiders have eight. We have only one lens and limited peripheral vision; insects have compound eyes with many lenses and can see almost 360 degrees. The fly's eye works five times faster than the human's, a fact that explains why we often miss when we try to swat a fly (www.cam.ac.uk/research/news/surprising-solution-to-fly-eye-mystery).

Vision evolved so animals could both perceive and respond. Vision and movement work in tandem because these two brain functions became more complex and intertwined in their capacity to respond to threats. Over eons, the two systems branched in greatly varied ways in responding to threats. But as our species developed, movements also became influenced by cultural forces. Consider today's movements: manipulating robots, bungee jumping, maneuvering through rapidly moving traffic. Disparate and complex actions result from coordination between the brain's visual and movement systems, and the range of movements across species is one of nature's great spectacles. The movement/vision axis evokes predictable responses: Persons with muscle spasticity unnerve us as they flail to grasp an ice cream cone. Comedians evoke laughter when an ice cream cone misses their mouth and hits their forehead. We cringe at acts of violence, marvel at Olympic feats, cheer at infants' first steps.

Paleontologists suggest that the relatively small number of animals without sight—like those living in deep caves—lost the capacity for stimulation by light as an evolutionary response (Erichsen & Woodhouse, 2014). Evolutionary zoologist Andrew Parker (2003) suggests that prior to the Cambrian era, 543 million years ago, sight as we know it did not exist. There was *only* light sensitivity, a sort of rudimentary proto-sight. Parker theorizes that the evolution of full vision, 538 million years ago, resulted in (1) the diversification of species from 3 to 38 phyla, and (2) the diversity in eye structures from light-sensitive areas to full-blown visual systems. Since this 5-million-year-long "Cambrian explosion" in evolution, no new phyla have emerged.

However, being able to see does not mean that we use the full or even partial capacity of our eyes. Nor does it mean that any two people see in the same way, use their eyes with equal efficiency, or make the same interpretation of what they see. The reason is that mind—our emotional/cognitive systems—and vision intersect in a limitless number of ways so that how and what each person sees is unique.

✦ Exercise 1: Observe the diversity of human eye movements.

- Study different eye movements as people read. How many ways do their eyes move across a printed page or computer screen?
- Ask people the meaning of "the man in the moon." Some see a rabbit, not a man. My husband cannot "see" the man in the moon (but he reads print much faster than I do). What are other different answers?
- Present a series of illusions to several people. Keep track of how many can "read" every illusion, some illusions, or none. *Note:* If everyone reads all, choose less familiar sets.

The differences are not as surprising as the many visual perceptions we agree on. For instance, we can recognize any letter of the alphabet no matter how fancifully or minimally it is elaborated.

*Interpreting What We See. Seeing* is a biological function. *Looking* is a cognitive act. Looking involves an effort to focus on an object in our direct line of sight or peripheral vision. We look in many ways.

- *Gaze*—look long and steadily, as children staring in toy store windows
- *Contemplate*—gaze with thoughtful attention, as children looking at Richard Scarry drawings
- *Glance*—look momentarily or in passing, as children becoming distracted when concentrating
- *Stare*—look intensely, possibly rudely, and perhaps in surprise or alarm, as 18-month-olds responding to the roar of a caged lion
- *Scan*—cast the eyes on every detail. *Note:* Children with weak or undeveloped scanning skills have great difficulty dealing with the printed page, either finding a particular item in a crowded visual field (e.g., detecting details in drawings by Mitsumasa Anno, the Japanese illustrator) or finding a word or phrase on a page of type.
- *Inspect*—look below the surface to uncover the full meaning, as Laura (page 27) looking at the watches
- *Behold*—fix in mind what is before the eyes, as children looking at still or moving images of action figures or fairy princesses
- *Survey*—comprehensively view a scene or text with exactness, as children meeting a challenge; for example: determining what lives in the soil at the base of the tree

- *Watch*—look over time and possibly warily, as a shy child considering whether to join an activity
- *Discern*—discriminate nuances, as toddlers refusing to eat oatmeal that does not look like their mother's
- *Observe*—look with thoughtful attention, as children examining realistic photographs of different life forms (babies and older) or Lego schematics (3 years and older)
- *Distinguish*—recognize by some outward sign or special mark, as children, from babyhood, responding to uniforms, flags, or other symbols that identify groups or nations
- *Discriminate*—look to see particular features: What is different about [a particular child] today? A new coat? A Band-Aid? A haircut? Feeling sad? Children often spot details adults miss.
- *Discover*—see what existed but was unknown, as spotting a gerbil toy or new plant added when children were not present
- *Detect*—perceive something faint, as children noticing a track made by an animal's footprint. Two 5-year-olds found a seed pod, believed it was an unknown species, and thought it could be named for them.
- *Ascertain*—examine or experiment in order to know for sure, as when adding different amounts of baking soda and vinegar and keeping track of the effects as you vary each trial
- *Expose*—visually uncover something not obvious, as Enid saying, "I think a fly landed here; I see a little black dot."

There are two points to the above list: one concerning teachers, the other, children. When teachers make a commitment to observe children through notes, photographs, video, or any other means, they have many ways of looking. Virtually all combine (1) directing one's attention; (2) engaging in cognitive acts such as comparing (that is, retrieving a stored memory), analyzing, interpreting, or synthesizing, to name merely four; and (3) feeling—emotion is the motivating factor that causes teachers first to look and then to act on what they observe.

When children look in some particular way, teachers can use a word that captures *precisely* how the child is looking: "Charles just *discovered* that a shell is missing from our collection." Or, "Nanette *detected* a tiny bud forming on the cyclamen." Giving children precise names for many ways to look enlarges their ability to observe with care, sparks interest in the world around them, and enlarges their cognitive repertoire.

✦ Exercise 2: Hone your observation skill.

On each of 17 days, practice one of the above 17 ways of looking at children.

- Reflect on your responses, noting particularly what mode(s) of looking enabled you to see things about children that had escaped your notice.
- Keep track of ways of looking that sharpen your understanding of children's behavior.

- Increase the effectiveness of observation by incorporating ways to look that provide the most insight about children.
- Engage colleagues in doing this exercise and share your findings.

*Tip:* Glancing enables you to continue a lesson with a small group while simultaneously monitoring the entire classroom.

✦ Exercise 3: Sharpen your ability to make comparisons.

- Choose two children who differ greatly.
- Watch them frequently for a week.
- Determine: Which ways of looking tell you the most about these children's behaviors?
- Reflect: Do different ways of looking change your understanding of what motivates these children's behaviors?
- Keep records of your changed perceptions to see your intentional, reflective capacities grow.

✦ Exercise 4: Hone children's awareness of how they are looking.

For a month, whenever you see a child looking in some particular way, make note of it and call it to the child's attention.

*Example 1:* "Jan, you just *distinguished* how *m* and *n* are different."

- Ask Jan to tell the class what she distinguished (or tell the class if Jan does not want to).
- Be sure to use the word *distinguish*.

*Example 2:* "Rob *ascertained* exactly how much water to put on the cactus so the water would not overflow."

- Use the same procedures as with Jan.

*Example 3:* "Henri, show us what you *detected* while digging."

- Use the word *detected* with the child and in reporting to the class.

---

**KEY POINTS:**
- Introducing children to an array of ways to look establishes dispositions to (1) observe carefully and (2) be excited by the world around us.
- You can significantly enlarge children's vocabulary by using a wide range of precise words for a common act, such as looking.

*Conveying an Intent.* *Conveying* means to use visual/cognitive/emotional signals to communicate something specific to an individual or group. Teachers convey:

- *Directions*—Store your work in the purple folder. Don't forget to wash your hands. Carry the pitcher with two hands.
- *Specific information*—This symbol makes the sound "ah." The author of the book is A. A. Milne. This is an oval.
- *Commands*—Scan the page and find a kitten. Close your eyes and don't peek. Discover something new in the classroom.
- *Approval*—Good noticing that Linda needed help! Nice expression of sympathy when your friend fell! You did the top button yourself!
- *Disapproval*—Don't stare at his crutches. Don't watch while she is crying. Don't laugh if someone falls.

The essence of conveyances is to express meaning. The following techniques are effective in conveying meaning to young children without words and mainly with your eyes.

1. *Point.* Using a prominent gesture, move your pointing finger into the child's direct line of sight. Then use your finger to direct the child's eyes to what you want her to see. Pointing is a universal human means of communicating. Infants share emotions soon after birth, and infant pointing can be seen as early as 3 months as a proto-linguistic act. By 9 to 12 months infants read others' intentions, and by 12 months infants point with what Tomasello and colleagues (Tomasello, Carpenter, & Liszkowski, 2007) call "shared intentionality" to inform, request, direct, or express feeling; or, in other words, to influence or share something with another person. Throughout life we use pointing to share information.
2. *Lead a child's eyes.* Catch a child's eyes with your own intent gaze and hold the child's eyes as you shift both your gazes to what you want the child to observe or enact.
   *Tip:* The more highly focused your intention, the more successfully you can lead a child's eyes.
3. *Stare.* With great interest, stare at what you want a child or group to notice. A staring person's gaze causes most people at any age to follow it. Notice this behavior when you are in a group.
4. *Focus.* Peer intently at an insect, a picture, or whatever you want children to notice. Your intensity rouses children's interest and tendency to imitate.
5. *Detect.* Pore minutely but sedately over whatever object you want children to study, then startle: Widen your eyes and register surprise at finding some particular thing. You are conveying how to examine something carefully in a way that children can imitate.
6. *Play Tom Sawyer.* If the reference is unfamiliar, read in *The Adventures of Tom Sawyer* (Twain, 1876/1936, pp. 23–29) the scene in which Tom whitewashes a fence (see Figure 2.4).

Figure 2.4. Tom Sawyer adopts a demeanor that makes others beg to become engaged in his work.

© MBI, Inc., reprinted by permission.

> Carry out a sequence of action.
> Pay utmost attention as you exaggerate every movement.
> Stand back and appreciate your result.
> Continue with enthusiasm.

Your attitude will arouse children's desire to perform the action; your exaggeration will help children remember the sequence of actions and techniques.

*Tip:* "Tom-Sawyering" is a good way to introduce something new that requires movement control, for example, using balance toys, take-aparts, 3-D puzzles, sharp-pointed pencils, delicate markers, and hard-to-carry items.

✦ Exercise 1: Increase your ability to use your eyes to convey information facilely.

Practice each of the techniques on page 46. Reflect: Does increasing the ways in which you look enlarge your children's "content, narrative, theory-making, or skill"—Gardner's (2004, p. 61) words for mental representations?

✦ Exercise 2: Build children's repertoire of different ways to look.

Once you have mastered different ways of looking, introduce them gradually to your class. Encourage children to notice the differences in what they see when they look in different ways.

✦ Exercise 3: Build children's skill in looking in different ways.

Play looking games. At different morning meetings, tell children:

- "Gaze out the window sometime today. Later we'll have a conversation about what you noticed."
- "There is something new in the classroom. If you discover it, come and whisper to me. We'll all have a conversation about it later."
- "Glance at the trees outside. At meeting we'll talk about what your glance revealed."

After children have had different experiences gazing, discovering, or glancing, have a conversation, either one-on-one, with a small group, or with the entire class, about their reactions to these different ways of looking.

*Tip:* Be sure to engage in a whole-class conversation to bring acts of looking to everyone's attention.

After playing looking games for several weeks, reflect on whether the children:

- Are more focused
- Pay more attention to their surroundings
- Notice subtleties you might not have expected them to see or you might have missed
- Use more words to describe ways of looking

Once children use the words *gaze, discover,* and *glance* spontaneously, introduce another three ways of looking.

## The Power of a Look

I have observed teachers in crowded school corridors use a look to suppress a child's incorrigible behavior. The look is powerful—commanding, directive, forceful, and, sometimes, withering. No child failed to respond.

In different cultures, certain looks are considered rude—staring, making direct eye contact, watching, or gazing. Ask parents of different cultures to help you understand their culture's different ways of looking. What ways are rude, common, effective in stemming children's disruptive behavior, or special in other ways? Ask whether this particular family or its native region has its own ways of looking or customs that involve how, when, at what, and for how long people look. Invite parents from other cultures to participate when you use looking exercises and to demonstrate their culture's (or family's) looks. If you notice cultural differences, talk with parents about them. Converse with children about other cultures' behaviors and how they are similar or different from ours.

> **KEY POINTS:**
> - The eyes are a powerful tool for expressing intention.
> - Analyzing the effects of using your eyes in different ways is a reflective process.

## INTENTIONAL FACIAL EXPRESSIONS

Crying, laughing, and other emotions that we see in facial expressions "are hard-wired into the brain. They are present at or appear soon after birth without any training" (Ratey, 2002, p. 228). Facial expression often controls meaning. "Wonderful!" said with a smile conveys approval. "Wonderful!" said with a smirk implies disdain. Darwin remarks on the involuntary nature of facial expression:

> Seeing how ancient these expressions are, it is no wonder that they are difficult to conceal.—a man insulted may forgive his enemy & not wish to strike him, but he will find it far more difficult to look tranquil.—He may despise a man & say nothing, but without a most distinct will, he will find it hard to keep his lip from stiffening over his canine teeth. (Darwin, 1838, p. 93)

One of Darwin's great gifts was his unusual capacity to notice subtle detail in whatever he studied.

### Confronting Cultural Differences

Cultural differences trigger what Gardner (2004) calls "intuitive theories of mind"; these theories exist everywhere and are attempts to make sense of the world even though they may not be correct. Here is one of Gardner's examples: "If you look like me, then your mind is like mine and you are good. If you look different from me, then your mind must differ as well, and we are enemies." This theory supports prejudice. "Early theories prove especially difficult to alter" (p. 57).

The jury is out on whether humans are born with a disposition toward prejudice or learn from prejudiced people that it is "wrong" for children who look different to be friends. My grandson Sheppy, age 5 at the time, and I were at the airport meeting our cousin and her toddlers, who needed car seats. Sheppy knew we also were meeting the toddlers' father on a later plane. The rental car representative—a Black man with the darkest skin—helped the toddlers' mother install the seats. Shep, mistaking the representative for the toddlers' father, greeted him with a huge smile, big hug, kiss, and no recognition that the toddlers' mother was White and the man was Black.

Whether innate or learned, prejudice is best confronted in early childhood. The most effective lessons grow from teachers' thoughtful listening and observation in order to:

- Distinguish "overt behavior—what one actually says or does at a given moment . . . [from an] underlying belief system" (Gardner, 2004, p. 58)
- Erase biases before they become "engraved" (p. 58)

Bell (2014) describes 1st-grader Madisyn Jones, "a typically quiet little girl," on seeing the miniature train exhibit at the Muncie (Indiana) Children's Museum, who asked, "Why aren't there any Black people in the train exhibit?" The student teacher "pointed to a figurine of a darker complexion and said, 'Do you think that one could be African American?' 'No, it doesn't look like me,' Madisyn answered." A big discussion followed. "Yeah," said one of Madisyn's classmates, "we should be able to see ourselves in the train exhibit because it's not fair that I can't see anybody that has my skin or someone that looks like me." The children wrote to the museum and embarked on a search, at first unsuccessful, for miniature Black figures. There were none in Muncie; a set they found online turned out to be prisoners in orange suits. Finally they found "people of color engaging in various recreational activities and wearing a variety of clothing, including business attire," which Madisyn and her classmates used to revise the exhibit (pp. 56–58). The best antibias lessons are not in curriculum guides but lie in children's own experiences in environments where adults listen, note children's observations, discuss them with the full class, hear how children would right wrongs, and then, with the children, take the actions that children themselves suggest.

---

**KEY POINTS:**

- Changing only children's (or one's own) words and actions may have no effect on underlying beliefs.
- Teachers whose culture differs from their children's must be vigilant in noting children's observation of and reactions to social injustice.
- Children's actions or comments provide the best material for lessons.
- Intuitive theories of mind are "prevalent among young people everywhere, and none of them proves easy to change" (Gardner, 2004, p. 55).

---

### Facial Expressions and Feelings

Facial expressions can be more truthful than words. They convey intention, and we *read* other people's meaning in their faces. How can we intentionally use facial expressions to inform, evoke, shape, or express feelings?

Infants are prewired to recognize a human face. Elizabeth Spelke, director of the Laboratory for Developmental Studies in the Psychology Department at Harvard, is a preeminent researcher on the infant brain and behavior. She calls abilities that are present at birth "core knowledge" (Spelke & Kinzler, 2007). Ratey (2002) says, "We come into the world expecting to see human faces and ready to respond with our own prewired facial expressions" (p. 300).

Of utmost importance to infants' development is the bonding between mother and infant through reciprocal facial interactions. That is, mother initiates contact, for example, smiles; the infant responds; mother responds in turn; and the engagement continues. It is in this earliest give-and-take that infants learn to regulate their emotions and develop trust. If the mother intuitively understands how to disengage, the infant also learns social boundaries. This early communication builds the neural circuitry that is part of language and that psychologists call "theory of mind," the understanding that others have separate mental capacities and use their minds intentionally to contemplate, gaze with thoughtful attention, and carry out planned actions. Autistic children lack socially integrating skills such as awareness of others' minds or recognition of what one's face shows about one's feeling (Feuerstein, Falik, Feuerstein, & Rand, 2006; Gelman & Au, 1996; Greenspan & Shanker, 2004; Spelke, 2002).

## Reading Facial Expressions

Facial expressions are "important social cues that the child must learn in order to navigate the environments of day care, school, and playground" (Ratey, 2002, p. 302). Facial expressions are numerous and varied. Common facial expressions can be read by a careful observer.

A short inventory of facial expressions, with examples, includes:

- Furrowing the brow, a sign of worry or deep thought—when children whose mothers value cleanliness get mud on their clothes
- Raising eyebrows, a questioning expression—children observing a magnet for the first time
- Squinting, an aspect of concentration—2½-year-olds working intently at buttoning
- Wrinkling the nose, to show surprise, uncertainty, or disgust—any age person looking at images of snakes
- Curling the lip, to show dislike or disrespect. (See www.thesaurus.com/browse/curling%20one's%20lip?s=t for 47 synonyms for curling one's lip.)
- Pursing the lips, shows disapproval or distaste—a baby spitting out spinach
- Biting the lips, indicates fear—backing away from the source of a loud noise
- Turning the mouth up or down, displays happiness or sadness. Upward positions can be part of laughter; downward positions, like a grimace, can show fear, displeasure, or disgust.
- Setting the mouth, indicates resolve or stubbornness—a child refusing to do something
- Jutting the chin, expresses aggression—children having an altercation
- Pouting, a manipulative expression to get one's way—acting petulant, threatening tears, crying to get someone's sympathy
- Blushing, an involuntary response, reflects embarrassment—a shy child unwilling to perform
- Scrunching the entire face, shows extreme displeasure and may precede an emotional outburst—having a tantrum
- Sticking out the tongue, a strong oral response, which may occur unconsciously when young children concentrate intently, or may be done consciously to show disdain as in directing the sing-song-y "nah-nah-nah-nah-nah-nah" at another child

These mainly involuntary acts provide obvious clues to someone's feelings. Young children rarely disguise their feelings by controlling their facial expressions, as older children learn to do. In a comprehensive review of 20 years worth of studies, Keltner and Ekman found that "select emotions have distinct facial expressions [and] more emotions may be expressed than previously thought" (2003, p. 412). Psychologists who study facial expression recognize micro-movements of the facial muscles that reveal emotions, even in those practiced at disguising their feelings.

*Tip:* Enlarge the above list of facial expressions through your own observation.

✦ Exercise: Increase your awareness of the meanings of facial expressions.

Photograph children's faces when their expression reveals an intense feeling. Reflect on the photos:

- What was the child doing?
- Was she or he alone or with another child(ren)?
- What actions or interchanges provoked the facial expression?

Train yourself to be aware of children's facial expressions as an indication of their state of mind. *Note:* The same facial expression may mean different things at different times or in different children.

---

**KEY POINTS:**

- Learning to read facial expressions and developing expertise in making facial expressions are important skills in intentional teaching.
- Reflecting on the meaning of facial expressions brings new layers of understanding to teacher/child interactions.
- Teaching children to read facial expressions develops their awareness of others, one aspect of being empathetic.

---

## CONCLUSION

Intentional/reflective teachers master the use of subtly distinct movements that comprise a host of powerful techniques. When used with intention, teachers' movements stimulate children's use of nuanced movements and thus expand the cognitive and emotional capacities of the senses, actions, mind, and emotions. When children are engaged in activities that challenge them to perceive nuance and to express themselves in shades of meaning, their minds, movements, emotions, and perceptions become integrated. Teachers can develop the skill to be both intentional and reflective in using nuanced expressions with subtle distinctions. Equally important, teachers can help children learn these skills.

# CHAPTER 3

# The Voice and Hand in Intentional/Reflective Teaching

It takes the human voice to infuse words with deeper meaning.

—Maya Angelou

> **TECHNIQUE 3**
> Use language exuberantly: Build on children's love of
> language by playing with words and hands to express meaning.

In Chapter 2 we looked at micro-actions of the body—movement that conveys demeanor, eyes that *look* in numerous ways, and facial expressions that reveal meaning and emotion. We considered the importance of micro-actions in intentional/reflective teaching. In this chapter we first explore multiple uses of language, with an emphasis on understanding the human voice, using the sounds and structure of the English language, and playing language games. We consider the vocal system, which, like the body's other systems, is a complex, sophisticated assembly of moving parts and of interactions throughout the brain. We harness this system in using our voice mindfully. We then study the hands by looking at American Sign Language as a means of communication. And we read a parable about the consequences of losing one of the senses.

We begin here by pondering the conclusion of the book *The Hand* by the "Hand Doc," neurologist Frank R. Wilson. His thinking sets the stage for many of the ideas in this chapter:

> Self-generated movement is the foundation of thought and willed action, the underlying mechanism by which the physical and psychological coordinates of the self come into being. For humans, the hand has a special role and status in the organization of movement and in the evolution of human cognition. (1998, p. 291)

## INTENTIONAL AND REFLECTIVE USE OF THE VOICE

The structure and physiology of speech involve how words convey meaning and what makes speech audible. I suggest games to help children decipher word meanings and use their voices with intention as they build awareness of words' meanings and sounds. Games are meant to be used often with the full class, small groups, and individual children, even several times a day. Games are designed to be short—2 to 3 minutes at most. As they reflect on the games, teachers will observe growth in children's language capacities.

## How English Works—A Combinatorial Language

Phonemes and morphemes are keys to how the English language works. Here I examine the roles of phonemes and morphemes in children's ability to use English facilely.

It is estimated that U.S. college graduates know about 60,000 words. Imagine having to make a different sound for every word! The English language works because the brain uses phonemes—44 sounds represented by 26 letters—to utter or think all English words. And the brain uses morphemes—bits of sound that contain meaning—to understand speech, writing, and thought. Because phonemes and morphemes can be combined in endless ways, psycholinguist Stephen Pinker (1994) refers to English as a "combinatorial" system that is economical: With merely 44 sounds we can express an infinite number of ideas.

The English language is also efficient: With merely one, two, or three letters, we can change a word's meaning. Add the morpheme "a": The word *typical* becomes *atypical* and changes to the opposite meaning. Or tack the morpheme "un" on the front of a word: It means the *removal* of a part or mass—uninstall, unearth, unhook. The morpheme "ed" at the end of many verbs means an action has been completed—cooked, canned, crated. The three-letter morpheme "dis" at the beginning means something is taken apart—disconnect, disassociate, dismantle.

Consider the 11-syllable, 28-letter word *antidisestablishmentarianism*; it means a movement against those who want to separate church and state.

- **Establish**—bring together
- **Dis**establish—separate
- Disestablish**ment**—the fact of the separation
- Disestablishment**arian**—a person who believes in this separation
- Disestablishmentarian**ism**—many people's belief in the separation—the morpheme "ism" turns an idea into a movement
- **Anti**disestablishmentarianism—being *against* those who are for the separation

The meaning of the base word, *establish*, changes each time one of five morphemes is added. But if you know the base word and the meaning of each morpheme, you can figure out this long word's meaning.

Now consider the 14-syllable, 34-letter word *supercalifragilisticexpialidocious*. The mixture of unrelated words (super, fragil) with nonsense syllables (cali, expi) shows that this word is made-up. Only the first and last morphemes—"super" and "ious"—convey meaning, but without a base word, the long string is nonsense—beloved by children because it is used in a cheery song about the ultimate nanny, Mary Poppins. The combinatorial aspect of English enables us to distinguish real words from nonsense, and to extend words, twist or change meanings, and grow the language endlessly.

*Teachers' game:* Play with English's combinatorial aspect. Find a dozen or more morphemes that, when added to a word, change its meaning. For each morpheme, find a dozen or so examples of changed words and their meanings. Make the game harder: Find words (like *atypical*) where adding a one-letter morpheme makes a new word with the opposite meaning.

*Note:* Playing with the language makes teaching literacy more enjoyable and intentional.

Contrast English's 26-letter alphabet with Chinese, which has about 5,000 "letters." They are *not* phonetic but must be memorized. A person needs to know about 3,000 characters to read a Chinese newspaper, and Chinese college graduates are tested on about 7,000 characters.

## How English Works—Phonemes and Morphemes

I am thankful my native language is English. Because the structure of English is invisible, it is unlikely I would have learned to speak English as a second language. It is also unlikely I would have understood English grammar had I not studied Latin, where rigidly defined word endings make the structure clear. Understanding phonemes and morphemes helps to unpack meaning in English. Here I explore how English-language words are spoken and voiced. Throughout I suggest exercises or games to play with children to develop basic literacy skills.

*Phonemes.* Put simply, phonemes enable us to speak. Almost from birth, infants practice making phonemes. First they isolate and repeat vowel sounds and, at around 11 months, intentionally say their first meaningful word. In the ensuing months, babies become noun fiends, hungry to know the name of everything they see. I watched two children self-scaffold their use of language through noun hunger. My niece, Alexandra Cruickshank, learned the names of 31 fish. My grandson Sheppy asked and remembered the names for over 20 heavy construction vehicles. The intense quest for nouns, at around age 18 months, is a step in language acquisition.

In English, phonemes assemble with extreme precision into either meaningful bits or words. Consider: Knowing the sounds *p, o,* and *t,* we can say the words "pot" or "top," choosing specific phonemes and ordering them so that we boil water in the "pot" or put the "top" on the "pot." We know we cannot cook in a "top;" nor can we put something on "pot." "Pot" and "top" are morphemes and thereby embody specific meaning. As Steven Pinker (1994) says of the following three morphemes, "*Dog bites man* differs from *Man bites dog,* and believing in God is different from believing in Dog" (p. 158). The difference between phonemes (sound) and morphemes (meaning) is that while individual letters or letter combinations can be assembled in countless ways, the meaning of morphemes remains constant.

English homonyms are curve balls. The brain stores words in two ways, by how they sound (lexical) and by what they mean (semantic) (Pinker, 1994). Psycholinguists are not sure whether children learn a second meaning for a homonym more easily than they learn a novel word (Storkel & Maekawa, 2005). This point aside, by age 3 or 4, children can distinguish homonyms, words that sound alike—*Which* mean *witch*? A *male* brings our *mail*. Can you *hear* from *here*? *Flu flew* through the city—and readily grasp the meaning (semantics).

**Speech and Comprehension.** Consider: We can think without speaking but cannot speak without thinking. (Well, some do, but we have names for them!) To communicate by speaking, we must make phonemes audible and *combine* individual bits into a long stream of sound. To comprehend, we must do the opposite: *separate* a long stream of sound (phonemes) into individual bits of meaning (morphemes). As Pinker (1994) says:

> Speech is a river of breath, bent into hisses and hums by the soft flesh of the mouth and throat. The problems . . . are digital-to-analog conversion when the talker encodes strings of discrete symbols [the phonemes] into a continuous stream of sound [the morphemes that make up words and sentences], and analog-to-digital conversion when the listener decodes continuous speech back into discrete symbols [phonemes and morphemes]. (p. 159)

To converse, the speaker's brain must:

- Contain an inventory of phonemes,
- Sample and manipulate what it wants to say to make recognizable words, then
- Make the phonemes pronounceable, and finally
- Speak them (Pinker, 1994).

Among the world's languages there are thousands of phonemes. All are formed by different combinations of five speech organs (throat, nose cavities, mouth cavity, lips, tongue), the range of movements these organs can make, and how movements combine. In English, gleaning meaning from phonemes is difficult because "actual sounds are different in different contexts" (Pinker, 1994, p. 187): *d* can sound like *t*—example: *snapped*; or consonants can change the way vowels sound—example: *rage* and *ram*. The reason is that the muscles that enable us to speak assume different shapes depending on what sounds precede and follow one another. It is no wonder that children take several years to learn to speak articulately. It is evidence of humans' innate capacity for language that we master such complexities.

✦ Exercise: Experience how hard it is for an adult to reproduce a sound in a foreign language.

Invite a child who speaks a foreign language to stump you by saying a word in her own language that you must reproduce. The children in your class may be able to do this more easily because younger children are more facile at imitating the sounds of speech.

*Tip:* If children make fun of a foreign child's speech, use this game to show that the foreign speaker is as clever as English speakers, only different.

Psycholinguists agree: The abilities to hear phonemes, to combine them into morphemes that have meaning, and to use them to send, receive, and make meaning from sound are hard-wired human capacities. They are part of core knowledge, the brain's basic equipment, and will develop in reasonably predictable ways from birth through age 4 or 5, regardless of children's native culture.

**Voicing.** Voicing refers to the vibrating sound waves that "the vocal tract sculpts into vowels and consonants" (Pinker, 1994, p. 160). Voicing is possible because when the diaphragm moves, air is compressed into different volumes, then squeezed into different shapes by nasal and mouth cavities, and shaped further by the tongue and lips. Example: The rhyme, "How now brown cow" is voiced so that the *ow* sounds are made by rounded lips forming circles, and deep, regular breathing. The *ow* sound contrasts with the line, "grazing in the green, green grass," where the mouth forms two parallel lines on *graz* and two parallel lines that are closer together on *ee* (green), and a third different shape on *grass*. Speech organs change position or shape for each different syllable or word. These moves are possible because the vocal system, represented in Figure 3.1, is capable of complex interactions with both the brain's word-making/retrieval systems and the mind's capacity to express ideas.

When teachers intentionally emphasize the musculature that is integral to voicing, they help children (especially those who have trouble articulating) perceive how different sounds are made. When teachers exaggerate the movements of the vocal system in a game-like way, children are delighted: They enjoy aligning a precise movement with a precise sound.

Figure 3.1.
The vocal system

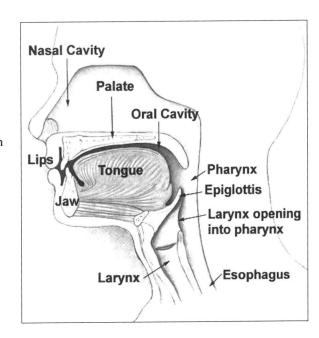

*Games with Voicing.* There is no limit to the games you can create to play with children almost from birth. Here are examples for children from age 2 on.

✦ Exercise 1: Feel the muscles that make sounds distinct.

Say a word with sounds in which lips, throat, or diaphragm make distinct movements (see examples in Exercise 2). Have children repeat the word, then feel lips, then throat, then diaphragm, as you repeat the word together. Ask children to describe what they feel.

✦ Exercise 2: Use the muscles that make sounds distinct.

Build children's sound vocabulary using a collection of words that require the mouth to assume different shapes. The purposes are for children to:

1. Practice hearing and making a wide range of sounds
2. Distinguish individual sounds
3. Utter sounds articulately

*Examples:* Moon, wire, pickle, bumpity, sneeze, giggle, amazing, zigzag, popsicle, lonesome, squeal, yoo-hoo, jittery, doodle, blowhole, squish, tuba, wiggle, thwack, chopsticks, singular, cackle, frostbite, hip-hop, even-Steven, lollipop, quicksand, abracadabra, shipshape, chatter, prickly pear, Yosemite.

Start the game with a single word. After a day or two, when all children articulate the word well, add a word. The game should be very short, less than a minute. Keep adding words as the children master pronunciations. After 6 or 7 words, start a new group of words to keep children alert. Important: The purpose is *not* to teach vocabulary. Unless a child asks, do not define the words. If a child asks, keep the definition short and simple. The purposes are to help children fall in love with the variety of sounds in our language and masterfully articulate sound combinations.

*Tips:*

• Draw out the long vowel sounds: Moooooon. Sneeeeeeze.
• Hit the consonants precisely, as if your vocal movements were striking a small drum.
• Exaggerate the movement of your lips.
• Emphasize the shape and position of your tongue body and tongue tip.
• Communicate an awareness of your breathing.
• Savor the distinctiveness of each word.

If children laugh at a word, enjoy laughing with them. *Play* with the sounds of words.

✦ Exercise 3: Enjoy sounds that abound in children's literature and common expressions.

Read aloud (or recite by memory) from the vast collection of traditional English sayings and verses. They are traditional because their sounds are pleasing, amusing, strange, or humorous, and have thrilled generations of children. Let your voice emphasize the different organs of speech:

- "Park the car in Harvard yard." (Say this with a broad Boston accent: "Pack the caa [as in "cab"] in Haavad yaad.")—regionalism
- "Y'all comin' back tuh see us?"— regionalism
- "Pussy said to the owl, 'You elegant fowl, how charmingly sweet you sing . . .'" (Eugene Field)
- "The rain is raining all around . . ." (Robert Louis Stevenson)
- "Hickory, dickory dock . . ." (Mother Goose)

*Note:* I've used a few words of the first stanza; read children each full poem. Bring Mother Goose into the classroom. Use its time-honored rhymes to help children learn 1) the nuances of clear pronunciation and 2) the relation between voicing (use of the various organs that make sound) and pronouncing (use of various muscles to correctly produce words) the 44 (some linguists say 46) sounds in the English language.

✦ Exercise 4: The vowel sounds—numerous games to play with the sounds of vowels.

- Use a consistent sound, such as the long sounds when vowels "say their names": *ay* (examples: gate, aim, say, lake, hey, neigh); *eee* (examples: free, Marie, flea, either, donkey); *i* (examples: high, my, ride, spied, eye, buy); *o* (examples: go, boat, snow, bureau, home, oh, sold); *u* (examples: blue, hoop, pool, chew, glue, do, new). Say each word in turn, drawing out the sound for several seconds. Then have the children say each word with you several times.
- Many days later, play the same game but use the short sounds of the vowels: *a* (examples: hat, wham, ax, pack, flat); *e* (examples: bet, men, pet, step, flex); *i* (examples: hit, him, pin, flit, sip); *o* (examples: hot, palm, top, cot, sock); *u* (examples: but, rub, cup, bump, slug).
- Make a vowel sound, such as short *a* (hat); have the children make it after you; make it together several times. Then embed the sound in a string of words: at, bat, brat, cat, chat, fat, flat (and so on). On different days, use different sounds (*bet* and a string of words; *it* and a string of words, and so forth).

*Tips:* These games are meant to be played:

- Often, at least once or twice a day
- For 2 or 3 minutes at most
- With the whole class, a small group, or a single child
- So children isolate vowels' and consonants' individual sounds and thereby form clear speech patterns

Do *not* give lessons on vowels! If the games are short and varied, and have content or sounds that tickle the ear, children will fall in love with words and sounds and thus have a leg up on learning to read. The games are especially useful in helping foreign-language speakers become facile at manipulating the sounds of the English language or in ameliorating speech problems.

Explain the games and play them with parents. Ask parents whether children play the games on their own; if so, what do parents hear? Reflect: Is there a connection between what you do in class and what parents report?

## Using Speech Effectively

Of particular interest to intentional teachers are the many ways of manipulating the voice to communicate meaning. Here are several, with ways of using each as a game.

- Stress—how a syllable, word, or phrase is emphasized in contrast to the sounds that precede or follow. Use familiar words so the children can show what they know: You use the *wrong* emphasis and they correct you.
  - ➤ *Game:* Intentionally stress the wrong syllable in a familiar word or sentence—Hide the en-VEL-ope under a table. Time to eat car-ROTS. Insist there is nothing wrong. Pretend that you don't understand when children correct you.
- Prosody—variation in inflection, dynamics, speed, timbre, and so forth that "infuses speech with emotional content and often influences its meaning" (Mithen, 2006, p. 55). Examples: I would LOVE (stressed and drawn out) to see the cow jump over the moon. (In an extremely quiet voice) Let's be quiet as mice until it's time to hunt for (very loud) CHEESE! Trade sentences with colleagues and use Mother Goose rhymes to expand your list. If the children particularly enjoy certain sentences, reflect on why.
  - ➤ *Game:* Make your voice go up when it should go down and vice versa—Good morning? (a rising tone like a question). As rapidly as possible: I'm going to sneeze so I'd better hold a tissue in front of my (make a make-believe sneeze). Crying (as with tears): "I'm so happy to be sucking a lollypop." The more humorous your examples and the more the children laugh, correct your intentional mistakes, and decipher the meaning, the more they will enjoy language, which is the purpose of this game.
- Syntax—how we order words in a sentence and combine thoughts. Classic example: The difference between Dog bites man and Man bites dog. The first is commonplace; the second, newsworthy (Pinker, 1994, p. 75).
  - ➤ *Game:* Mix up word order but pretend you are speaking normally: Let's our coats in their cubbies hang. Let's drink the milk and open the carton. Eat dessert, then we'll have lunch. The aims are for children to:
    - Be word police
    - Revel in telling you that you are not making sense

- – Laugh at your absurdities
- – Show that they know how language works
- Parsing—a mental process "involved in sentence comprehension . . . [in] determining who did what to whom from the information in a sentence" (Pinker, 1994, p. 511).
  - ➤ *Game:* Mix up direct and indirect object:
    - – Roll him to the ball.
    - – Give a dog to the bone.
    - – Hand me to a napkin.
  - ➤ *Game:* Use the wrong word:
    - – Let's rain to the store.
    - – Daddy's umbrella-ing the grass.
    - – Tommy is buttoning his teeth.
    - – Sweep the crumbs onto the table.
    - – How slow can the plane fly?
    - – The butterfly's wings are flapping noisily.

As you play the games, pretend there is nothing wrong in what you are saying. Invent names for the games or encourage the children to do so: Silly Sounds, Inside-out Sentences, Word Police, Upside-down Talk. "Riffing" on English builds children's enjoyment of and competence with the language.

- Pitch (sometimes called intonation)—controls emphasis, emotion, and meaning; determines loudness and softness; defines tranquil or agitated expressions.
  - ➤ *Game:* Vary pitch:
    - – Start a sentence very softly and end loud.
    - – Make your voice very loud in the middle of the sentence and bring down the tone at the end.
    - – Speak in a fast, nervous squeak.
    - – Announce an emergency in tones that are deep, long, and drawn out: The milk truck broke down and milk will be very late today.

Playing with pitch builds the capacity to speak with expression and changes speech patterns from singsong, atonal, or nasal so children learn to color their speech with tone.

- Amplification—the development or expansion of a sound, producing different vowel sounds such as *ah* or *aw*, *uh* or *eh*. Amplifying requires combining all five speech organs: throat, nose cavities, mouth cavity, lips, and tongue. Consonants form when a barrier (the tip or body of the tongue, the lips) obstructs the air.
  - ➤ *Game:* Mix up sounds:
    - – Switch sounds s and sh: Sut the pairsh of shishorsh and shtick them in the bashket.
    - – Switch sounds t and m: Tother gom pomamoes to eam with dinner.

The purpose is, through humor and analysis, for children to become facile in hearing and speaking the sounds in more and more words.

- Rhyming, the exact correspondence in sound and stress of two 1-syllable words (hat/cat), 2-syllable words in which the last syllable is stressed (upset/forget), or entire longer words (breakable/shakable, hickory/ dickory, higgildy/piggildy, banister/canister, Beverly/cleverly, cheeriness/dreariness).
  - ➤ *Game:* Choose a simple 1-syllable sound (*at, em, up, ix, off,* etc.) and make every possible 1-syllable combination. Examples:
    - At: bat, brat, cat, chat, drat, fat, flat, gnat, hat, mat, pat, rat, sat, scat, slat, splat, stat, tat, that, vat. Spelling and meaning are irrelevant. The purpose is learning to isolate the sounds in common words. Do not turn this game into a vocabulary lesson.
  - ➤ *Game:* (1) Say any 2- or 3-syllable sound (even, sister, utterly)—it does not have to be a word; (2) in order from *a* to *z*, precede each sound with every consonant that will make a pronounceable word or sound (ignore meaning!); (3) add a random ending sound, for example:
    - ly: utterly: butterly, chutterly, clutterly, crutterly, cutterly, flutterly, frutterly, glutterly, grutterly, gutterly, mutterly, nutterly, plutterly, prutterly, putterly, rutterly, sutterly, scutterly, shutterly, splutterly, strutterly, stutterly, tutterly, trutterly, twutterly, etc.

Some of the words are hard to say because some of the vowel/consonant blends are rarely, if ever, used. The purposes are *not vocabulary expansion,* but (1) learning precise articulation, (2) stringing sounds together, and (3) distinguishing sounds and blends in order to reproduce them.

*Tip:* Going through the alphabet yields more possible combinations.

- Alliteration, use of the same kinds of sounds at the beginning of a series of words, often in a poem.
  - ➤ Example 1: "James, James, Morrison, Morrison, Weatherby, George Dupree . . ." (A. A. Milne, 1924/1950)
  - ➤ Example 2: "By the shores of Gitchee Gumee, By the shining Big-Sea-Water . . ." (H. W. Longfellow, 1855/2003)
  - ➤ Example 3: "Jellical cats come out tonight . . ." (T. S. Eliot, 1939/1982)
  - ➤ Example 4: "Rats! They fought the dogs and killed the cats and bit the babies in the cradles . . ." (R. Browning, 1888)
  - ➤ Example 5: "When I was sick and lay a-bed I had two pillows at my head . . ." (R. L. Stevenson, 1885/1944)
  - ➤ Example 6: "So the sun came up and the sun went down. So summer changed from green to brown." (J. Ciardi, 1963)

*Note:* If the poems are short, as in examples 1, 3, and 5 above, recite the entire poem. Otherwise, recite two or three stanzas. Read some of the English language's great poems. If you have children from foreign-speaking families, invite them to read poems or traditional children's rhymes in their language and from their culture. It is not necessary to translate. Children can appreciate rhyme and meter in any language. The purpose is to expose children to the range of sound, the richness of language, and its vast ways of expressing ideas.

- Metaphor, use of one word to mean another without using the words *like* or *as*. Examples:
  - ➤ He has a golden heart.
  - ➤ Her teeth are pearls.
  - ➤ His eyes are ice.
  - ➤ "The fog came on little cat feet . . ." (Sandburg, 1916)

Tell children these are metaphors, and invite them to make metaphors and tell you the meaning. If you use the word *metaphor*, the brain will categorize this type of speech pattern. Humans use metaphor extensively. Current research suggests a strong relationship between the use of metaphor and regions of the brain that process sensations (Lacey, Stilla, & Sathian, 2012). Metaphor is so common that we are unaware of the extent to which the senses influence speech. Examples:

- Sense of touch—a scratchy voice
- Sense of taste—a sour note
- Sense of smell—a burning remark
- Sense of hearing—a brassy manner
- Sense of sight—a sea of green

Encouraging children to use metaphor enlarges their capacity to express themselves in varied, picturesque, and original ways.

- Idioms, common sayings in which word combinations bear no relation to the meaning of individual words. Examples:
  - ➤ He is a dog in a manger.
  - ➤ She slept like a log.
  - ➤ Time flew.
  - ➤ All that glitters is not gold.
  - ➤ That takes the cake.
  - ➤ He let the cat out of the bag.
  - ➤ You're pulling my leg.

Because English is heavily salted with idiomatic expressions, learning their meanings increases children's comprehension.

- Analogy, comparing two things using the word *like* or *as*. Examples:
  - ➤ She is as stubborn as a mule.
  - ➤ They are rich like King Midas.
  - ➤ He runs as fast as a deer.
  - ➤ It's like finding a needle in a haystack.

Have fun as you make a game of analogies. Children love to play with analogies. Game variation on analogies:

Teacher: "Blue is to sky as green is to _____." Children supply the word.

*Examples:*

- Fast is to run as slow is to _____.
- Fast is to _____ as slow is to walk.
- Dark is to night as _____ is to day.
- Dark is to _____ as light is to day.
- _____ is to night as bright is to day.
- Huge is to elephant as _____ is to mouse.
- Huge is to _____ as _____ is to mouse.
  Challenge children to say either the noun or the adjective. Nouns are easier.

*Tips:*

1. Do not name the parts of speech.
2. Don't correct children's mistakes. Simply move to another example and another child. In time, children correct themselves or learn from other children.
3. Vary the examples, as shown above. It is easier for children to supply the adjective when the noun is given and much easier to fill in only one blank. Save the harder versions for when children are facile using analogies.

The purpose is not to elicit "right answers" but for children to use language as they use clay, as an open-ended, versatile, malleable "material." Making analogies enables teachers to hear what children know, how large their vocabulary is, and what attributes they associate with nouns.

- Chant or call, which uses the voice in a dropping third (understood in music as the fifth note of a scale followed by the third note). Example: Nan (high)-cy (low)! Where are (high) you (low). Children love hearing their names chanted. One-syllable names can be split by holding the vowel sound for a few seconds. Examples: Bob: Baah (high)-ob (low); Dan: Daaa (high)-an (low).
- For a full day, chant the children's names when you address them.

The purpose is to attune children's ears to pitch, a fundamental capacity of the human voice. The game can help children learn to use the voice with increased range. When teachers chant, children listen with increased attention.

*Tip:* Chant when you want to quiet the class as you make a transition from a raucous to a calm activity. Examples: Time to come to meeting. Wash your hands for lunch.

*Tip:* Be sure that routines are well-established before chanting transition instructions. Examples:

- Putting work away before meetings
- Limiting the number of children (in the bathroom, at the sink, wherever)
- Getting coats
- Singing a simple tune with children's names. Example, to the tune of "A tisket, a tasket": Alonzo's shirt is red today. Shameka has some new shoes. Isaiah's eating cheese and bread. Dottie's sipping cold milk. *Note:* Fit the words you use by stretching or compressing the syllables or slightly altering the tune, whichever is easier.

The purpose is to make routines varied and playful, and thereby focus children's attention.

The more word games teachers play with children:

- The better children become at hearing individual sounds, blends, rhymes, and other forms of speech.
- The larger children's vocabulary grows.
- The more facilely children use the syntax and grammar of English.
- The more readily children use metaphor, analogy, and idioms.
- The more poetry children carry through life.

Manipulating the voice arrests children's attention, keeps them focused, fosters literacy, engages cognitive skills, and provides emotional pleasure.

✦ Exercise: Make games with phonemes and morphemes a regular part of each day.

For a week, vocalize in one of the above ways every day for a couple of minutes with the full class, individuals, and small groups of children. After a month or so, reflect on whether the children's vocabulary and their ability to speak articulately have increased. Consider which games are the most fun for the children and which do most to build their language prowess.

---

**KEY POINTS:**

- Language is complex. Playing with language breaks down the complexity.
- Frequently playing short language games builds children's love of sounds and words.
- There is no end to the variety of language games you can make up.
- Repetition of the games enables children to master rhyming, isolate letters, pronounce blends, grasp meaning, speak colorfully, and a multitude of other functions that define literacy.

## Summary

Preschool years are the optimum time to develop children's love of language. The first 4 years are a sensitive period for language acquisition. The games I suggest should be played with the full class, small groups, and individual children. Because most of the games are auditory, when you play with small groups or individuals, other children will absorb whatever you do. Ears do not have lids; children hear and learn even when not directly involved. Repetition, brevity, and enjoyment are critical.

If teachers fall in love with the wonders and playfulness of the English language, they will transmit their feelings to children. The games are not a "curriculum" to be done on schedule, "covered," and left as you move on to the next item. The games are exercises that bear daily repetition because they address the deep structure of language in the brain. Be intentional in using the games often; be reflective in observing the flowering of language in the children. Above all, be enthusiastic, playful, creative, and buoyant in using these games. If you have fun, children will adopt your love of language.

## USING THE HANDS INTENTIONALLY AND REFLECTIVELY

Here we look at the hands, the vehicle for limitless means of expression—gesture, drawing, writing, sculpting, protection, stroking, making music. We look at use of American Sign Language and an entire culture—with new kinds of movement and hand skills—created by the blind. Again, I set the stage by quoting Frank R. Wilson:

> The hand is so widely represented in the brain, the hand's neurologic and biomechanical elements are so prone to spontaneous interaction and reorganization, and the motivations and efforts which give rise to individual use of the hand are so deeply and widely rooted, that we must admit we are trying to explain a basic imperative of human life. (1998, p. 10)

### Communicating with Hands

Sit with hearing-impaired people who speak American Sign Language (ASL). ASL is its own language, not a translation of spoken language. Shut your senses to all but the moving hands of the hearing-impaired group. First watch their body language; they lean toward and away, choreographing as if dancing. Watch their faces, full of intention and exhibiting a range of emotionally charged movements with forehead, head angle, and mouth. Especially watch their eyes. Deprived of one sense, the hearing-impaired move their bodies in original and varied ways. If left to themselves, children born deaf will invent sign language in order to communicate (O. Sacks, 1989).

Now turn your attention to the ASL speakers' hands. They are alive, hovering, flying. They are attached to wrists and arms that define gestures, some small and discreet, some dramatic; arms are driven by shoulders so they can make broad and sweeping moves. Finger movements are varied and precise; when they spell, they skim effortlessly and rapidly through bends, extensions, curves, straight lines, and angles, flexing, straightening, and spreading effortlessly. Hands display a certainty of movement that suggests top athletes.

I made myself blind to everything but the group and felt I was in a no-man's land, intentionally divorced from all but the deaf and simultaneously shut out of their world. Because I could not read their hands, I could neither join their conversation nor glean meaning from their intense, rapid, joyously emotional communication. Their eyes were intently focused, moving effortlessly from one another's hands to their faces, scanning one another's bodies to catch meaning in movements and gestures. Their expressiveness integrated the depth of emotion found in great dancers and the hunger to communicate that all humans share.

## A Parable: Hand, Eye, and Culture

My experience with ASL speakers reminded me of H. G. Wells's story "The Country of the Blind" (1904). The story shows the power of sensory perception and how it influences both individuals' behavior and society's culture—history, beliefs, mores.

The Country of the Blind is trapped between treacherously high mountains with precipitous peaks that defy access and exit. There, following a horrendous earthquake, the population became isolated and eventually, through illness, congenitally blind. After 14 generations, they knew nothing of eyes, lost words for vision, and had no sight-based metaphors. Carefully proscribing their movements, the blind created new means to obtain food and shelter, invented their past, imagined a geography, and developed a new mythology, all to accommodate sightless existence.

An accident brings Nunez of Bogata, a mountain climber, to the Country. He falls through a terrifying avalanche down successive long cliffs and lands bruised but miraculously alive on a mountain ledge. Watching from his perch, Nunez realizes he has landed above the fabled Country of the Blind. His head redounds with the phrase: "In the land of the blind, the one-eyed man is king." But on meeting the blind he finds:

> Their senses had become marvelously acute; they could hear and judge the slightest gesture of a man a dozen paces away—could hear the very beating of his heart. Intonation had long replaced expression with them, and touches gesture, and their work with hoe and spade and fork was as free and confident as garden work can be.

Only when Nunez seeks to assert himself and become king does he learn how precisely they move. Attempting to strike one of the blind, and thereby show the superior advantage of sight, Nunez realizes:

> You cannot even fight happily with creatures who stand upon a different mental basis. . . . He could not find it in himself to go down and assassinate a blind man.

Finally a fight ensues. Nunez is cornered, threatened, and helpless. Incredulous and subdued, he abandons his ambition to be king, submits to becoming Yacob's servant, and does heavy, menial work.

Succumbing to his fate, Nunez eventually falls in love with Yacob's daughter, Medina-sarote. Her eyes, less red and sunken, made her shunned by others of the blind but beautiful to Nunez. At the thought of her marrying Nunez, Yacob tells Medina-sarote:

> "You see, my dear, he's an idiot. He has delusions; he can't do anything right."
>
> "I know," wept Medina-sarote. "But he's . . . getting better. And he's strong, dear father, and kind. . . . And he loves me—and, father, I love him."
>
> Distressed by his inconsolable daughter, Yacob tells the other elders: "He's better than he was. Very likely, someday, we shall find him as sane as ourselves."

Still thinking Nunez strange, the aged religious leader proposes to make Nunez suitable by removing his eyes. All agree: This solution is wise.

Read the story. You will see the details of a blind society, the hand's role in shaping culture, and Nunez's response to having his eyes removed.

## Meaningful Gesture

The congenitally deaf group I observed had created their own "country." There, with one another, they conversed and shared a life that was as full for them as that of hearing persons. Their hands were the vehicle for their humanness.

Linguists agree that ASL is as robust a language as English: Speakers can express the most abstract and complicated thoughts. The syntax, albeit different, is as regular as any spoken language, and language development in deaf infants follows the same timetable as in hearing children. Frank R. Wilson notes that Petitto's research shows that no early finger movements are "individually executed or articulated" (1998, p. 354):

> Neither in speech nor in sign do extended sequences or complex grammatical constructions occur before individual finger movements are developed! A simultaneous explosion of grammar and of finger movements begins in the third year. (p. 354)

Dr. Laura Petitto, cognitive neuroscientist, heads the Brain and Language Laboratory at Gallaudet University, a major research, education, and training institution for the hearing-impaired. In a 1992 study, Petitto compared hearing and nonhearing children's acquisition of language. She found that if language exposure begins very early, preferably at birth, *all* children will acquire the essential structures of their native language. As part of the study, Petitto isolated hand gestures of babies between 7 and 24 months, shown in the chart in Figure 3.2. She says there is a universal timetable for the development of meaningful gesture, just as there is a universal timetable for spoken language.

Harlan Lane, Distinguished Professor of Psychology, Northeastern University (Boston) and founder of the Center for Research in Hearing, Speech and Language, focuses his research on speech, deaf culture, and sign language. He is a MacArthur

Figure 3.2. Six types of manual activity in children between 7 and 24 months.

| Age in Months | Type of Activity | Examples |
|---|---|---|
| 9 to 15–18 | Motoric Hand Activity | Banging, scratching |
| 7–9 to 18–24 | Pointing | To objects and locations |
| 12 months and beyond | Social | Waving hello, bye-bye. Yes–no head nods  Routinized manual gestures of games such as patty-cake, peek-a-boo, pease porridge hot. |
| 12 months and beyond | With Object in Hand | Brushing with a brush  Driving a "block" car |
| 12 to 15–18 | Instrumental Gestures | Raising arms to be picked up |
| 14–18 to 18–24 | Symbolic Gestures | Empty-handed downward movements at side of head while gazing at a comb |

*The first number or number pair is the age the activity is first seen; the second number or number pair is the age of peak activity. *Source:* Adapted from the work of Laura Petitto.

Genius and recipient of many other awards. Lane says that while sign and gesture may appear the same to onlookers, they are profoundly different. Gesture is specific to the person making the movement. Sign is a code shared by anyone who speaks ASL. So, for example, one could gesture"Take the dog for a walk" through a clever pantomime of fetching the dog, putting on the leash, going out the door, and so on. For a good charades player, it might take just a few seconds. But, for the ASL speaker, it would take the same fraction of a second as the spoken phrase.

Consider that words are arbitrary: The sound *table* could mean anything, but English speakers agree on a specific meaning. So it is with ASL: "Everyone says the same thing in more or less the same way" (Lane, quoted in F. R. Wilson, 1998, pp. 185–186). This is what Lane means by the phrase "the arbitrariness of sign" (p. 197).

Lane described to Wilson his epiphany about language when, in 1973, psycholinguist Ursula Bellugi (quoted in Wilson, 1998) translated into English what deaf people were signing and explained: "There are rules for making up words and rules for making sentences out of the words, but the rules have to do with space and shape—it's an entirely different way of doing language" (p. 198). Lane said he was "stunned . . . like being told there's another ocean that you had never heard of." After digesting the information, Lane realized the implication: "Language was not about speaking and hearing. . . . It meant that the brain had the capacity for language, and if you can't put it out through the mouth, you put it out through the hands" (p. 198).

The work of Lane and others has changed the world for the hearing-impaired. Once it was considered unacceptable for deaf children to talk with their hands, and they were forced to try to communicate solely by lip-reading. The controversy over lips versus hands is not completely resolved, but most "lip" advocates now believe it is advantageous to use both hands and lips.

> **KEY POINTS:**
> - Even the deprivation of senses as central to human existence as hearing and sight does not preclude the drive to communicate and to form community.
> - While there are enormous variations in languages created by hearing and non-hearing cultures, mechanisms in the brain forge language that emerges on a predictable trajectory, whether through voice or hand.
> - The underlying similarities in humans dwarf the differences and provide evidence of language and hand use as innate and powerful forces in our species.

## CONCLUSION

In this chapter you have learned:

- Phonemes and morphemes underlie the structure of the English language.
- Games can help children to become adept users of phonemes and morphemes.
- Playing word games encourages children to use language fluently and facilely.
- Sensory perception has a strong influence on culture, including language.
- The hearing-impaired provide evidence that language is an integral part of the brain's structure.
- The hand plays a major role among the micro-actions that are the hallmark of intentional and reflective teachers.
- Hand movements offer powerful ways for teachers to help children become intentional and reflective.

# CHAPTER 4

# The Influence of Belief on Teachers

Belief creates the actual fact.

—William James

**TECHNIQUE 4**
Examine your beliefs honestly:
Search for mindless habits and replace them with determined actions.

My readers recall that near the beginning of every book I write about teachers' beliefs. Everything we do is based on belief, yet we often lack awareness that our beliefs impact our actions. Beliefs influence our thoughts and feelings about being intentional/reflective teachers. In this chapter, I describe some of the many influences—family, where we live, the tenor of the times, corporate marketing, political forces, educators' theories—that determine what we believe about children and education. I give examples and pose questions that challenge us to think about our beliefs.

By the end of the chapter, you should be able to determine what you believe; what has influenced your beliefs; whether you believe you can use the techniques of being intentional and reflective; or, if you are already intentional and reflective, whether you believe you can become more so.

Many factors determine what we believe about children. Some include culture, the Zeitgeist, industries that sell products. Beliefs are influenced by the teacher down the hall, the discussion in the teachers' lounge, the speaker at the last inservice session. Some beliefs are influenced by politicians; others by research. We live in a noisy culture with a cacophony of voices vying for attention. These voices relay numerous and often conflicting ideas (see Figure 4.1). Frequent strident messages make it difficult to know, much less to change, what we believe. Amid the noise, teachers struggle with what will work in their classroom: The most recent voice on TV? radio? the movies? from a book, a peer, a blog, a chat room, or Pinterest? How do we sort it all out? Here I try.

## BELIEFS INDUCED BY FAMILY, LOCALE, AND THE ZEITGEIST

A pundit said, "We don't know who discovered water, but we know it wasn't the fish." Like fish, we cannot see, much less understand, what surrounds us. Our surroundings include families, locale, culture, and the times in which we live.

**Figure 4.1. Who has shaped your image of a child?**

| | | |
|---|---|---|
| **Politicians** | Industrial production models work in schools. One-size-fits-all testing provides accountability. Learning occurs by rote. |  |
| **Early Educators' Mantra (Piaget)** | Development occurs "naturally." Children learn when they are "ready." "Teachers should not intervene." |  |
| **Marketers** | All media are sales tools. Infants and children are markets worth billions of dollars. Anything goes if it sells. |  |
| **Recent Researchers** | We're born driven to learn. We have multiple intelligences. We learn through relationships with intentional adults. |  |
| **Neuroscientists** | We are cognitive and competent at birth. Classrooms are operating theaters for the brain. | 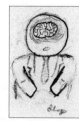 |

## The Influence of Family

Bertha served ham every Sunday. Before baking it, she dutifully cut off the ends. Askance at the waste, Jim ventured to ask why. "I don't know," she replied. "I guess because Mother did." So she asked Mother. "Well," Mother said thoughtfully, "my mother did." So Bertha called Granny: "Cut the ham?" repeated Granny, "The only pot I had wasn't big enough."

Likewise Alfred: His wife tried but could never get the goulash right. At dinner with Alfred's family, his mother served goulash. It tasted distinctly burnt. "Ah," beamed Alfred, "goulash the way I like it!" We find these stories humorous because we recognize that our actions may be based on behaviors we have learned but never thought about.

I find no humor in abusive childrearing that is influenced by family patterns. (Names and identities have been changed.) Stan was a shy child and utterly bashful around girls; he did not date until after college. His brother Ron was antisocial and, as his first marriage broke up, lived with a wife to whom he did not speak for months on end. Their father was alcoholic, a large man, 6'5", with huge hands that affirmed his star position as left guard on the college football team. Not only his size terrified Stan and Ron; he also used his hands as punishment, to hit the boys or occasionally wield his belt. Moreover, their mother was mean. Her sons recalled remarks like, "No child that ugly could have come from my body." Or, "You'll eat everything on your dinner plate if you have to sit until breakfast." She would not countenance the distaste many young children have for certain foods. Stan remembered when Ron, age 5, started to voice his distaste for liver. As Ron said, "I don't like . . .," his father's hand slammed across his mouth. Neither brother ever complained about food again—except for Stan's complaint about spinach, which he could not tolerate. Once, when his mother forced it on him, he projectile vomited. Covered with spinach, his mother never served it to him again. The home culture was permeated by fear and meanness. Teachers saw boys who were intent on doing well, who would speak in class only when they knew they had the right answer, and who were easily disciplined by the threat of calling a parent.

At an Orthodox Jewish school where I consulted, I noticed a 3-year-old sitting in the hall with the classroom aide. All that day and the next morning, whenever I passed the room, there they were. I questioned the teacher, who explained, "He bolts from the room; we can only stop his running wild by having Julia sit with him. He is the first-born and in the Sephardic culture, the first-born male is considered a prince. He can do no wrong. His every whim is honored." The home culture was permeated by adoring permissiveness. Teachers saw a willful, demanding child whom they were afraid to cross.

Toby, age 4, was a classroom terror—punching or physically tackling other children. His parents, billed as Alphonso and Jasmine, were star wrestlers, their bouts well-advertised, their earnings high. They were rarely at home, but when there, Alphonso played with Toby by wrestling him to the floor, pinning him down, and punching him. Alphonso believed that he was toughening Toby, that the younger Toby was when he began to wrestle publicly, the larger the audiences he would draw and the sooner he would bring home income. The home culture was permeated by acts of physical bravado and selfishness. Teachers saw a child who knew how to relate only by acting violently.

Teachers are not always privy to the reasons for children's behavior. Usually they know only what they observe and little of family circumstances. Yet teachers are responsible for mediating difficult behavior that may be evident even in toddlers or infants. For Stan and Ron, their parents' own difficult personalities and beliefs about childrearing accounted for their sons' repressed social relations. The culture of a particular religion accounted for Sam's self-centered behavior. The ethic of his parents' workplace, along with their beliefs about what would make them stars, accounted for Toby's pugnacity. Where causes of children's behavior are less obvious, psychological help may be required in order to find a diagnosis and prescribe interventions.

Old platitudes or personal needs inform some parents' beliefs about childrearing:

- Spare the rod and spoil the child—belief in corporal punishment
- Children should be seen and not heard—belief that what children have to say is not worth listening to
- Do as I say, not as I do—belief that children can be influenced by words
- Do it because I say so—need to control others

Our actions tell children what we believe about them and are children's blueprints for their own actions.

Harvard psychologist and professor emeritus Jerome Kagan (1986) defines conditions that determine a child's personality. One he calls identification with role models:

> A parent's most important influence on a child originates in his or her status as a role model with whom that child can identify. One problem is that most parents find it difficult to hide their deep qualities, especially if these are undesirable. If a child perceives that the mother is competent, kind, nurturing and attractive, then, fair or unfair, that seven-year-old girl will feel better about herself than she would otherwise. But if the mother is incompetent, not liked, and perceived to be unjust, then the child, even though she possesses none of those qualities, will feel bad, perhaps guilty . . . [and have] anxious feelings about [her]self . . . a result of identification with a parent whom one perceives as bad. . . . Even though parents have limited control over how they present themselves to their children, it is their strongest power for it will influence the child's conception of self for many years. (pp. 12–13)

Children become what others believe about themselves or about the child. The tendency is reflected in the platitude, "I have the name, I may as well have the game." Some teachers believe that if they learn the realities of children's lives, they can use the information to understand difficult children and perhaps help them overcome problems. Other teachers believe that children's personalities are immutable, unable to change: "That's just who Carla is."

---

**KEY POINTS:**

- Parental actions have a stronger influence on children than their words.
- To change a belief, first understand what formed it.

## The Influence of Locale

In the early 1960s, I was a social case worker administering federal government economic assistance programs, including Aid to Dependent Children (ADC), usually referred to as welfare, and recently as Temporary Assistance for Needy Families (TANF). My caseload had 200 families; my territory was half a rural southern county. Snapshots of my clients show:

- A mother living in a one-room cabin in a clearing in the woods. She had just had a tenth baby, and I was required to see the newborn in order to increase the welfare payment.
- A family of nine living in a trailer, 8 feet wide by 20 feet long. There had been considerable incest; their average IQ was below 80.
- A family with five children farming 1 acre with a single crop—tobacco. Setting out plants, weeding and hoeing, picking leaves, tying bundles, and going to market took from early spring to late fall. Children were kept out of school to help. The farmer borrowed from the bank in the spring, repaid the bank when the tobacco was sold, and borrowed from the bank for next spring's planting.
- Several clients who were prostitutes and lived in shanties on a dirt road without electricity or running water. Their children played on the road, a running sewer when it rained. The Clerk of the County Court owned the shanties and received the welfare checks. He took out his rent and returned the leftover pittance to the prostitutes.

Welfare payments were calculated according to a formula: Take the number of children times the government-allowed stipend per child and award 75%. If they grow collards or sweet potatoes, subtract the value. Families who owned a vehicle or television were ineligible. My caseload was about 50/50 Caucasian and Negro (the word then used for African Americans).

The common factors were that every locale was bleak, sterile, joyless, and all family members had an air of resignation. They were beaten down by ceaseless repetitive cycles—an infant every year, ongoing incest, borrow/plant/harvest/repay/borrow, the spiritual and financial poverty of prostitution.

In the ensuing 5 decades, sociology bloomed, welfare recipients were studied, and the causes of poverty were endlessly documented. Studies have not broken the welfare cycle. Documents have not facilitated ways out of poverty. In an online article in *The Atlantic* ( 2013), reporter Eric Schnurer quotes the Hon. D. Cameron Findlay, Deputy Secretary, U.S. Department of Labor, before the Subcommittee on Human Resources of the House Committee on Ways and Means, Hearing on Unemployment Fraud and Abuse, on June 11, 2002. Findlay testified that "fraud accounts for less than 2 percent of unemployment insurance payments." Schnurer continues:

> It's seemingly impossible to find statistics on "welfare" (i.e., TANF) fraud, but the best guess is that it's about the same. A bevy of inspector general reports found "improper payment" levels of 20 to 40 percent in state TANF programs—but when you look at the

reports, the payments appear all to be due to bureaucratic incompetence (categorized by the inspector general as either "eligibility and payment calculation errors" or "documentation errors"), rather than intentional fraud by beneficiaries.

Schnurer concludes: "Entitlement programs, from food stamps to Medicare, don't see unusually high cheating rates—and the culprits are usually managers and executives, not 'welfare queens'."

Endless studies have bulletproofed the belief that children's locale and economic status determine what they can achieve. Studies conclude that children from poverty locales have lower test scores than more affluent children. The potential of economically impoverished children is straightjacketed by studies that become self-fulfilling prophesies.

## The Influence of the Zeitgeist

The word *Zeitgeist* is made up of two German words, *Zeit* meaning time and *Geist* meaning spirit. Zeitgeist refers to the tenor of the times, the trends, mores, styles, and beliefs. The Zeitgeist of the Roaring Twenties meant freedom: Women bobbed their hair, shortened skirts, smoked and drank in public—shocking their mothers and violating their Victorian grandmothers' "shoulds" for women's behavior.

Many factors influence the Zeitgeist: Whether the economy booms or busts, as it did in the Great Depression; what kind of leader dominates: Hitler, Gandhi, Mandela, Stalin, King, Castro; what messages mass media broadcast; how today's world opinion is impacted by individuals' messaging.

Since the advent of mass media, a Zeitgeist's prevailing period has shortened. The United States quaked, fearful and paranoid, for several days—a very short Zeitgeist—on hearing Orson Wells's 1938 radio broadcast *The War of the Worlds*. Believing it was being invaded by aliens, the nation panicked; soon panic was replaced by anger—how could CBS be so irresponsible! Public reaction is shown in Figure 4.2, Les Callan's 1938 political cartoon.

Nobel–Prize–winning psychologist Daniel Kahneman (2011) says that media shape public interests and in turn are shaped by public response. Events

> are warped by media coverage . . . [that] itself is biased toward novelty and poignancy. . . . Unusual events (such as botulism) attract disproportionate attention and are consequently perceived as less unusual than they really are. The world in our heads is not a precise replica of reality; our expectations about the frequency of events are distorted by the prevalence and emotional intensity of the messages to which we are exposed. (p. 138)

Kagan (1986) considers the Zeitgeist a "chance factor" in children's lives, like "historical events that influence the entire society" (p. 15). World wars, the Civil Rights Movement, a Great Depression, or the 2008 bank fiascoes have "little to do with [parents'] kindness or meanness . . . [they] were events totally outside familial control" (p. 15). Yet the adult behavior of people who were children during such events was "influenced profoundly": "Many who were adolescents in Europe

Figure 4.2. Public reaction to *War of the Worlds* radio broadcast.

Copyright Torstar Syndication Services. Reprinted with permission.

after World War I, the spiritual war that was to solve all of the world's problems, became skeptics for the rest of their lives" (p. 15).

## Summary

The influences of parents' nature, home locale, the Zeitgeist, and the sweep of current events are beyond control. Parental influence may be open to change. But rarely can teachers change parents. Teachers, however, can examine their own beliefs and seek to understand the relationship between what has influenced them and how they relate to children.

---

**KEY POINTS:**

- Diverse and powerful variables mean that each child is unique.
- Teachers can begin to examine their own beliefs by noting whether they use the word *they*, a depersonalizing word that denies a child's or group's individuality.

---

✦ Exercise: Consider what influences you.

Have parents, locale, or the Zeitgeist influenced what you believe about children? Think of how your beliefs might influence each child in your class. Briefly describe a child, your beliefs, and whether you see a relationship between the two.

## BELIEFS INDUCED BY MARKETERS AND POLITICIANS

America is inundated by messages from marketers and politicians. These messages are insistent, incessant, and invasive. Marketing and political campaigns are shaped with counsel from experts steeped in the latest research on how to influence the brain. Campaign designers know the importance of repetitive messages, the value of embedding emotional content in ads, the eye-catching effects of color and movement, and the attention-getting capacity of musical sounds, vocal tone, auditory effects, and emotional and sexual allusions. Here we examine the influence on children and teachers of marketing and politically motivated educational programs.

### The Influence of Corporate Marketing

By age 18, over 50% of American youth have been diagnosed with ADHD, and drugs have been prescribed for over 70% of them. In 1999, when Ritalin was the best-known ADHD drug, the National Institute for Mental Health (NIMH) published the results of its $11 million study on early ADHD drugs. Tracking 600 children, experts compared four different ADHD treatments—drug therapy, behavioral therapy, a combination of both, and no therapy. The study concluded that the use of drug therapy without behavioral therapy was the "winner." The media pounced on the finding, and use of ADHD drugs became commonplace. Now, many years later, as reported in a lengthy article by Alan Schwarz (2013a) in *The New York Times*, researchers on the 1999 study have second thoughts about the study's results and their roles:

- We "lost the opportunity to give kids the advantage of both [drugs and behavioral therapy] and to develop more resources in schools to support the child—that value was dismissed." (Dr. Gene Arthur, psychiatrist, Ohio State University, principal researcher)
- "If you don't provide skills-based training, you're doing the kid a disservice. I wish we had had a fairer test." (Dr. Stephen Hinshaw, psychologist, University of California, Berkeley, researcher)
- "I hope it didn't do irreparable damage. The people who pay the price in the end are the kids. That's the biggest tragedy of all this." (Dr. Lily Hechtman, McGill University, coauthor)

Schwarz writes, "Looking back, some study researchers say several factors in the study's design and . . . [how the drugs were marketed] disguised the performance of behavioral therapy, allowing many doctors and drug companies to discourage its use."

The NIMH study is widely considered the most influential study ever on ADHD. It is disconcerting that the researchers "worry that the results oversold the benefits of drugs, discouraging important home- and school-focused therapy and ultimately distorting the debate over the most effective (and cost-effective) treatments." A factor in drugs' winning over therapy is the huge price differential—$200 for a year's worth of drugs versus $1,000 and more for a year's worth of behavioral therapy (Schwarz, 2013a).

In a second lengthy front-page Sunday *New York Times* article, Schwarz (2013a) notes that Keith Conners, psychologist and professor emeritus, Duke University, for years fought to legitimize ADHD as a neurological problem. Yet today, Conners calls the increase from 600,000 children on medication in 1990 to 3.5 million today "a national disaster of dangerous proportions. The numbers make it look like an epidemic. Well, it's not. It's preposterous. . . . This is a concoction to justify the giving out of medication at unprecedented and unjustifiable levels."

The increase is due to advertising by drug companies who target doctors and parents. "Marketing," reports Schwarz (2013b), "has stretched the image of classic ADHD to include relatively normal behavior like carelessness and impatience, and has often overstated the pills' benefits." The FDA has targeted every ADHD drug for "false and misleading advertising since 2000, some multiple times" (Schwarz, 2013a). Drug companies pay doctors to publish research, make presentations, and encourage other doctors to make diagnoses; these doctors-for-hire call ADHD medications "safer than aspirin" (Schwarz, 2013b). The "disorder is now the second most frequent long-term diagnosis made in children, narrowly trailing asthma" (2013a), a fact that testifies to the success of drug companies' marketing.

Mass market magazines run ads that tout benefits of ADHD drugs with statements like, "schoolwork that matches his intelligence," an emotional pitch aimed directly at parents' and teachers' fears about school performance. Convinced by infomercials that ADHD pills work and are safe, parents and teachers find it easier to give a child a pill than to do the hard work of channeling children's challenging actions into productive behavior. Moreover, addressing behavioral change may require specialists—teachers or psychologists—for whom school systems or parents have no funds.

Schwarz (2013b) reports that Roger Griggs, the pharmaceutical executive who introduced Adderall in 1994, calls ADHD stimulants "nuclear bombs, warranted only under extreme circumstances and when carefully overseen by a physician." Schwarz quotes Griggs, who said in 1994: "There's no way on God's green earth we would ever promote" stimulants directly to consumers. Pharmaceutical giant Shire

> bought Griggs' company for $186 million and spent millions more to market [Adderall] to doctors. . . . As is typical among pharmaceutical companies, Shire gathered hundreds of doctors at meetings at which a physician, paid by the company, explained a new drug's value. (Schwarz, 2013a)

Today, as Schwarz documents extensively, handsomely paid doctors-for-hire:

- Write "research" papers used to train other doctors on the benefits of ADHD drugs
- Make regular presentations to physicians at conferences
- Write the content used in drug companies' brochures and ads

For example, Dr. Joseph Biederman, "a prominent child psychiatrist" at Harvard and Mass General, was paid "$1.6 million in speaking and consulting fees," a fact revealed in a 2008 Senate investigation. Doctors-for-hire claim that their fees do not influence their conclusions (Schwarz, 2013a).

With the youth market securely in its grips, big pharma is going after adults by promoting adult ADHD as a condition that requires lifelong treatment, an assertion "not supported by science" (Schwarz, 2013a). Many promotions, some delivered by TV personalities, neglect to mention the risks of side effects associated with using stimulants. Dr. Conners, who has attended many drug-company–sponsored meetings, refutes their messages: "Perhaps half of ADHD children are not impaired as adults, and little is known about the risks or efficacy of long-term medication use."

It is well known, and psychologists, including Griggs, concur, that ADHD occurs in 5% of children. Schwarz's in-depth reporting sheds light on the facts that

- Side effects can be dangerous and, if mentioned at all, are downplayed by drug companies.
- "ADHD drugs are regulated [by the FDA] in the same class as morphine and oxycodone because of their potential for abuse and addiction." (Schwarz, 2013a)
- Market leader Shire marketed directly to children, with comic book superheroes telling children: "Medicines may make it easier to pay attention and control your behavior!" (Schwarz, 2013a)
- There are no studies, aside from those that are pharma-sponsored, on the risks of long-term use.
- Drug company ad campaigns are misleading at best and generally false.
- "Dr. Aaron Kesselheim, a Harvard professor, analyzes several [drug company] ads and discusses how many of them play on parents' common fears about their children" (Schwarz, 2013a).
- Patient advocate groups, whose operating expenses are underwritten by drug companies, have lobbied to loosen restrictions on ADHD drugs.
- According to Brian Lutz, a Shire sales rep who markets Adderall directly to doctors, the company told him "to acknowledge risks matter-of-factly for legal reasons, but to refer only to the small print in the package insert or offer Shire's phone number" (Schwarz, 2013a).
- ADHD profits have soared: Sales in 2002 were $1.7 billion and in 2012 were more than five times that, $9 billion.
- Shire's FDA-imposed fine for "improper sales and advertising of several drugs, including Vyvanse, Adderall XR and Daytrana, a patch that delivers stimulant medication through the skin," was $57.5 million. (2013a)

Sadly, for 20 years drug companies have honed the belief in many doctors, parents, and teachers that many children have ADHD and therefore need drugs. The belief is now so strongly embedded that evidence against using ADHD drugs is ignored or belittled.

Emotion is an integral part of every cognitive act. Fear is one of the strongest emotions surrounding ADHD. Consider these fears of teachers:

- Will these rambunctious boys prevent me from covering the material mandated in the curriculum?
- Will my evaluations be negative if I cannot keep these children under control?
- Will the disruptive behaviors "infect" other children in the class?
- I have no effective means to get these children to focus.
- Others will consider me a bad teacher because of the noise and movement in my classroom.
- Will I be fired if these children perform badly on tests?

Ads have created a Zeitgeist that makes it seem natural to have many children on drugs. Individuals can rarely counter a prevailing sentiment that has been fostered with millions of advertising dollars. If teachers' fears are eased when drugs calm children, it is hard to admit that using drugs is wrong, much less to stop using them. Moreover, neither teachers nor parents are able to determine which children are among the small percentage of those whom the drugs really may help.

✦ Exercise: Examine what has influenced your attitude about ADHD drugs.

When parents tell you that drugs have been recommended because their child has ADHD, ask yourself whether this child seems like a candidate for drugs or whether the behavior may be symptomatic of something other than ADHD. Ask parents:

- How was the diagnosis made?
- Did the physician recommend drugs to the parent? Or did the parent ask the physician to consider drugs?
- What tests or other means were used to determine the diagnosis?
- How much time did the physician or psychologist spend interviewing the parents? What kinds of questions were asked?
- How much time did the physician or psychologist spend with the child?
- Did the parent consider using behavior therapy rather than drugs?

Children are a market worth billions in potential revenue to merchandisers of drugs, clothes, electronics, and other products galore. Ads for clothes prey on children's fantasies just like ads for drugs play on adults' fears. A key question is what teachers believe their role is—to remain silent, or to disclose the impact of false advertising? To play it safe, or to stick out one's neck?
What you can do:

- Beware and help parents beware of being pawns of drug companies.
- Educate yourself and parents on the facts about ADHD and drug use.

- Be sure you identify the source of your information and shun information provided by drug companies or identify the source if you use the information.
- Be proactive in turning the tide on drug treatment for ADHD.
- Know what the behavior therapy resources are in your school and community and provide a list to parents.

**Key Questions:**
- Should teachers play a role in shaping families' responses to marketing?
- Do educators have a responsibility to counter deleterious and false cultural influences by providing sound information?

## The Influence of Politics on Education

The political climate that has evolved since 2001 is a departure from earlier times by virtue of its vitriolic nature—a red and blue nation divided. Education is neutral turf for politicians. No matter what their ideology, all politicians can agree that we need better schools, more money for education, new ways to motivate teachers to produce high performers, and better tests to measure the success of our methods. Both sides of the aisle agree on such needs. Two successive administrations, Bush and Obama, each funded signature education initiatives—Bush's No Child Left Behind (NCLB) and Obama's Race to the Top (RTTT). NCLB's centerpiece was the mandate that all children would read on grade level by 3rd grade. The amounts of money spent on these initiatives are staggering: an estimated $20 billion in 2013 alone for NCLB (febp.newamerica.net/background-analysis/education-federal-budget). It is hard to find references that separate spending on No Child Left Behind from all Title I spending, but reports of the National Bureau of Economic Research (Dee & Jacob, 2009) suggest that the total is over $1 trillion. Race to the Top awarded $4 billion for the 12 winning states to be spent over 5 years (McNeil, 2014).

Along with specific academic goals, NCLB mandated new requirements for standardized testing of all children and penalties for schools with low test scores. A study by the National Bureau of Economic Research (NBER) concludes:

> NCLB generated statistically significant increases in the average math performance of 4th graders (effect size = 0.22 by 2007) as well as improvements at the lower and top percentiles. There is also evidence of improvements in 8th grade math achievement, particularly among traditionally low-achieving groups and at the lower percentiles. *However, we find no evidence that NCLB increased reading achievement in either 4th or 8th grade.* (Dee & Jacob, 2009, emphasis added)

The NBER study also found that under NCLB, teacher pay increased, as did the number of teachers with graduate degrees, and that instruction time increased for math and reading.

Detractors believe that NCLB's emphasis on testing caused teaching to the test and all but eliminated arts and other "superfluous" subjects. NCLB heavily publicized its centerpiece—that by 3rd grade children would read on grade level. The program failed to meet that goal but succeeded in driving out of education many excellent teachers who could not or would not deal with performance standards that many considered rigid, inimical to good education practices, and detrimental to children's development.

Race to the Top provides "incentives to States to implement large-scale, system-changing reforms that improve student achievement, close achievement gaps, and increase graduation and college enrollment rates" (www.ed.gov/open/plan/race-top-game-changing-reforms). Given the slow start the 12 winning states have had, it is too early to determine whether RTTT will meet its goals or what its other effects might be.

Politics drives many educational reforms. As with drugs, the money loosed by big federal programs is too much to be ignored. Bevies of consultants emerge to feed on the funds and to meet regulations for which states have neither expertise nor staff.

In reviewing the interaction between politics and education, Peter Sacks, educator, writer, and Pulitzer Prize nominee, finds a long history of politicians' using education to advance their careers. Sacks (1999) says: The "unavoidable lesson from history [is] that politics and power rather than strictly educational concerns have driven the use of testing" (p. 70). Horace Mann (1796–1859) is credited as the first advocate for universal public education in the then-young United States. Sacks unpacks the reality:

> Mann's educational stewardship in the state of Massachusetts underscored early on the basic contradiction inherent to state-mandated, external examinations of public school-children in a democratic society. On one hand a free society required an open system of public education for all citizens. Yet, according to Mann's view, such an educational system had to be controlled, efficiently managed, and held properly accountable to the public. (1999, p. 70)

The dichotomy was set as American public education began: An efficient system would be measured by test results. But standardized tests have little to do with fairness or sound education, despite test designers' efforts to convince us otherwise.

The question is what an individual believes: Do you believe that test results are the only basis for knowing whether education works? Or do you believe that education works best by fostering development of each individual's strengths? Sacks says:

> Watching in horror, the progressive educational philosopher John Dewey once remarked, "Our mechanical, industrialized civilization is concerned with averages and percents. The mental habit which reflects this social scene subordinates education and social arrangements based on [measures of] average gross inferiorities and superiorities. (1999, p. 73)

Tanner (1997), revisiting Dewey's ideas in her book *Dewey's Laboratory School: Lessons for Today*, uses the following quote by Dewey to explain why the move toward standards was misguided:

> Individual effort is impossible without individual interest. . . . However hard [the child] may work at it, the effort does not go into the accomplishment of the work, but is largely dissipated in a moral and emotional struggle to keep the attention where it is not held. (p. 160)

Tanner recalls that the national goals for standards, set by state governors in 1989, were expressed as children "*will* learn" (emphasis added) with 2000 as the target year by which children would have learned. When it became clear in the late 1990s that the target would not be met, standards were more rigorously defined (pp. 159–160). We keep tightening the screws, laboring under the delusion that learning can be accomplished by fiat and measured by tests.

The Bush and Obama educational programs have each added another layer of accountability to an educational system already awash in testing.

✦ Exercise: Experiment with an alternative to testing.

Make a quick evaluation of children in your class to determine whether you would give them a Pass or Fail in overall development. Then, for 1 week put aside the mandated curriculum, occupy your Pass students with self-directing activities, and spend your time with children whom you marked Fail. For each Fail child, plan one-on-one activities in the area you consider the child's weakest. It could be weak verbal ability, awkward movement, misreading social cues, or cognitive difficulties, such as failure to select specific objects when scanning a page dense with information. Choose any single task you believe will enable you to help this child move from Fail toward Pass. At the end of the week, compare what the curriculum might have accomplished for your Fail children with what your one-on-one time accomplished. Analyze what your comparisons show about your beliefs, specifically: (1) your role as a teacher and (2) the ways children learn.

---

**KEY POINTS:**

- In an educational system overburdened with testing, teachers can be a critical force for using authentic assessment instead of standardized tests.
- Test objectivity is an illusion; teachers know children's strengths and weaknesses as well as if not better than tests reveal.
- Teachers who assess children reclaim a responsibility that is rightfully a teacher's.

## BELIEFS HELD BY EDUCATORS

The mantra in early education is that teachers should perform "developmentally appropriate practice." The National Association for the Education of Young Children judges whether practice is developmentally appropriate by using over 500 measures. Meeting those measures is onerous, and using them to explain the meaning of "developmentally appropriate" is impossible: How do you describe a child's development in terms of 500 objectives? Even with one-word answers, how could you summarize the fulfillment of 500 objectives?

Harvard psychologist Howard Gardner (1983, 1991, 1993, 1999, 2014) has offered nine ways to judge quality education in the theory he proposed called Multiple Intelligences, which he formed through his own firsthand observations and research of what cultures throughout the world value. Each intelligence reflects a capacity of the human brain. Classrooms for young children, ages 0 through 8, could be judged by whether they foster all nine intelligences.

Israeli psychologist Reuven Feuerstein offers three ways to determine the value of what we offer children in his Theory of the Mediated Learning Experience. Every teacher/child interaction should be based on a meaning the teacher selects to convey to the child, the intention with which the teacher conveys the meaning, and an act Feuerstein calls transcendence, by which he means encouraging children to find relationships between the meaning at hand and something children remember or can envision in the future. Classrooms for young children, ages 0 through 8, could be judged by whether teachers teach with meaning, intention, and transcendence.

Lev Vygotsky, the Russian psychologist who is considered the father of sociocultural theory, proposed that children learn because of their connections with others and through the use of language that, as it develops, changes from self-talk to fully conversant discourse with others. Classrooms for young children, ages 0 through 8, could be judged by how much opportunity there is for interaction and the quality and quantity of conversation among teacher and class, teacher and small groups of children, teacher and child one-on-one, and children among themselves.

David Hawkins (1974), the physicist and educational philosopher, believes that children learn through an "I, It, Thou" relationship. That is, I, the teacher, must provide an environment rich in "its"—diverse stimuli imbued with their own languages, concepts, and relationships. Teachers' role is to build a relationship between I (the teacher), it (the stimulus), and thou (the child). Classrooms for young children, ages 0 through 8, could be judged by the number and quality of the I/it/thou relationships that occur on any day.

Maria Montessori, Italian physician, anthropologist, and educator, developed a method in which the teacher creates a well-prepared environment—using materials Montessori herself developed ("it" in Hawkins's parlance), introduces children to the materials, observes to determine which materials are of deep interest to a child, and structures the time so that children can spend long, uninterrupted periods with the materials that interest them. Classrooms for young children, ages 0 through 8, could be judged by the richness of the materials, the amount of time children can work without interruption, and the quality of the children's focus.

Loris Malaguzzi, the Italian educator who founded the Reggio schools, created an educational system in which the environment is highly aesthetic, open-ended materials for making things abound, and teachers engage children in learning the qualities of diverse materials and the skillful use of tools to shape materials. Teachers in Malaguzzi's system collaborate with children on creations the children envision, stimulated by interaction with both teachers and peers. Classrooms for young children, ages 0 through 8, could be judged by their aesthetic quality, the availability of diverse materials, the extent of teacher collaboration, and the quality of what the children produce.

✦ Exercise: Experiment with alternative assessment.

Using one of the above theories or practices, imagine what you would do as a teacher, how your classroom would look, what the children would do, and how you would put the theory into practice. How would using your chosen theory reflect what you believe about early education? How might it change what you currently believe about early education? How might it shape your interactions with children and how you assess children's development?

## CONCLUSION

Our beliefs are influenced by so many factors and are so deeply embedded in our mind and emotions that it is difficult to articulate what we believe, much less where beliefs originated and how they became embedded as the drivers of our thoughts and actions. In this chapter, I have tried to expose some of the factors that shape beliefs. I have intentionally used controversial examples and challenged established ideas. Knowing that the only way to define a belief may be to defend it, I have gone after some sacred cows. I hope this chapter inspires you to challenge established "isms" on your own.

The conclusion I draw is that it is not possible to be an intentional teacher without knowing what you believe, what accounts for the belief, and how fiercely you are wedded to the belief. Nor is it possible to be a reflective teacher without taking the time to examine the relationship between what you do, what happens as a result, whether you like the result, and how/what you would change if you do not like the result. Intentional/reflective teaching is about change in teaching behaviors. It is not possible to change our behavior without first determining what beliefs drive our practices.

# CHAPTER 5

# Choosing Words That Speak with Intention

The right word may be effective, but no word was ever as effective as a rightly timed pause.

—Mark Twain

---

**TECHNIQUE 5**
Choose words strategically: Understand the impact of words on children.

---

Words have two functions: They are a tool of the brain that we use to think and talk to ourselves, and they are the means by which we communicate with others. The wonder of language is how well it works to share information. Even if words are mispronounced, wrong, mixed up in an idiom, or omitted, we usually grasp enough meaning to respond sensibly. Speaking with intention means imbuing words with meaning and feeling. Listening with intention means to reflect on meaning and feeling to form a response. This chapter is about making listening more focused and speaking more thoughtful by using diverse techniques; some are drawn from the psychotherapeutic discipline called *mindfulness*.

The first section, on intention and reflection in choosing and using words, contrasts intentional and unintentional word choices, depicts words' impact on children, and shows how to choose words *with* intention. The second section, based on Kelly Wilson's book *Mindfulness for Two* (2008), provides many techniques for adopting patterns of word use that make communication more *mindful*. A short third section shows mindful communication between infant and parent, and among teacher and parents. By the end of the chapter, teachers should be:

- Intentional about choosing statements, phrasing questions, and forming responses that foster children's thoughtful communication
- Able to reflect on how to continually expand children's cognitive and behavioral skills through precise word choice
- Employing more techniques for mindful speaking and listening

This chapter is based on the reality that we don't spend much time listening and that young children are often recipients of the least attentive listening.

I watched as 3-year-old Roger tried to engage his mother. She was focused on her computer, Roger on the floor nearby. He asked quietly, "Mommy?" and received no response. He asked again, just as quietly, "Mommy?" and again received no response. He asked a third time. Mommy remained unresponsive. She did not look at him, or hold her hand in a stop-like gesture that, while not responding verbally, at least would have acknowledged that she heard. The fourth time, Roger raised his voice and declared: "Mommy!" Still no response. With that, Roger stopped asking, half-ran toward the dining room, where he sat down hard on the floor and launched into singing "The Alphabet Song" as loud as he could, all the time his eyes on his mother, who may as well not have been present, so intently was she working, and so totally did she ignore Roger.

Some parents find it difficult to foster their career and their children's development equally well. Some teachers find it overwhelming to listen wholeheartedly to the 20 or more children in their care. As overburdened adults, we can empathize with the pressures of unresponsive parents and teachers. But children may interpret nonresponse as the adult's saying, "I don't like you." Or "You're not important to me." Or "My teacher likes the other children (or Mommy likes her work or my brother) better than she likes me." Such feelings, when consistent in the early years, undermine children's self-image.

Consider the following alternatives to no response:

- "I hear you, Roger. I'll answer soon."
- With one finger raised: "In a minute!"
- A glance, a smile to acknowledge the child's request, and the word, "Soon."
- A quick explanation: "I'll listen as soon as I finish (this thought, answering Charlie, this phone call . . .)."
- "Thank you for asking quietly; it will be your turn next."

Young children interrupt for many reasons:

- They need a quick answer, explanation, or some other content that will enable them to pursue their activity.
- They are hungry or need to go to the bathroom.
- Something is not right and they want an adult to mediate (e.g., the dog is drinking from the goldfish bowl; their siblings are fighting; poop is unflushed in the toilet; their pants are wet).
- They have seen something scary and need an adult's comfort—a violent action through a window; something frightening on TV.
- They hunger for a hug, lap time, a story, or simply human exchange.
- They are ignored frequently and need affirmation that the adult in charge cares.

Some children might be far more vociferous than Roger in their demand for attention; others might have learned never to ask.

A large repertoire of nonverbal responses can show that adults are aware—and care—even when they cannot respond at once. Adults, however, are far removed from their own childhood feelings of being ignored. Hopefully, Roger's mother's response was an isolated instance in Roger's life. When ignoring children is typical, consider that you are:

- Teaching children that it is all right to ignore others' requests, a behavior children may adopt
- Seeding doubt in children about whether they are valued
- Possibly establishing a basis for children's lifelong hunger for responsiveness and love

✦ Exercise: Read and recommend to parents Albert Cullum's books, *The Geranium on the Window Sill Just Died But Teacher You Went Right on Talking* (1971) and *You Think Just Because You're Big You're Right* (1976).

The publisher's note (1976, p. 5) says:

So many of us have forgotten how powerless and ineffective a small child can feel. So many children cannot imagine that the adults in their world were ever children like themselves—children surrounded by adults who perversely ignore some of their deepest concerns and deal out tragedy and elation seemingly at whim. This author, these artists do remember—with astonishing recall. Because they do, they can bring young readers the comfort of understanding how hard it is to adjust their lives to the powerful world of the adults around them. The [authors and artists] re-create for adults the emotions that move and consume the children. By saying and showing—and publishing—these poems, we tell the truth to one another.

## INTENTIONAL WORD CHOICE

Word choices both show teachers' intention and are the means by which teachers reflect. Words have a major impact on motivation and cognition in children and adults. Here we look at words heard frequently in classrooms, their impact on children's responses, and possible alternative choices. Then we consider how to use words to resolve altercations about sharing.

### Words That Trigger a Range of Behaviors

Teachers' words influence children's responses. Here I examine word choices from classrooms, describe responses provoked in children, contrast intentional and unintentional word choices, and suggest how to choose words with intention and reflection.

Consider examples frequently heard in ECE classrooms. For each pair, I explain why the first is not intentional and why the second is.

**Requests.** Query: "Will you put away the blocks?" vs. declarative statement: "Let us put away the blocks."

*Unintentional:* Asking children, "Will you . . ." offers the option to refuse. Some children, age 2 or 3, latch onto the word *no*. Initially they might not know its meaning, but they quickly learn that it can evoke big responses from adults, responses

that too often turn into power struggles. Rephrasing from, "Will you . . ." to "Let's
. . ." puts the child in a frame of mind to cooperate.

*Tips:*

- Say "let's" in a firm voice.
- Hold out your hand to invite the child to come with you.
- Let your demeanor say, "We *will* do this together."
- Have fun as you put away the blocks.

*Intentional:* Saying, "Let us . . ." positions you to be a collaborator. Collaboration
builds children's trust in you and gives you an opportunity to observe their capabilities at close hand:

- Can they lift and position blocks precisely?
- Do they know vocabulary—rectangular solid, cylinder, triangular prism,
  square, half-arch, long, thin, flat, and other geometric words intrinsic to
  blocks?
- What is their attention span?
- What is their disposition?

These are some things you can learn about children when you work one-on-one.

**Directions.** Work time is over. Teachers ask children who don't stop work on
their own by giving them an unlimited choice or a direction. Unlimited choice:
*"Do you want to stop?"* vs. direction: *"Put it away now, please."*

*Unintentional:* Asking a child, "Do you want . . .?" is an open-ended question
with more latitude than some children can handle. While it is the norm in some
schools to ask children what they prefer in regard to most, if not all, options, some
situations require action . . . *now*. Children who find transitions difficult:

- May resist switching, even when they like the next activity
- May not know how to disengage
- May be overwhelmed by shifting gears
- May have fallen into a pattern of engaging in willful contests

Questions with unlimited choice give children permission to be willful. Asking
"Do you want . . ." invites children, who as preschoolers are naturally self-focused,
to be more self-focused.

*Intentional:* Telling children, "Put it away . . ." is a clear statement that you
expect this to happen. Try these responses:

- When children request help putting work away, help them. Children who
  ask for help give you an opportunity to collaborate, with all the above
  benefits.

- Engage another child: "Tim, please help Nan put the blocks away." If Nan says emphatically, "No! I want to do it myself," you have achieved your goal of Nan's stopping work. Moreover, Nan is taking responsibility for putting her work away on her own. If Nan chooses to have Tim help, that is fine, too. Your goal is that work stop, not that Nan put things away by herself.
- When children ask to leave work out, talk it over. A teacher's objections may be legitimate, or the child's desire may be reasonable. At times leaving work out is a good option. Be sure you and the child listen to each other's reasons.

In using declarative statements, choose words that state your intention precisely.

*Tips:*

- With young children, age 2 or 3, request just one action ("Please stop now," not "Please stop now and put your work away") unless you are certain the children are capable of following two-part instructions.
- Resist being arbitrary: Does it really matter if children put work away themselves, with you, or with a friend?
- Request what you believe a child can accomplish in what Vygotsky calls the "zone of proximal development," that is, an act that both builds on and stretches current abilities.

**Choices.** Unlimited: "What do you want to do?" vs. limited: "Do you want to use the blocks or a puzzle?"

*Unintentional:* Asking children what *they* want to do can overwhelm children who are not self-directed or who have no experience making choices. These children may:

- Have something in mind but not know an item's name or location
- Not have developed enough focus or sense of self to know what they want to do
- Need guidance in learning how to make choices

*Intentional:* Offering two choices gives you a chance to remind children:

- Where something is
- What its name is
- Of something they have enjoyed but have forgotten

If a child says no to the options you offer, offer another two: "Do you want to use the puppets or the tracing stencils?" Think carefully so you offer choices that are likely to interest the particular child. If among several choices nothing sparks interest, try one of these options:

- Say, "Come watch . . ." Bring the child to a lesson you are giving to another child or small group.
- Say, "I have something special just for you," and bring out a new material.
- Take the child to an activity that you recall interested him in the past.

Give more one-on-one time to children who do not know how to choose than to children who easily make choices. Making choices is one of the most salient characteristics of being human, and children who cannot choose need support to learn how. These children benefit from your planning in advance and keeping notes of what to offer:

- Erika might like to set out the place mats for lunch.
- Derrick might like to make a Lego helicopter; he was fascinated when the helicopter hovered over the playground.
- John spends a lot of time watching the gerbil; he might like to clean the cage and refill the water bottle.

Being first to use a new material or to have an out-of-the-ordinary experience can impel reluctant children to choose.

*Tip:* Review Exercise 6 in Chapter 1, on making lists of choices for individual children.

**Taking Turns.** Top-down: "Tell him it's your turn," vs. bottom-up: "Ask him if he is finished."

*Unintentional:* Because turn-taking limits the time children spend on an activity, it may interrupt children's focus and interfere with repetitive activity. Repetition is one of the most powerful aids to learning because repetition leads to mastery. Removing an engaged child so another can use a material destroys focus and eliminates repetition.

*Intentional:* Children have the right to finish what they start. Insisting that they take turns violates that right.

Rather than using turn-taking when everyone wants to use particular materials:

- Consider whether your classroom has enough compelling materials and, if not, add more interest-provoking materials.
- Train children who want a "turn" to *ask* whether the other child is finished. This builds the ability to collaborate.
  - ➤ Asking protects the right of the child using the material to say no and thus complete a cycle of activity on his own.
  - ➤ Children who ask, learn to be respectful of others' rights.

Children using the material may invite another child to join, but if they want to continue on their own, the right to do so must be protected. Consider: If someone said it was her turn to use my computer when I was concentrating, I would be furious! Children have the same right as adults not to have their material taken from them. Turn-taking is arbitrary because some children may want to use something

for a few minutes and rapidly lose interest, while others may be deeply engaged. *Tip:* Don't sacrifice focus
for turn-taking. Eventually everyone will have a turn;
the turn does not have to come at the expense of another child's concentrated engagement.

✦ Exercise: Sharpen your ability to make
intentional requests.

- For 1 week list everything you ask children to
  do in exactly the words you use.
- Review your list alone or with a colleague.
- Determine which of your questions or
  statements are not intentional.
- Rephrase what you have said to make it
  intentional.

> **KEY POINT:**
> Subtle differences
> in how questions
> and directions are
> phrased have big
> effects on children's
> willingness to
> comply and on
> their ability to
> concentrate, to
> use judgment,
> and to function
> independent of
> teacher interaction.

If you are puzzled about this exercise, email me (ann@annlewin-benham.com)
your questions about word choices and I'll engage in a dialogue with you to try to
clarify intentional vs. unintentional use of language.

## Words That Resolve Altercations About Sharing

Altercations are a regular feature of early childhood classrooms. One of the most
common altercations is over sharing. Problems will occur, but whether they escalate
and how they are resolved depend on what teachers believe about sharing and what
words they use to help children reach resolution. Consider the following examples.

**Directives.** Directive: "Ask her to share (whatever)" vs. choice: "Ask her if she
wants to share (whatever)."

*Unintentional:* Asking children to share imposes an adult's sense of fairness.
Problems about sharing occur most frequently when there is only *one* of a desirable object or piece of equipment or when something new and alluring has been
added to the classroom.

*Intentional:* Children who ask one another whether they *want* to share rather
than hearing an arbitrary rule that they *must* share, take charge of a social interaction. Allowing children to make such choices demonstrates teachers' trust in
children's judgment. Children are innately fair and have a strong sense of right
and wrong. Moreover, children are empathetic and can relate to another child's
desire not to share. Teachers' trust strengthens children's sense of fairness, their
understanding of right/wrong distinctions, and their feelings of empathy.

**The One-of-Something Problem.** Top-down: "I have a list . . ." vs. bottom-up,
"Let's make a plan." In top-down solutions, teachers develop a list of who will
have access to the desirable item and when. The list has children's names, the time
limit, and a chart showing who uses the item at what time on what day.

In the bottom-up solution, the teacher involves the *full class* in the question of how everyone can have access to the item.

***Generating Rules.*** When classroom rules are formed in a process that involves children, rules are likely to be followed. Using such a process, the teacher:

- Gathers the full class and begins, "We have a new (whatever). There is only one. How do you suggest we share it?"
- Listens carefully to children' answers, writes down what they say, and reads answers back to the children. If the answers are complex, the teacher asks the children to think about what the best solutions are. The key to the success of this process is the teacher's accepting what the children agree is the best way to share.

*Tips:* Children are most likely to arrive at a workable solution if:

- The conversation is not rushed
- Solutions are truly proposed by the children
- There is adequate time for the children to reflect—several conversations over several days with lots of digestion time between discussions
- The item is not put in the classroom until the children have agreed on how to share it
- Each conversation is unhurried so children's ideas have time to develop

The teacher returns to the conversation after some time has elapsed, a day or two, perhaps a week. Before reading ideas generated at the last conversation, the teacher:

- Asks children to raise their hands whenever they hear an idea they think will work
- Explains that she will keep track of the ideas children consider workable
- Reads the children's previous ideas: "In our last conversation about how to share the (item), you made many suggestions. I'll read them to you. Walter said, (quote); Dorothea said (quote)."
- Quotes every child's idea and has the children discuss each one

*Note:* Conversation means:

- Encouraging the children to talk to one another, not just to the teacher
- Listening carefully to record the children's ideas
- That day or another day, repeating the children's ideas back to them

In these ways teachers orchestrate conversation. They do not offer solutions or comment on the children's ideas with facial or other expressions. They help children reflect by reporting back what children have said and ensuring that everyone listens to each speaker.

Once the children have suggested, thought, conversed, winnowed, reconsidered, and conversed more—a process that might last 2 weeks or more—the teacher asks the children to:

- Summarize how the (item) should be shared
- Decide whether they think the plan will work
- Consider whether they want to think more and discuss the matter again

If the children disagree about what to do next, the teacher explains the process:

- "I'll read the plan as you developed it."
- "There are two choices: You want to discuss the plan more. Or you want to test the plan now."
- "We'll vote. I'll count hands. The majority rules."
- "Remember: You will either discuss more *or* test the plan now.
- "Raise your hand if you want to discuss more."
- The teacher counts the hands.
- "Raise your hand if you want to test the plan now."

The teacher counts the hands, reports the outcome, and does as the majority ruled.

---

**KEY POINTS:**
- Children remember and respect rules they themselves generate.
- A successful outcome depends on teachers trusting a process and allowing adequate time for the process to evolve before arriving at a solution.

---

### Summary

Words influence children's behavior. The key to changing dysfunctional behavior is teachers' analyzing word choices and their impact. Keys to classroom management are teachers' listening, helping children learn to choose, and involving all children in collaborative rule-making.

## TECHNIQUES IN MINDFUL COMMUNICATION

Mindfulness grows out of a tradition based on the teachings of the Indian spiritual leader Gautama Buddha, who is thought to have lived around 400 B.C.E. Writings based on Buddha's teachings were transcribed from oral tradition long after his death and date from about 100 B.C.E. to 300 C.E. These writings exist in 27 birch-bark manuscripts held by the British Library (wikipedia.org/wiki/Gautama_Buddha). First I explain mindfulness, which some consider the current leading edge of psychotherapy; then I adapt mindfulness to ECE.

Teachers who make a conscious effort to examine the patterns of the words they use are being intentional in their word choices. Borrowing techniques from the practice of mindfulness can improve the quality of both listening and respond-ing. This section is informed by Kelly Wilson's book *Mindfulness for Two* (2008). Wilson says:

> Words have an amazing capacity to make monsters present. We confuse words with the things that the words point to. We do this sometimes when the thing pointed to doesn't even exist. There was a time when many people wouldn't sail far out to sea for fear of falling from the edge of the earth. (p. 51)

Children's fusing fears into real things is captured in the traditional Scottish prayer:

> From ghoulies and ghosties
> And long-leggedy beasties
> And things that go bump in the night,
> Good Lord, deliver us!

When verbal utterings are taken literally and invested with authority and con-sequence, psychologists say "fusion" has occurred (Wilson, 2008, p. 51). In the extreme, fusion disrupts normal functioning, as when people have severe phobias. A goal of psychotherapy is to *defuse* patients' delusions. The analogy for education is to defuse patterns of thinking that could be improved through mindfulness.

### What Are Your Patterns?

Without pattern, daily life would be impossible; we quickly would be stymied by tasks of rising, dressing, breakfasting, packing lunches, and getting everyone to their destinations. Routines make life possible. But paradoxically, routines also shut down thinking, close avenues for new approaches, create ruts, and stymie possibilities for awe and wonder to enter the classroom. Consider your routine beginning with morning meeting: Is it routinized, dull, repetitive? Do children chatter, poke, or engage in other nonattentive behavior? Or does the meeting ad-mit change, surprise, and long, open-ended, unscripted conversation?

Wilson (2008) again: "Humans are great at being physically present but psy-chologically absent" (p. 80). In conversations, "all of us have had at least some trouble with listening. This difficulty is in large part due to the fact that, without active and focused attention, we can literally miss half or more of what people say to us" (p. 79). With brutal honesty, Wilson describes his one-on-one therapy with patients in which his mind wanders.

How honestly do teachers look at their interactions? When teachers go through the routines of greeting, calendar, letter-of-the-day, flannel board, and whatever else they do with the full class, are they simultaneously reworking the argument with their spouse that morning, the grocery list for tomorrow's dinner party, an al-ternate route home to avoid construction . . . ? You get the idea. Are teachers really present when they face the full class, give lessons to individuals or small groups, or talk with peers?

A 2nd-grade teacher I knew told me with pride that when she settled her class into silent reading, she wrote Christmas cards or thank-you notes, or attended to other personal work. While it is unlikely that an early childhood teacher could do that, we can be just as absent if our mind is on one topic and our lesson on another. And if our lessons are boring, children's behavior will tell us: Their minds will focus on something they find interesting, as shown in Figure 5.1, and/or their bodies will move.

What of the children when teachers' minds wander? I imagine that children know the adult is not listening. Are we letting them down as Roger's mother let him down? Kahneman (2011) says, "Many parents have discovered, perhaps with some guilt, they can read a story to a child while thinking of something else" (p. 23). In the first years, when they are still mastering the mechanics of speech, children are especially aware of adults' emotions—their unspoken feelings, their attention or lack thereof, their presence (or absence) in the moment of an interaction. It is much easier to "fool" adults into thinking you are present than it is to fool children. Wilson (2008) says: Notice "that while you're not listening, you're somewhere else and often somewhen else" (p. 79). He suggests trying the following experiment:

> When speaking casually to another person, just toss random words into your sentences. Don't change inflection or pace; just drop them in like they belong there. People will often hear what fits and not necessarily what you said. (p. 79)

Wilson advocates bringing your wandering mind back to the present by taking a "mindful moment." He offers this exercise called "Just Sit Still":

> Simply stop reading at the end of this paragraph. Go find something that you can use to keep time for three minutes. Start the timer, and let your awareness come to rest on your breath. Let go of any problem solving until the timer goes off. See what happens.

Figure 5.1.
Boring lesson =
distracted children.

> If you found yourself getting busy [mentally], welcome to the human race. Minds hate unemployment. If there's nothing to do, they're happy to generate make-work projects. And they don't ask our permission when they do. (p. 82)

Evidence of mindfulness is seen in "body language, eye contact, interactions with . . . objects close to hand. But . . . the spoken word [is paramount so] . . . let's focus on two aspects of our talking, namely our voices and the content of what we have to say" (p. 82). In putting word skills to work for children, the voice is teachers' best tool—its tone and pitch, pacing, tempo, and pauses.

*Tone.* Wilson advocates a "soft, steady, deliberate voice," in the midrange of your normal speaking pitch. With such a tone, you have someplace to "go" for emphasis. Watch how Wilson uses tone and pitch in the following description of a mindfulness activity:

> Begin to notice the temperature of your hands [pause and notice]. See if you can notice that there is slight variation in that temperature [pause and notice]. See if you can notice that one hand is just slightly [with voice just a bit higher and a bit softer, like you're telling a secret] warmer than the other hand [pause and notice]. See if you can notice any tiny sensations that go along with that warmth [with voice a bit higher and softer—and then pause and notice]. See if you can notice that, right—at—this—very—moment [said with just a bit more force—and then pause and notice]. (p. 83)

The continuous "slow, soft, steady speech" (p. 83) draws both teacher and children to the exercise and keeps them in the present moment.

*Pacing.* Wilson advocates going slow! He paces himself by engaging in whatever he asks others to do. Having children keep their eyes closed to shut out visual input helps the children slow down and also puts intention into your direction to the children. Your own involvement in giving and following the directions is the best guide for pacing. Moreover, in following the directions yourself, you might notice something, such as, in the above hand exercise, an itch or a tingle. Teachers can bring anything they notice into the exercise and ask children to notice the sensation in their hands. Wilson says that mindful exercises foster "conscious, non-judgmental attention to things as they are in the here and now" (p. 84).

Wilson's instruction pattern typically is:

- "Notice
- Speak
- Then notice again, just a bit more mindfully
- Then speak
- Then notice
- Speak again
- Notice one more time" (p. 84)

This pattern sets a calm, consistent, mindful pace. In a mindfulness exercise with a slow, steady pace as background, if children's attention has wandered, any variation in the teacher's voice will bring children's attention back to the voice. The slow pacing provides "depth to moments where the pace speeds up just a bit," and the soft background "brings into relief the places where particular words are given a bit more emphasis" (p. 85). In other words, your voice creates almost a hypnotic state, not in the sense of sleep but of attention and hyperawareness of the moment.

*Pauses and Tempo.* "The more consistent the backbeat, the more clearly we note the variations. . . . In daily conversations our attention drifts in and out, and the unexpected changes draw our attention back to what's being said" (p. 85). The variation also short-circuits the habit of "half listening" in both teacher and children. Wilson suggests putting pauses in where they don't belong, not where you would expect commas and periods. Too many would be annoying, but something unexpected maintains attention.

Wilson listens to his own words to determine the length of a pause:

> When I can feel a bit of anticipation, I pause just a bit longer and then let the next word drop. I hold these pauses as long as I can comfortably tolerate—and then I hold them just a little longer. I notice my urge to move ahead. (p. 86)

As you brought your awareness of the itch or tingle in your hand to the children's attention, you can bring the urge to move on to their attention. Ask the children whether they notice themselves trying to move ahead. The time the leader (clinician, teacher) takes to notice impulses gives children the time to do so also. "Our natural inclination is almost always to move more quickly than is useful. As a general rule, slow down just a little more than you think is enough" (p. 85). Analogies to pauses in speech are rests and held notes in music, light in deep shade or shadows in bright sun, negative or void spaces in art—blanks on a canvas or hollows in a sculpture.

Wilson suggests practicing mindfulness exercises by yourself. He says that your mind won't like the pauses, but to keep at it and attend to the void. With tone and pitch, pacing, and pauses, he advocates practice, more practice, and more practice. Practice, Wilson finds, enables you to be more direct and powerful—or, in our work, intentional and reflective.

## Tips for Mindfulness Exercises

Noticing anything—a bit of nature, a scene, trees blowing in the breeze, leaves rustling, streams flowing, clouds forming, or sensations in a part of our body—is a powerful way to focus. But Wilson has found that focus on real things co-opts the mind and draws us into thoughts about what we are imagining. Instead, he advocates focusing on:

- Our breathing
- Sensations in our hands
- One prominent sound in the room
- A spot on the wall
- Detail in "white noise"

In other words, draw yourself and the children away from distractions or day-dreaming and into the present moment.

The example Wilson gives is to "notice a host of subtler details in the breath:

- The coolness at the back of the throat as air moves into the lungs
- The peculiar sensation of air coursing in through the nostrils
- The rise and fall of the belly
- The tightness in the chest as the lungs reach their full capacity
- The warmth that rises in the back of the throat on exhalation" (p. 88)

He calls this a "winnowing of more prominent aspects of experience to more subtle ones [that] can be done with tactile sensations" (p. 89).

Wilson also suggests concentrating on the feeling of your body in contact with the chair or the floor, or the "tiniest details of sensation that tell where clothing touches and where it does not" (p. 89). He suggests imagining tracing the margins "between touching and not touching. Small details, that require a great deal of attention, assist in bringing intentional, focused awareness to the present moment" (p. 89).

If you are using unfamiliar content with young children, such as nostrils or lungs, introduce the vocabulary apart from the mindfulness exercise. Use only one word at a time, for example, nostrils:

- Feel your own nostrils, then say, "I felt my nostrils."
- Have children copy your movements.
- Place a hand beneath your nostrils.
- Focus on the gentle breathing in and out (in Tom Sawyer-like fashion).
- Ask children to focus on the breath from their nostrils on their hands.
- Listen to children's comments about what they feel.

In introducing new content to children, follow the techniques you are practicing in mindfulness—regulated pitch varied for emphasis, and pacing with pauses.

Practice mindfulness techniques alone and out loud before bringing them into the classroom. Notice whether these delivery techniques cause children to pay closer attention. Reflect on the differences you notice in children's attentiveness. If you see no change, choose different content and practice again. Or work with a second adult—one leads the mindfulness exercise; the other unobtrusively observes the children.

Keep practicing until your performance becomes smooth and natural. Be aware that what you are doing is not new or a fad. Mindfulness techniques are grounded in practice over millennia by some of the world's greatest teachers. What is new is that you are bringing the practice of mindfulness to very young children and that mindfulness may be new to you, unless you are a student of yoga, tai chi, or other ancient Eastern traditions. The essence of mindfulness is that it is nonjudgmental. What you think and feel is neither good nor bad, it just is. Mindfulness techniques still the constant voice, and especially the critical voice, that hampers intention, reflection, and the capacity to be truly present with the children in your care.

Finally, consider the problems that your mind races to solve all day long and in wakeful periods at night. Over and over you go, worrying about the past, ruminating about the future as your mind makes up reasons for what did happen and creates scenarios of what might happen—all of them stories, make-believe because we can neither change the past nor control the future. Kahneman (2011) reports: "The ease with which ideas of various risks come to mind and the emotional reactions to these risks are inextricably linked. Frightening thoughts and images occur to us with particular ease, and thoughts of danger that are fluent and vivid exacerbate fear" (p. 139). "Worry and rumination are examples of fusion [those 'things that go bump in the night'] because the storied version of events dominates over the potential richness of experience" (Wilson, 2008, p. 100) in the here and now.

## Summary

Using mindfulness techniques can increase teachers' and children's listening capacity. Mindfulness is the essence of teaching that is intentional and reflective. Techniques require no purchases, only a willingness to bring an ancient practice into preschool classrooms.

## MINDFULNESS IN CONVERSATION

The use of words evolves over the first year of life. In the first weeks, infants learn to associate emotions with experiences. Conversation begins early, long before the first word at age 1. Here I discuss the development of communication in infancy and how infants "converse." I describe communication with family, and I show how to grow the ability to converse beyond the classroom.

### Infant Communication

From infancy, children want to converse. In the book *The First Idea*, Greenspan and Shanker (2004) describe processes that evolve almost from birth as infants experience the drive to make contact with other humans.

> The biological potential for learning from experience . . . includes our rudimentary capacities to perceive, organize, and respond. . . . In human beings . . . even the tools of learning must be learned and relearned by each new generation. These include the ability to attend, interact with others, engage in emotional and social signaling, construct complex patterns, organize information symbolically, and use symbols to think. (pp. 4–5)

The "rudimentary capacities" are integral to human biology; the "learned" "tools of learning" are "determined by variations in each individual and time period, that is, they express the near infinite variations of human groups" and are "embedded in our cultural learning processes and not in the structure of our genes" (p. 5). Three simple examples are English language vocabulary and grammar for children born into English-speaking homes, clay-cutting tools, and scooters.

✦ Exercise 1: Find "learned" "tools of learning"—tangible.

Everything man-made and all natural materials are potentially "learned" "tools of learning." Use this exercise to raise your awareness of the virtually infinite number of readily available "tools" that can be used to engage learning processes.

✦ Exercise 2: Find "learned" "tools of learning"—intangible.

1. Be creative in listing the intangible"learned" "tools of learning."
2. Consider whether to put customs, manners, and mores on your list—some of the intangible "tools" of culture.
3. If you are familiar with a culture other than that of the United States, list "learned" "tools of learning" for that culture.
4. Engage parents from other cultures in this exercise.

Cultural patterns of adult/child interactions form the basis for learning that is "reciprocal, co-regulated, [and] emotional" (p. 30). As defined by Greenspan and Shanker:

- "Interaction" is generally thought of as the social interactions between child and caregiver(s).
- "Reciprocal" relates to the "back-and-forth nature of preverbal interactions between infant and caregiver" with a "conversation-like pattern to their interactions" (p. 31).
- "Co-regulation" is the continuous influence infant and caregiver have on each other in which they "together create new behaviors and meanings" (p. 31), with the infant not just responding but initiating interactions.
- Emotion refers to feelings of pleasure, surprise, annoyance, disgust, anger, to name merely five, as well as overwhelming feelings of "rage, fear, or emotional hunger or neediness that press for direct discharge in fixed actions" (p. 28).

Involved, responsive caregiver(s), through co-regulated interactions, help infants and young children tame their catastrophic emotions. During the first month, infants learn to regulate facial muscles, a function of the developing nervous system. The relationship with the caregiver provides the impetus for the infant to make facial expressions and other movements intentionally (p. 29). This stage begins in the first weeks of life. At this stage, "conversation" begins—the regular back-and-forth responses that are mutually pleasurable and intentional, and involve increasingly complex sounds, gestures, and facial expressions.

Greenspan and Shanker believe that these early interactions build babies' ability to regulate their mood. When babies realize that caregivers understand their intentions, they gradually learn to modulate overwhelming emotions and to trust that their needs will be met. "There is, therefore, less of a tendency to explode into desperate action" (p. 32). It is in the multitude of minute-by-minute interactions that babies learn to regulate their emotions: mother who smiles and coos on hearing an infant's distressed cry; dad who changes the poopy diaper and gently cleans his child; the caregiver who is there with a warm bottle, with talk, song, and smiles. These seemingly small events multiply and lead to infants feeling secure.

✦ Exercise: Change an infant's mood through co-regulation.

1. Approach an infant who is in a state: agitated, fussy, disengaged, overstimulated.

2. Make your own behavior match the infant's state.
3. Gradually change your behavior to calm agitation, redirect fussiness, dispel disengagement, or compose overstimulation.

As the emotions grow, conversations become part of long exchanges in which toddlers use gesture and complex social interactions, taking an adult by the hand, leading him where the toddler wants to go, pointing, and using what Maria Montessori (1963, p. 126) calls "fusive" talk (see Figure 5.2)—the combination of two or more syllables to stand for an entire thought: mama-go-coo, meaning, "Mommy, let's go to the kitchen and get me a cookie." By age 2½, children are capable of speaking in fully grammatical sentences and have a vocabulary of 1,200 to 2,400 words, a number that can expand to several thousand by age 6 (Brown, 1973; Montessori, 1963; Pinker, 1994).

## Communication with Families

Many teachers believe that conversation stops with "good-bye" at day's end. Here I discuss conversation that involves families.

At stoplights, peer into the car in the next lane. Is there a parent and young children? What are they doing? Often I see everyone on a handheld device—mom or dad on the cell phone, children from toddlers on using pads. Or watch family groups in restaurants. Often everyone is in his or her own electronic world during this "shared" time. Unlike Roger, the children are too absorbed to ask for their parents' attention. Conversation? Rare! When I do see parents interacting with children, I often stop to comment on what good parenting (or grandparenting) I have observed. The response is always surprise and delight.

✦ Exercise 1: Observe family conversation with children.

For a month, observe out-of-school family interactions. Take notes. Use your notes to examine what you believe about your role. Consider: Should you talk with parents about drive time or restaurant meals? What would you say?

Figure 5.2. The toddler wants to know the name of an unfamiliar object. He points and, in fusive talk, asks, "Lus lat?" ("What is that machine?")

✦ Exercise 2: Talk with families about conversing with children.

Hold a parent meeting on family communication. It might go like this:

T: "The topic tonight/today is family communication. Let's begin by describing what you do during drive time or meals at restaurants or whatever situation you want to describe. Who will begin?"

Let the silence remain until someone breaks it. Throughout the meeting, restrain all impulses to comment or lecture. Make sure that anyone who wants to speak is heard and that no one interrupts a speaker.

If after 10 or 15 minutes no one speaks, reintroduce the topic, saying exactly what you said initially. And wait.

If after another 10 or 15 minutes no one has spoken, comment: "Yes, this is a weighty topic and requires lots of thought. We'll return to it at another meeting. Today/tonight I will read an unedited transcript of a classroom conversation." Choose one that is rather long and be sure to read it verbatim and without comment. When you finish, offer copies for parents to take home and read. Announce that your next meeting will be their comments on the conversation.

### Summary

Parents need as much help as children—albeit different help—in reflecting on their beliefs, patterns, and conversations. While it might stretch teachers' sense of their role, talking with families about parent/child communication could be a force for some families to recast the substance of family time.

## CONCLUSION

I have tried in this chapter to dissect word choices, to explain intentional versus unintentional choices, to convey the impact of silence, and to show how to stop the mind's word clatter. I have also returned to the all-important period of infancy and introduced mindfulness techniques for parent meetings. In Chapter 8 I will show how to hold conversations with young children that let their voices be heard, not in random, run-on expression, but in respectful give-and-take on topics of importance to them.

I am an author and a teacher. I love words. I hope every teacher loves words. In their choice of words, teachers exert profound influence over children, for better and worse. Words have the power to make spirits soar or to deflate them, to soothe hearts or wound hearts. Word choice determines the quality of intention and reflection.

I close this chapter with words by the poet John Keats (1884):

"And they shall be accounted poet kings
Who simply say the most heart-easing things."

# CHAPTER 6

# Intentionally and Reflectively Connecting Hand/Eye

Twist, turn, make, model, click, drag, hack, push, pull, mold, hold, but don't poke; don't ever poke.

—Sheppy Lewin, age 13

---

**TECHNIQUE 6**
Manipulate materials purposefully: Provide diverse materials
to stimulate increasingly skillful eye/hand coordination from birth on.

---

It is unlikely that in non-Reggio–inspired schools, focus on the development of children's hands has matched the intensity seen in Reggio teachers. This becomes clear as you look at children's work from Reggio schools which reflects:

- Skill far beyond our expectations for what young children can do
- Competent use of tools and materials

Some Reggio works are well known because of two large Reggio-created exhibits that travel internationally: "The Hundred Languages of Children" and "The Wonder of Learning." Moreover, Reggio publications, including extensive exhibit catalogues, contain high-quality images of children's works. Study the images and essays in the book *Everything Has a Shadow, Except Ants* (Sturloni & Vecchi, 2000): The thick book, studded with photos of children's ventures with light and shadow, is rich enough to be a 0-through-6 curriculum in using light and shadow to teach observation, problem solving, and drawing. Delve into *Children, Arts, Artists* (Reggio Children, 2004) to read extensive documentation of diverse projects from infancy through age 6. All Reggio publications show evidence of hand competence.

At a minimum, browse the website www.ReggioChildren.com. Ignore photos of adult crowds and teachers at the Loris Malaguzzi Remida Center. Instead find images of children and their work. There are not many and they are small. But peruse each: The images reflect children's intention. Look at body positions, facial expressions, and especially hands. Look at the children's drawings, paintings, and sketches in diverse colors and media. Because I made a dozen trips between 1992 and 1995 and observed in classrooms in about 15 of the (then) 32 schools, I can put the small images in context: I read the images as a reminder of what I witnessed—extensive explorations; robust, complex constructions; and sophisticated hand skills in using tools and shaping materials.

While teachers are virtually invisible in Reggio publications, they actually exert strong influence over what projects are undertaken, how they evolve, and the final results. Reggio teachers:

- Direct the flow of children's work
- Ensure that work is purposeful
- Suspect, from experience, what children might accomplish
- Reflect critically to determine whether what was accomplished is what was intended

While children's hands have indeed done remarkable work, the teacher has been a not-so-silent partner throughout—observing, listening, chivvying, cajoling, inviting, urging, insisting, and pushing past "sticky" places. The role is opposite of laissez-faire teaching and the notion that "it-all-comes-from-the-child-if-we-(teachers)-stand-by-and-watch." Confusion in American Reggio-inspired schools stems from a misunderstanding of teachers' pivotal role.

Reggio teachers' intention is based on:

- How much they see when they observe children
- Confidence in their role in projects
- Ease in knowing they cannot predict, much less control, project outcomes
- Expertise in using techniques that both exploit children's potential and inspire them to perform to the utmost
- Extensive study and discussion of diverse works by educators, philosophers, artists, scientists, and technologists

The rhythm of work in Reggio classes is simultaneously relaxed and intense.

This chapter applies the ideas of intention and reflection to the hand—possibly the most important part of the body in which to develop competence. In Howard Gardner's (1983) concept of intelligences, use of the hand involves both the visual/spatial and kinesthetic (movement) intelligences. To understand the hand, I look at the role of materials in hand development, the hand's evolution, and the use of increasingly complex materials from infancy through age 6. The role of materials is the first topic.

## MATERIALS AND THE BRAIN

Materials are to hand development what food is to the body—the substance that makes action possible. Without food the body dies, without materials the hand cannot develop. First I discuss why materials are important. Then I discuss the two lives of materials: In the "first life," children explore materials' properties; in the "second life," children exploit materials' potentials. I show the "first life" in the context of children from 0 to 3 and the "second life" in the context of children from 3 to 6. The age division is arbitrary because exploration can take place across the life span, whenever someone uses new a material or whenever a child becomes deeply engrossed in a material. Psychologist Mihaly Csikszentmihalyi (1990) calls such engagement being "in flow."

## Mastery of Basics

The first thing children must learn about materials is how they behave. This stage often is overlooked when Reggio-inspired schools are new. Frequently I see works by children in U.S. Reggio-inspired schools that lack the complexity, originality, or depth of things made by children in Reggio schools. Why? Teachers jump too quickly to make some "thing" before children have fully explored a material. What is too quickly? I opine that the more time children spend in the company of a teacher or other children with no end in mind other than open-ended exploration of materials, the more competent the work will be when children make some "thing," that is, when they use the material for a specific purpose. Why? Through repetition the hand comes to understand the nature of a material and how it can be manipulated.

Imagine trying to read before you have learned what sounds the letters make. While there are still proponents of teaching children to read by recognizing whole words, "research has repeatedly shown that the intensive teaching of phonics brings on greater gains in primary reading than does the use of any kind of look-say methodology" (Groff, 1977, pp. 323–332). In their role in literacy, letter sounds and shapes are the "material" from which reading evolves.

Or, imagine trying to solve a multiplication problem without knowing the times tables "cold," or being able to zip correctly through multiplication "facts" ($2 \times 7 = 14$; $9 \times 6 = 54$; $12 \times 8 = 96$). Without mastery of the 156 multiplication facts for numbers $1 \times 0$ through $12 \times 12$, your performance will be substandard. In their role in mathematics, number facts are the material from which arithmetic operations, primes, properties of the number 9, the Fibonacci series, algebra, many games, and other areas of mathematics evolve. Singapore Math (see en.wikipedia.org/wiki/Singapore_math) is successful because before children manipulate abstract numerical symbols, they explore mathematical concepts by handling concrete objects. Tolstoy railed against education that trained children to perform calculations by rote at the expense of their understanding anything about how numbers function:

> Not one boy knew how to solve, that is how to pose, the simplest problem of addition and subtraction. However, they were able to operate with numbers in the abstract, multiplying thousands with dexterity and speed. (Tolstoy, quoted in Pinch & Armstrong, 1982, p. 78)

So it is with materials—mastery of basics comes before applications. The difference between proficiency with materials and with letters and numbers is that use of materials combines hand skills *and* brain skills, while reading and arithmetic are largely brain-skill based. Early number concepts are best understood by manipulating objects. Montessori understood that a trimodal approach—sight, sound, and touch—is the best way to learn letters. Our culture deems letter and number work "important" and hand skills "artsy-fartsy." Nothing could be more untrue.

The Italians—in fact, Europeans, Chinese, Japanese, Indians, and numerous other cultures—value products of the hand. These cultures, far older than ours, have long traditions of hand production that have yielded timeless sculpture, tapestry, jewelry, mosaics, furniture, painting, and more. Reverence for centuries-old, hand-wrought treasures has embedded the desire to educate children's hands. Many Americans don't share this value. And while Americans gasp at Reggio children's sophisticated work, they miss the facts that this work results from highly analytic thinking, scientific process, sophisticated cognition, powerful hand skills, and hand/eye coordination that resonate throughout the brain. Many Americans fail to understand the processes, time, or value in producing much of anything other than good test scores.

## Materials and Brain Organization

What is the relationship between materials and the brain? And what is the role of materials in how the brain organizes content, concept, and context? Teachers need to convince parents that when the hand is working, the brain is engaged. Using materials is not about learning to make things, but about making things in order to learn. The materials children use either limit or expand what children think about, and thereby determine what relationships the brain can make. The examples that follow explain a few higher-level thinking skills children can acquire from using materials.

*1. Hand Skills.* Children can develop extraordinary manual dexterity. Consider the competent drawing in Figure 6.1, the dome of the U.S. Capitol by a child 4 years, 8 months old. The proportion and regularity of the lines are strikingly like the photo the child is using as a model. Brain functions include:

Figure 6.1. The young child's copy of a complex image is amazingly accurate.

- Focusing
- Ensuring that the hand does what the visual system perceives and what the child intends
- Maintaining one-to-one correspondence
- Holding an image in mind in order to reproduce it

These are all higher-level brain skills. Brain networks develop when the hand is challenged to acquire skills in using such diverse materials as cardboard, wire, clay, paper, fiber, looms, fine-point markers, scissors, pencils, rulers, and fasteners, to name a few. Consider: Research shows that

> neuronal networks in musicians' brains have increased volumes of gray matter in motor, auditory, and visuospatial areas of the cortex, as well as in the cerebellum. . . . The anatomical changes they [researchers] observed . . . were strongly correlated with the age at which musical training began [the younger the better] and with the intensity of practice and rehearsal. (O. Sacks, 2008, pp. 100–101)

We can expect similar findings when hand training in the graphic arts has been examined as carefully as hand training in music.

*Brain skills acquired*: Dexterity and precision in using a wide variety of materials and tools that require hand/eye coordination in tasks that increase in complexity and demand for accuracy.

**2. Pattern Recognition.** Children from 2 years on begin to make realistic drawings from random lines and shapes. For example, when using black markers with extra-fine nibs, 3- and 4-year-olds have drawn and named clearly recognizable images by combining lines and shapes in intentional and highly specific ways (see Figure 6.2).

*Brain skills acquired:* The ability to use content (circles, lines) to form concepts (man, train).

**3. Problem Solving.** Children can learn that there are many ways to approach a problem. For example:

- Making a model may be the best way to begin to build something complex.
- A model is based on an idea.
- The idea can be sketched.
- A 3-D representation can be made from paper.
- A more detailed rendering can be made from clay.
- A preliminary working model can be made from cardboard.
- Further models can be made from plastic, metal, wood, foam core, brick, or other materials.
- A final working device can be made from those materials that will best achieve the idea that evolved from concept to reality.

**Figure 6.2. The brain seeks patterns, as is evident in the drawings of very young children.**

Age 3

Age 3

Age 4

Age 4

The brain grows when it is required to transform something from one material to another.

*Brain skills acquired:*

- The ability to put *content* (the idea of a concrete "thing") into a *context* (the materials from which to make the "thing")
- Analytic capacities of planning and implementation
- Capacity to use increasingly sophisticated tools and materials

**4. Symbolic Representation.** Children from 0 to 6 can learn that objects can be used as symbols. For example, consider representations in which children chose subject and material:

- Translucent blue paper for water
- A worked piece of clay for a boat
- Cork (bottle stoppers and/or flat sheets) for a river bank
- A ladder made of toothpicks

The brain grows when it makes connections between an actual object or feature of the world and its representation.

*Brain skills acquired:* The abilities:

- To think about something without having the thing at hand
- To think metaphorically:
    ➤ A rippled, glassy surface as a body of water
    ➤ A piece of shaped clay as a boat
    ➤ An arrangement of toothpicks as a ladder

**5. Motivation.** Children can learn that someone appreciates their work. When children's work is displayed so that other children, parents, and visitors can see it, the "authors and makers" are pleased. Others' affirmation motivates children.

*Brain skill acquired:* The motivation to achieve whatever one sets out to do.

**6. Classification Skills.** Children can refine their perception of what distinguishes one thing from another; in other words, they can learn the properties of objects, including:

- Size
- Shape
- Color
- Texture
- Sound
- Form
- Olfactory attributes
- Gustatory attributes

The brain grows when materials cause children to engage their sensory perceptions, to distinguish subtle differences, and to apply what they perceive to achieve specific goals.

*Brain skills acquired:*

- Acquisition of content that undergirds all thinking
- Diverse knowledge of attributes that are the basis for categorizing, classifying, and ultimately realizing anything in three-dimensional form

**Content, Concepts, Context: Brain Organizing Systems.** *Content* is everything that exists in the world. *Concepts* are ideas (psychologists call them "schema"), a mechanism in the brain that organizes content so we can make sense of the world.

*Context* means the situation, time, place, event, people, and circumstances in which content is embedded. For example:

- Cows, beetles, eagles, and thousands more creatures are *content*; the word *animal* is a *concept*.
- Silk, burlap, wool, and hundreds of other woven items are *content*; the words *textile* or *fabric* are *concepts*.
- Protractors, yardsticks, and rulers are *content*; the words *measuring device* are a *concept*.
- The representations 1, 11, 111, and 1,111 are *content*; the word *number* is a *concept*.

These relationships are shown in Figure 6.3.

We could not think if the brain did not form concepts. Moreover, content and concepts are context-dependent; that is, the meaning—or how the brain interprets content—depends on the context in which the content is embedded. For example, color does not exist in the world. "Color" is a concept the brain uses to identify a specific attribute of a particular object, namely, the way the object reflects or absorbs light waves. Consider:

- The human brain can distinguish about 2 million colors. Color is a factor of how light waves behave and how the human brain interprets light waves. The eye detects and the brain interprets the *content*, for example, what we call vermilion, rosy, ruddy, crimson, scarlet, ruby, burgundy, cherry. The brain registers these perceptions, classifies them as "red," and stores them as "colors." Color is a *concept*.
- Understanding may depend on *context*. Consider the word *ruby*: When applied to a hummingbird, it denotes a particular species. When applied to a stone, it denotes a precious gem. When used as a name, it denotes a specific girl. These are examples of "lexical" (what words mean) memory.
- The brain interprets sounds that are alike but have different meanings by using *context* to understand the *content*: "I read an exciting book" vs. "I saw an unusual red hat." These are examples of "semantic" (time/place) memory.

Children gradually learn to use content, concept, and context to make sense of the world. For example:

- The 1-year-old learning to speak, who loves orange juice, points to the rain and calls it "onj joos." The baby is using a particular instance of liquid (the *content*) as the *concept* for all liquid-like substances.
- The 4-year-old, riding for the first time in the front car of a subway train, sees the train's powerful headlight illuminating the pitch-black tunnel and says: "The light is swallowing the night." The child is applying familiar content—the effects of light at nighttime and of food leaving the mouth

Figure 6.3. The brain builds relationships because it organizes information according to the content, concept, and context.

## CONTENT

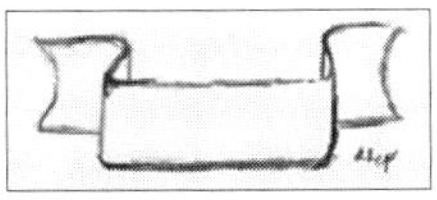

Banner 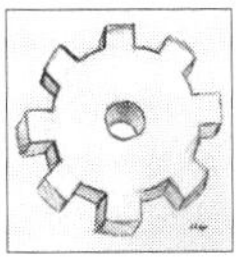              Gears               Lock

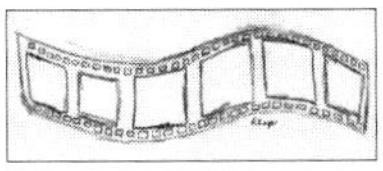

Film Strip           Cloud           Light Bulb 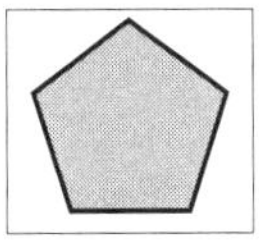          Pentagon

The world has an endless amount of *content*.
Shape—or color, texture, and other concepts—help the mind recognize content.

---

## CONCEPT

# S H A P E

The world does not contain *concepts*. *Concepts* are created by the mind.

---

## CONTEXT

Shape classifies objects. 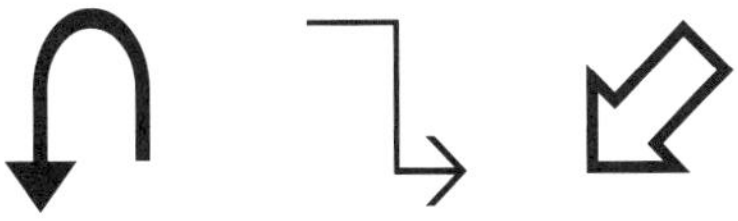          Shape makes it easy to follow directions.

Shape defines life forms.           Shape alerts the mind to warnings.

Humans build relationships—or think—by using content, concepts, and context.
These three types of mental organization enable the brain to construct meaning.

as we chew—to the unfamiliar sight of strong light in a dark tunnel. The child is using two familiar experiences (the *content*) to describe a new *context*.

A simple word for content is *idea*. Kahneman (2011) explains: An idea

> can be concrete or abstract and it can be expressed in many different ways: as a verb, as a noun, as an adjective, or as a clenched fist. Psychologists think of ideas as nodes in a vast network, called associative memory, in which each idea is linked to many others. In the current view of how associative memory works, a great deal happens at once. An idea that has been activated does not merely evoke one other idea. It activates many ideas, which in turn activate many others. (p. 52)

Figure 6.4 shows different types of links. Ideas are linked in the brain's networks. We express ideas abstractly, musically, concretely (nouns, verbs, adjectives), spatially (where), temporally (when), as images, actions, humor, feelings, symbols. We simultaneously link cause to effect (eat → grow); object to property (car → red); thing to category (milk → drink); feeling to action (snarling lion → run). Using materials establishes powerful links in children's associative memory.

✦ Exercise 1: Find examples of content, concept, and context in children's words and actions.

**Figure 6.4. The fact that "an idea activates many ideas" (Kahneman, 2011, p. 52) is called associative memory**

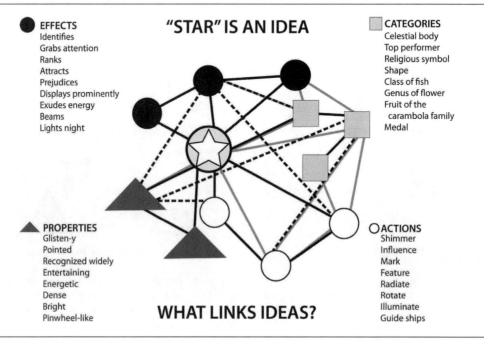

Observe and listen carefully to children of different ages experimenting with movement and speech—babies through 6-year-olds. Note all uses children make of content, concept, and context.

✦ Exercise 2: Reflect on how children are using content, concept, and context.

Classify your notes according to the relationships children make among content, concept, and context: Is the child:

- Substituting content for a concept (All liquids are "onj joos")?
- Using content as a concept (Pointing at dogs in the dog park: "Look! Snoopies!")?
- Making symbolic movements, such as pushing a block while saying, "Beep-beep!"
- Interpreting the meaning of homonyms correctly? "We read about a red witch in that book."

The purposes of these exercises are to (1) intentionally note when young children are making sense of the world and (2) reflectively analyze how young children build relationships.

Materials enable children to expand their content knowledge, form concepts, and put knowledge in context; that is, to understand experiences and express their thoughts. By using diverse materials children:

- Enlarge their knowledge of content
- Increase the number of concepts they use
- Build connections among the brain systems that are responsible for hand/eye coordination
- Expand the links in associative memory
- Strengthen connections among brain systems
- Think facilely and flexibly

> **KEY POINT:** Materials stimulate thinking.

**Summary**

During early years, *materials provide children with powerful ways to link content, concepts, and context,* vitally important skills for school and for life. As they use materials, children accumulate schema (conceptual thinking) and build the neuronal networks to practice and perfect hand skills. Representational skills and many other brain functions develop from early use of materials.

## MATERIALS AND THE HAND: 0 TO 3

Children become familiar with materials by handling them. Materials have two lives: The first life involves children becoming acquainted with the materials, a process that can take place at any age. The second life involves putting their knowledge of materials to use for specific purposes. Materials were vital to the development of the human hand as it evolved and have an important role in development from 0 to 3.

### Evolution of the Hand

Paleontologists use the precision grip of the human hand to determine which fossils are truly human. When proto-humans got up off four legs, their front legs were freed from locomotion and the life of the hand began in earnest, a change that neurologist Frank R. Wilson (1998) says altered "the repertoire of hand movements in ways that favored tool use" (p. 16). Sherwood Washburn, a pioneering scientist who is considered the "premier anthropologist" of the 20th century (Rock-Payne, 2013, p. 10), "insisted that the modern human brain came into being after the hominid hand became "'handier' with tools" (Wilson, 1998, p. 18). Pre-human hands could scratch, pick, dig, strip, and pinch small objects between thumb and index finger. Lucy, from 4,000,000 years ago, is considered the closest link between ape and human. By Lucy's time a wrist had evolved that today enables us to "grasp the handle of a hammer, a golf club, or a tennis racket and prepare to take a swing" (p. 25). Infants possess a hand with potential for amazing capacities that evolved gradually over millions of years.

But sophisticated though human tools are, Wilson (1998) proposes a role for the hand beyond toolmaker. Wilson suggests that while our ape heritage enabled us to map the world in order to "satisfy the brain's need for gravitational and inertial control of locomotion" (p. 59),

> a new physics would eventually have to come into this [human] brain, a new way of registering and representing the behavior of objects moving and changing under the control of the hand. It is precisely such a representational system—a syntax of cause and effects, of stories and of experiments, each having a beginning, a middle, and an end—that one finds at the deepest levels of the organization of human language. (pp. 59–60)

Wilson explains how hand use, in conjunction with the social context in which early humans made things, drove the evolution of language. The question for early education is how to leverage young children's simultaneous development of (1) hand skills, (2) social skills, and (3) language skills to maximize development of all three. Reggio schools provide evidence aplenty that these skills blossom when children use their hands to shape materials collaboratively with teachers and peers.

✦ **Exercise 1: Observe babies from 0 to 1 to identify maturational imperatives for language and the hand.**

Note instances:

1. When vocalization and hand action occur simultaneously
2. Of intentional hand use and intentional vocalization
3. Of the first intentional *and* simultaneous use of hand and voice

## The Hand: 0 to 1

In the first year, language and thought begin separately: Thought comes before language. The roots and the developmental course of the intellect differ from those of speech; initially thought is nonverbal and speech nonintellectual (Vygotsky, 1934/1986).

Wilson (1998) asks:

> What, then, were thought and intellect *before* language arrives? As far as we know, or can imagine, thought and intellect are the sum total of the organizing tendency of the child's entire, rapidly expanding collection of passive and active interactions with the world via touch, smell, sight, hearing, and kinesthesis. . . . [This takes] the form of a schedule of necessary developmental events in the child's body (which includes the brain), and the child's experience of that sequence begins in the form of the dawning, here and now, of *episodic awareness*. . . . At this state the heuristic and the child's awareness are working at breakneck pace to organize the child's active movements and sensorimotor explorations. (p. 195, emphasis in original)

In summary, the infant through the first year of life and into years 2 and 3 is driven by maturational imperatives (Wilson's "heuristic") to:

1. Use the senses
2. Move
3. Produce sounds that it hears
4. Interact socially using smiles, noises, and gestures to engage parent and primary caretakers
5. Use the meanings of words to communicate

The hand has a role in all these imperatives. Using sight, touch, taste, smell, and hearing, combined with movement, babies actively explore everything they can see or reach—much of it by hand. By 4 months, "infants notice, grasp, pull, roll, mouth, poke, stroke, and enlarge their capacities to handle and relate to materials" (Lewin-Benham, 2010, p. 55).

✦ Exercise 2: Observe infants concentrating on their hands.

Note everything the hand does and reflect on changes. Purpose: Follow the developmental path of hand movements (see Figure 3.2).

## Challenging Materials: 0 to 1

Educators' responsibility is to foster the development of maturational imperatives. Here we look at activities with infants before age 6 months in which materials play the key role. All ages are approximate, some months earlier, others months later. Development is not a race. Assure parents that no groom walks down the aisle in diapers.

*To Do with Infants.* Once viewed as a time when nothing happens, we now know that infancy is a period of intense brain-building in which experiences build the brain networks that determine many of our capacities. Consider the following suggestions as starting places to imagine diverse ways to stimulate infants' senses and movements and to reflect on infants' reactions.

Infants' reactions to stimuli are undifferentiated. This means that during the period when brain systems are potentials, before the networks of neurons that constitute different systems exist, and while systems are being built, stimuli may trigger responses almost anywhere in the brain. Thus, while not intended just for the hand, a stimulus may invoke a response from the hand as a side effect of the brain's not-yet-differentiated neuronal networks. The implication is that in the first year it is important to use a wide range of stimuli such as the examples described below.

1. Talk to, touch, and treasure infants, holding them often, and ensure that clothes and furnishings do not restrict movement. When infants are not sleeping, resting, or purposefully self-engaged, put them near you where they can imbue all their senses with the life of your home or school. Throughout, notice the hand's role in reaching and grasping, rolling over, sitting, crawling, pulling up, and walking.
2. Watch for and collect visually compelling lamps—lava, fiber-optic, color-changing, and more. Place them, one at a time, in the same location within infants' line of sight. At 3 months, watching a shiny brass ceiling fixture with many bulbs, an infant:
   • Became very excited
   • Gazed intently at the light fixture
   • Arched his back
   • Beamed a huge smile
   • Made cooing, gurgling noises
   • Extended his arms to both sides
   • Wiggled his fingers rapidly

*Tip:* Change a fixture when an infant tires of looking at it.

3. Provide books with illustrations by world-class artists:
   • Cave paintings and petroglyphs from around the world
   • African masks
   • Audubon prints
   • Agam's abstracts
   • Vasarely's kinetic graphics
   • Giacometti's sculptures
   • Albers's squares
   • Rothko's colors
   • Miro's figures
   • Mondrian's geometrics
   • Man Ray's surrealist ensembles

- Chagall's surrealist paintings
- Elliot Porter's and Ansel Adams's nature photographs
- Escher's spatial ambiguities
- Hnizdovsky's woodcuts

and other iconic works, including those from the culture(s) of children in your care. The list is endless. *Note:* The works I included have strong lines, large color fields, clear colors, and great variety. Borrow oversize art books so infants can look at large images. Change the books often. Be sure to place books in infants' line of sight. *Tip:* The clear plastic holders that support cookbooks on a kitchen counter make useful stands.

4. Hang a mirror—high-quality Plexiglas so the image is not distorted—wherever infants' gaze is most likely to fall when they are in cribs, on changing tables, and elsewhere at rest. *Tip:* Suspend mirrors from above and/or place alongside, close to where infants lie.
5. Hang mobiles and change them frequently. Make them yourself from objects with:
   - Unusual shapes
   - Exotic colors
   - Fresh flowers
   - Origami figures
   - Glisten-y beads

Visual interest, variety, and change are the guiding principles.

6. Read frequently. My favorite books for infants are T. S. Eliot's *Old Possum's Book of Practical Cats* (1939/1982), Mother Goose rhymes, and any of the narrative poems mentioned in Chapter 3. Read your favorite classic works. If you have always longed to read Mark Twain, now is the time—aloud to infants. Ask parents of other cultures to read their classic poetry aloud. Most important in the first year is for infants to hear *many* words. The number of words heard from 0 to 1 predicts reading ability (Huttenlocher, Haight, Bryk, Seltzer, & Lyons, 1991).
7. Find objects that make different sounds. Put them in shakers made from opaque PVC pipe; seal the ends securely. Containers should not stimulate the visual sense because the intention is to focus on sound/hand reactions. Fill containers with different materials (one material per container): rice, beans, small pebbles, grain (such as quinoa or couscous), salt, small bells, metal beads—objects with varied sound qualities. The hardware store will yield small wood, metal, rubber, and plastic items galore. Shake the container for infants not yet capable of holding. Hand containers to infants as soon as they can grasp them. Let infants discover for themselves how to shake the containers. As with other stimuli, change containers frequently.
8. Provide objects for infants to hold and feel that differ tactilely—soft, hard, squishy, firm, rough, smooth, and made of silk, netting, corduroy, wool,

burlap, fur, velvet—as great a variety as you can find. For example, collections of small:
- Soft, washable dolls
- Varied brushes
- Board books
- Sponges
- Dense foam (from which bits cannot be broken off)
- Homemade rattles (see 7 above)

9. Provide objects to hold that vary in shape—spherical, cubic, conical, pyramidal, rectilinear, ovoid, cylindrical. Provide some with projections, some with holes, others that are hollow in which, perhaps, an arm could fit (but not get caught).

✦ Exercise 3: Observe what infants' hands do with new stimuli.

What responses do infants make with their hands? Notice differences among infants' responses. Keep track of what the hand does in each case. Build your own record of stimuli/infant hand responses.

*4 or 6 Months to Before 1 Year.* Expanding use of the senses, increased social interaction, and new hand capacities characterize babies' next developments. Here we look at activities with hands, music, taste, and smell.

*Grasping Hands.* Initially infants may be spastic, knocking themselves in the head with their hand, poking their eye with their fist. They cannot mouth objects intentionally because they find their mouths only accidentally. Once they can reliably direct an object, mouthing becomes an important means of feedback. As soon as infants can grasp, fill all sizes and shapes of clear plastic containers with:

- Lightweight items of varied colors or shiny properties
- Seeds, cones, and other natural materials
- Beads, buttons, sequins, and other sewing trims
- Nuts, bolts, screws, and other small hardware pieces

Put the items in clear plastic bottles or fruit containers; seal with clear, strong packing tape so they will not open. Babies can reach for, grasp, lift, drag, hold aloft, shake, push, bang, taste, and manipulate the containers in any way their hands and feet can propel them.

Grasping hands also can hold clear plastic sheets (open ends sealed with strong clear packing tape) that contain an endless variety of visually stimulating flat items:

- Flower petals, leaves, grasses, feathers, insect wings
- Art reproductions
- Photos of animals
- Papers of different color, texture, and sheen

*Tip:* Calendars have excellent-quality images; cover the date side (with opaque construction, fadeless art, or typing paper).

When babies sit independently, seat two or three on a rug. Give them a large basket to share. Fill the basket with an assortment of related objects, the kinds named above and also plastic clothespins, nesting objects (measuring cups, drinking cups, blocks), fabric squares, and spoons. Put the basket within reach. When babies tire of exploring a basket, give them one with a different related assortment. Reggio teachers call these Treasure Baskets.

*Social Context.* Use social exchange to build babies' enjoyment of their hands—peek-a-boo, pat-a-cake, and other standards. Any nursery rhyme can provide a rhythmic background to gently "clap" a baby's hands, arms, legs, or feet in time. Vary the exercise by using right hand and leg, left hand and leg, or opposing hand and leg. Wikipedia has a short but good list of clapping rhymes with no commercials! (en.wikipedia.org/wiki/Clapping_game#Examples).

Babies' love of social engagement begins at birth. Encourage social exchange by bringing two or three babies together to be involved in any of the activities described. Watch different children's reactions to one another.

*Music.* Music stimulates hand movement. Like art reproductions, music can be drawn from the world's repertoire—Spanish guitar, African rhythm instruments, Gregorian chant, Irish lullabies, folk songs in any language, Bach, Brahms, Beethoven, Mozart, Schumann, Chopin. Avoid overly loud popular music. Provide complex and varied pitch, harmonic, and rhythmic structures. Folk tunes and classic nursery songs are good first choices for singing along. Expand selections beyond what babies are likely to hear.

✦ Exercise 1: Observe infants' hands as they listen to music.

Note how infants' hand movements change over time.

✦ Exercise 2: At 6 months or earlier, introduce hand movements to accompany music: clapping, waving, tapping, finger-flexing, pointing.

Clap hands to different parts of the body; with older babies, have pairs of children clap hands with each other. Be inventive in using varied wrist movements—bending, twisting, shaking, and articulated finger movements—wiggling, opening, closing, stretching, flexing. With older children, use individual fingers (from one or both hands) isolated from the other fingers. *Tip:* Take advantage of the deeply embedded drive to imitate to engage children in hand/finger movements stimulated by music.

*Taste.* The first year is a good time to expand babies' food tastes. Check first with families; many have strong preferences that must be respected. Within family limits, use many different flavors and textures. Avoid sugar and salt in accord with nutritional guidelines; these strong tastes can turn children against the unaltered flavors of fruits and vegetables. Accustom babies to the unadulterated taste of healthful foods, for example, orange wedges, dry Cheerios™, zwieback, or other hard, unsweetened teething biscuits.

For babies, food and hand are inseparable. By 6 to 9 months, introduce spoons. *Tip 1:* Use imitation to encourage use of eating utensils. *Tip 2:* Introduce utensils early to engage children who crave novelty and challenge.

✦ Exercise: Notice different reactions to the use of utensils

- Ways that different babies use their hands to eat
- When different babies want to use utensils
- How children differ in the desire to begin or master using eating utensils
- Whether children use utensils to make sound

*Smell.* Smells can stimulate hand movement and have powerful links in the brain to memory. Use liquids—vanilla, apple cider, almond, walnut. *Tip:* Walk grocery store aisles with your nose. Dried flowers, herbs, and roots are available in wide varieties and are sweet or pungent, with many complex aromatic overtones. Examples are lavender, dianthus, rosemary, basil, ginger, and celery. Put aromatic materials in small empty jars that are safe for babies to handle. Some spices or flavorings can be used as is; others can be smelled by saturating cotton; still others may need a perforated container from which items cannot fall. *Note:* Never let children inhale any powdery substance. *Tip:* A good read: *The Emperor of Scent* (Burr, 2002), a true account of the complex and not well understood olfactory sense, tells the story of a biochemist who could distinguish subtle differences in aromas and how this capacity made him a high-powered, in-demand consultant to the perfume industry.

✦ Exercise: Notice babies' reactions to scents.

- Do new scents stimulate babies' hand activity?
- How do babies use their hands to express interest, excitement, distaste, or other reactions?

Make records of reactions to inform future use of scents.

## Summary

A sophisticated product of evolution, hand capacities develop as infants use their hands to explore. Materials infants have access to, the social context in which materials are used, and sensory experiences that engage the hand determine whether hands fulfill their potential in building language and other brain systems.

## INCREASINGLY COMPLEX MATERIALS

With children from birth to age 6, *the environment IS the curriculum.* What I have just described is possible if teachers are intentional in preparing an environment and reflective about connecting children and stimuli. Starting at 6 to 8 months, the focus of activities can be materials that drive hand development. Reggio schools commonly use materials like paint and clay before age 1. Here I describe these ideas and discuss the role of materials from toddlerhood to age 6.

### Materials and Mobility

Sitting, creeping, crawling, pulling up, and walking give babies a new world perspective. Provide surfaces that offer tactile variety to crawl or walk on—smooth wood, bumpy rubber, knobby carpet, textured ceramic tile, cardboard with different corrugations, linoleum with raised patterns. Make texture "mats," areas where crawling babies touch different surfaces as they move. Read the Reggio publication *Children, Arts, Artists* (Reggio Children, 2004) for descriptions of inspiring visual/tactile mats in tones of black or white. For advanced crawlers, provide objects that babies can use as "hills," "valleys," and "tunnels."

✦ Exercise 1: Observe how babies' hands move in response to different tactile sensations.

Observe babies' hands as they sit, creep, or crawl (and eventually stand) on various surfaces.

- Be intentional in providing diverse surfaces to stimulate tactile exploration.
- Be reflective in analyzing reactions stimulated by different surfaces— excited, exploratory, receptive, cautious, timid, afraid.

Babies pull up before they walk. Install bars at different heights for babies to propel themselves along. The Reggio furniture catalogue *Play +* (Fontanili, 2007) pictures intriguing structures to entice babies to stand, crawl, and walk. Cardboard containers in various shapes and sizes can be configured in numerous ways as crawling and/or climbing structures. Tumbling mats or mattresses provide safe spaces for more boisterous physical adventures—rolling, tumbling, and intentional falling.

✦ Exercise 2: Observe hands' actions as movement develops.

- Observe how babies use their hands in mastering the abilities to sit, creep, crawl, pull up, and walk.
- Notice how the functions and competence of hands gradually change.

- Observe nuances in parts of the body connected to hands—wrists, arms, shoulders, fingers.
- Note differences among children.
- Reflect on which activities appeal to different babies and why.

### Paint, Clay, Mark Makers, and Drawing

Materials that are used throughout life can be used first in babyhood. Introduction proceeds at a gradual pace with no "right" time or time limits. Generally, introduce babies one, two, or three at a time to materials. This enables you to give as much physical, emotional, and linguistic support as needed. For example, teachers may hold a baby in their arms during a first painting experience. Two or three babies together will influence one another.

*Paint, a là Reggio.* As soon as infants can sit up, place them on the floor in the middle of a huge paper circle. In Reggio, a circle in which a baby can sit is cut from the middle of the huge circle (like a donut). The baby sits in the "donut hole" and paints on the huge surrounding circle. Begin with one pot of paint (non-tip) and one brush. Gradually increase the number of pots until babies are painting with three or four colors, each pot with its own brush. Some children immediately understand what to do; others understand only when shown. Some begin to paint in the company of other children, others when their hand is guided. Some may not like painting at all. With the latter, try at another time. Some children may never want to paint.

When toddlers stand comfortably, introduce an easel. Make the painting surface full-length, that is, as high and low as toddlers can reach. Since they have had experience with several colors, use several paint pots from the beginning. Around age 2, demonstrate the effect of mixing two different colors or adding black or white. When children make a shade, save it and add the jar to an increasing collection of colors mixed by children. Build up to 30 or more, as your space allows.

Reggio teachers sometimes attach an object, such as a beautiful fall leaf, to paper toddlers will paint. The object makes the experience novel as children paint around and over, attempt to match the color, cover it entirely, or ignore it altogether.

Introduce watercolors, first to toddlers whose fingers show some precision, and gradually to all toddlers.

*Clay.* When babies can sit comfortably, introduce low-fire artist's clay, a natural material. Provide a good-sized chunk.

Some babies dig right in. As with paint, others do so when shown, after watching or working with other children, and some may not like the medium. First experiences, which may last weeks, months, or a year, include poking, gouging, pulling off chunks, cutting pieces with clay tools, making holes with sticks, embedding natural objects (twigs, nuts, pebbles) or man-made items, rolling "snakes," coiling, stacking, and eventually using slip to fasten pieces. By age 3, encourage children who are experienced in using clay to make what they see: buildings, trees, animals, people, heads, parts of the face—anything. I watched Reggio 4-year-olds fashion clay horses with riders to sit on them. The teacher provided varied slats of wood to support the figures.

*Tips:*

1. Be sure explorations are unhurried and repetitive.
2. Introduce other materials with clay to encourage novel outcomes.
3. Challenge children who show affinity for clay to make increasingly sophisticated representations.

***Mark Makers.*** The variety of mark makers is huge—lead pencils that leave light, dark, skinny, fat, long, short, and colored lines of every shade. Ink markers come in a great variety of nibs, shapes, and colors. Brushes for many types of paint range from round, stubby, and coarse to exceedingly thin with ultrafine tips. Water-based inks, for use with pens or brushes, vary in color and texture. The oily texture of pastels leaves intensely colored marks. Colored chalk can be applied from the tip, rubbed on the side, smudged by hand, or lightened with an eraser. Crayons come in rich colors; be sure to sharpen them when the points are gone and to replace broken crayons.

Papers are equally varied. Weights range from tissue to card stock, sheen from dull to shiny, texture from smooth to heavily crinkled, and colors throughout the spectrum. Fadeless art paper comes in two dozen or more luscious colors. Graph paper comes in a dozen or more differently sized squares. Reggio 4½-year-olds use fine-tipped color markers to fill in the squares on graph paper cut into small 2″ × 3″ pieces. Later they may use the papers in an assemblage; sometimes children weave yarn or make needlepoints to match their paper colors.

***Drawing.*** Reading, a cultural invention, has been widespread for only 100 years or so. But worldwide, rocks show mark-making by early modern humans from 150,000 to 40,000 years ago. The connection between writing and human development is evident in children who, regardless of culture, follow similar developmental paths in writing as they do in language and movement. In most children, writing occurs spontaneously as a natural form of expression. Young children's mark-making is both a vehicle to develop skilled hand use and a means of personal expression.

From age 2, provide many 5″ × 7″ clipboards with blank paper to fit. Encourage children to have clipboards readily at hand in and away from the classroom. Show children how to use clipboards to record their experiences. Expect children's "writing" to follow a progression—random marks, scribbles, circles, and ultimately shapes that, in children's minds, are a concrete representation of objects and actions. In time, marks increasingly will resemble what children say they are drawing—*if* they have used mark makers regularly. Do not expect representations at any given age; children differ greatly in when and how accurately they draw. The important outcome is not drawing accuracy but written expression that is as facile and is used as often as speech.

## Summary

The variety of materials just described, along with natural and man-made objects, wire, and more, stimulate refined uses of the hand:

- Finger movements requiring different flexion as the joints bend up, down, and from side to side
- Finger grips requiring more or less pressure
- Actions with the wrist at different angles
- Arm and shoulder movements with more or less subtlety

The more experience children have using materials, the more adept they become.

## CONCLUSION

Hand skills are necessary for using tools and writing implements; are essential in design; underlie professions such as jeweler, dentist, surgeon, auto mechanic, musician, or magician; and provide satisfaction throughout life. Diverse hand activities satisfy humans' quest for novelty, complexity, and challenge. Varied materials motivate children who are not naturally facile with their hands.

The messages of this chapter are:

- Using varied materials develops hand skills, encourages self-expression, builds competence and confidence, and develops the hand's potential to execute many necessary functions capably, gracefully, effortlessly, and aesthetically.
- As with music training, the earlier hand training begins, the more likely children are to fulfill the potential for the hands' wide-ranging capacities.
- Classrooms that contain mainly blue-lined paper, fat pencils, and bulky crayons constrain what the hand can do and what the brain can imagine.

This chapter is not a comprehensive description of possible materials and their role in hand development. I have not discussed light and shadow, wire, hundreds of natural materials that cost nothing, found objects that abound in American homes, various glues, clips, string, and other fasteners that join and tools that shape materials—or the complex constructions that the hand can make when a classroom contains a plethora of materials.

I have tried to convey a sense of the heritage of the human hand. And I hope I have made a compelling case for teachers to find joy and excitement in providing materials, from infancy on, that entice children to use their hands with increasing skill.

# CHAPTER 7

# Behavior, Intention, and Reflection

> Far from being simply encoded in the genes, much of personality is a flexible and dynamic thing that changes over the life span and is shaped by experience.
>
> —Carol Dweck, 2008

---

**TECHNIQUE 7**
Engage children's cognition:
Use cognition to mediate disruptive or distracting emotions.

---

Children's behavior is an inseparable mix of who they are genetically, what they have experienced in utero and beyond, and what has provoked this moment's outburst of laughter, tears, aggression, or affection. Children's behavior is an indication of what Howard Gardner calls the personal intelligences, *inter*personal (how one reads others) and *intra*personal (one's insight into oneself). The personal intelligences determine how people control their responses, what emotional reactions are in their repertoire, and the balance between their emotional and cognitive control. Caltech neuroscientist John Allman is recognized for his research on cognition and on the brain's Von Economo neurons, formerly called spindle neurons, and commonly known as the "social" neurons. He says that our social intuitions "guide us through complex, highly uncertain, and rapidly changing social interactions . . . [that are] shaped by learning" (2007, p. 179). In this chapter, I explore teachers' vital role in children's learning to use the personal intelligences in their social interactions.

This chapter has three sections on behavior and temperament:

- What they are
- Their capacity to change
- The relationship among motivation, cognition, and emotions

Throughout are vignettes of teaching that supports the development of cognitive and emotional intelligence.

In no part of teaching are intention and reflection more important than in teachers' responses to children's behavior. So I interpret ideas about behavior through the lens of being an intentional/reflective teacher.

## BEHAVIOR AND TEMPERAMENT

If temperament is the broad outline of who a person is, behaviors are the minute-by-minute manifestations of one's temperament. All behavior is strongly influenced by one's beliefs. We read in Chapter 4 how teachers' behavior is influenced by their beliefs about the nature of intelligence. What results when teachers believe that children's temperament is changeable? How does teaching change when teachers adopt a cognitive approach to behavioral issues? Here I address these questions. I use the words *temperament* and *personality* interchangeably and also interchange the words *behaviors* and *states*. I define traits as indicators of one's temperament.

While some aspects of personality have been traced to specific genes, research on the link between genes and temperament is in the early stages. A perusal of PubMed's website on a range of genetic studies shows results that are suggestive, but not conclusive (see www.ncbi.nlm.nih.gov/pubmed/?term=human+temperament+and+genetics). Genetic factors are extremely complex, and studies focus not on broad characteristics but on highly specific behaviors. Some studies use samples that are too small to make generalizations; other studies have not been able to be replicated. Given the rapid advances in genomic research, we can surmise that in the future there may be more broadly applicable findings.

### Traits and States: Structure and Dynamics of a System

Teasing out what is driving young children's emotions at a particular moment is difficult. A guiding idea is to identify the trait underlying the behavior. *Traits* are givens of children's temperament and contrast with *states*, which are temporary, changing mental positions. So, when facing tantrums or karate chops, teachers can consider whether they manifest a child's temperament or are reactions to a singular happening that morning—a state. But, other than offering some insight, the question of trait or state is negligible because traits and states can be changed.

***Traits: Malleable Entities.*** Jerome Kagan, Research Professor of Psychology Emeritus at Harvard and pioneering developmental psychologist, said: "The concept of temperament refers to any moderately stable, differentiating emotional or behavioral quality whose appearance in childhood is influenced by an inherited biology, including brain neurochemistry" (1998, p. xvii). Kagan focuses on two traits that he calls *inhibited* and *uninhibited* and what happens "when a child confronts an unfamiliar person, place, or event" (p. xvii). Kagan observed that children with different temperaments "differ in the ease with which particular emotions and accompanying behaviors become habitual" (p. 29). Working with children of different backgrounds and ages and using fMRIs, then-new electronic technology, Kagan concluded that temperament has both a psychological and physiological basis (p. xxi), that there are different centers in the brain for different traits. Significantly for this book, Kagan countered much 20th-century research on personality by concluding that "temperamentally driven behaviors are not immutable; on the contrary, they can be unusually malleable" (p. 35).

*Trait/State: Two Sides of a Coin.* For the most part, despite accumulating research, beliefs in the 20th century remained locked in an outdated paradigm: Temperament is a fixed, lifelong determinant of who a person is. Yet, research was suggesting that

> individual differences in social behaviors tend to be surprisingly variable across different situations . . . [and] *when personality is conceptualized as a stable system . . .* it becomes possible to account simultaneously for both the invariant qualities of the underlying personality [temperament or traits] and the predictable variability across situations [states or behaviors]. (Mischel & Shoda, 1995, p. 246, emphasis added)

Mischel and Shoda conclude that using a *systems* perspective "allows one to pursue concurrently both personality dispositions and processes—structure and dynamics—as aspects of the *same unitary system*" (p. 263, emphasis added). In other words, there is both a macrocosm—the given personality—and a microcosm—the variable behaviors. Teasing out the influences on either personality or behaviors is extremely difficult, as Figure 7.1 suggests. One's personality and one's widely divergent behaviors are not only inseparable, but are equally important in defining who an individual is—and they are *both* amenable to change.

**Figure 7.1. Many paths in life shape one's personality.**

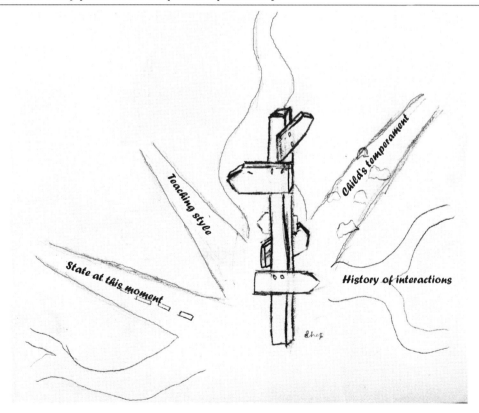

*"Person Praise" vs. "Process Praise".* Stanford University psychology professor Carol Dweck (2008) proposes that what Mischel and Shoda call the dynamics of personality are "in-between" parts, behaviors that take place "below the level of broad traits . . . such things as goals and construals . . . striving and coping strategies . . . and the way one perceives self, others, and events" (p. 391). Dweck says:

> Focusing on people's beliefs, as opposed to their simple preferences and habits or broad personality traits, helps us answer in more precise ways questions like: What personality factors allow people to function well in their lives—that is, to grow and learn, sustain satisfying relationships, achieve well in school and careers, be caring toward others, or recover from setbacks? (p. 392)

The reason we can answer such questions is that we can define beliefs "very precisely," measure them "very simply," and intervene so as to alter beliefs in such ways that we can see their direct impact (p. 392). Dweck concludes: "Beliefs lie at the heart of personality and . . . give us unique insight into how personality and functioning can be changed" (p. 391). People adopt a mindset that may lie anywhere on the continuum between open, at one extreme, and fixed, at the other.

The continuum of mindsets was subjected to research that examined persons with "fixed" mindsets (my intelligence is a given) versus persons with "growth"-oriented mindsets (my intelligence can increase). Gunderson and colleagues examined children from ages 1 to 3 to determine the effects of parents' praise on children's motivation 5 years later. They found that the more motivated children had received what the researchers call "process praise": "You used a good strategy," or, "You worked hard on that drawing," vs. what the researchers call "person praise": "You are smart," or, "You are a good drawer." The "person praise" instills a belief that I am who I am and cannot change. The "process praise" instills a belief that I can impact who I am and how I learn. The researchers conclude:

> Praise that emphasizes children's effort, actions, and strategies may not only predict but also impact and shape the development of children's motivational frameworks in the cognitive and socio-moral domains. Previous interventions have focused on changing the beliefs about trait stability that have already formed among older students. . . . However, our findings suggest that if you [want to change children's belief about themselves] and are using "person praise," change your language so that you use "process praise." (Gunderson et al., 2013, pp. 31–32)

✦ Exercise 1: Distinguish between "person" and "process" praise.

- Listen to what words you use when you praise children.
- Notice whether you are using "person" or "process" praise.
- If the former, change your words to "process" praise.
- Make a list of words you use in "process" praise.
- Compare your list with your colleagues' lists.
- Discuss your experiences using "process" praise with colleagues.

*Teachers' Beliefs About Intelligence.* Consider how teachers' beliefs determine:

- What teachers think intelligence is
- What teachers do to cultivate children's intelligence
- How teachers handle children's different behaviors

How might teachers teach if they realized that at the forefront of research on personality is the knowledge that personality can be changed? Viewing traits as malleable is a liberating idea. It negates the validity of statements such as: "He has his father's personality." "John is happy-go-lucky; he leaves everything to chance." "Alice has a lazy streak." Or, shrugging the shoulders, "That's the way all the McNeils are." Traits' malleability renders such statements meaningless. The malleability of traits is a hopeful belief, removes labels from children, and opens up limitless possibilities for change in behavior.

✦ Exercise 2: Analyze how you praise children.

- Write down what you say about children.
- Note if your statements reflect a fixed or growth mindset.
- If the former, change your words to reflect a growth mindset.
- Make a list of words you use that reflect a growth mindset.
- Compare lists with your colleagues.
- Discuss your experiences using a "growth mindset" with colleagues.

## Summary

Recall Chapter 5 on word choices. The research on change in temperament and behavior is clear: We can change words we use to praise children. Words in which we describe beliefs about our own mindsets provide a useful way to observe ourselves. Listening to our words is a reflective process and a first step toward changing what we believe. The research means: Change is possible! Changing language is possible. Changing beliefs is possible. The first step is reflection.

## COGNITIVE FUNCTIONS AND BEHAVIOR

Psychologist Reuven Feuerstein identifies "universal cognitive functions" that he considers important in many ways, including overcoming dysfunctional behavior. Replacing dysfunction with increasingly strong cognitive and sociocultural behaviors is the basis for his hopeful theory of mediation and its related set of practices. At the heart of Feuerstein's theory is his belief that the brain can change. Decades before brain plasticity was understood, Feuerstein used the words "modify cognitive function" to describe adult/child interactions that he knew were changing the brain. The implications for education are revolutionary. Knowing that teacher/child interactions can change the brain opens possibilities for education that differ radically from the current practice of "covering" a curriculum and teaching only the narrow body of specific facts in the curriculum.

Some ECE educators have rejected curriculum-based teaching. These teachers believe that a curricular approach in early education is inefficient, unproductive, and out of sync with current research in psychology on the enormous role of emotion as the basis both for motivation and cognition (Damasio, 1994; Feuerstein, Falik, Feuerstein, & Rand, 2006; Goleman, 2005; Greenspan, 1995). These seminal thinkers believe that personality can be changed.

Here I describe how Feuerstein's theory and others' research show that, especially in the early years, children are far more likely to gain control of their emotions and thus to regulate their behavior if they learn to integrate emotion with generalizable, universal cognitive functions.

## Human Factors in Learning

Feuerstein identifies two distinct facets of children's ability to regulate and control their behavior. One is an act of *inhibition*: eliminating "unwanted, dysfunctional, distracting behaviors." Example: "If I stop crying (inhibition), the teacher will understand what I'm saying." The other is an act of *initiation*: learning new ways to behave "that are blocked or insufficiently present in the [learner's current] repertoire" (Feuerstein et al., 2006, p. 77). Example: "I can water the plants (carry the pitcher, cut the paper—initiations) if I hold the watering can (any new behavior) just so."

Children's inability to inhibit undesirable behavior shows that they lack the cognitive structures "to self-regulate the internal (in the organism) and external (in the environment) tendencies toward impulsive action" (Feuerstein et al., 2006, p. 78). Feuerstein believes that regardless of what causes this lack—whether genetic, environmental, or both—current cognitive structures can be changed and missing cognitive structures can be built. "Intelligence," says Feuerstein, "is the dynamic expression of a complex interaction of biogenetic, cultural, experiential and emotional factors . . . [and is] characterized by the option, possibility, and propensity to become meaningfully changed by experience" (p. 27).

According to Feuerstein, what makes change possible is human interaction. While the dual impact of biological and sociocultural factors in forming intelligence and shaping personality has long been recognized, the specific role of teachers in changing cognitive structure is not widely practiced. Feuerstein calls this role "mediation," which he defines as adults' intervening in children's experience *with the intention* of changing children's cognitive functioning, motivation, and behavior—in other words, changing how children think, what they believe, and what they can do, including skilled performance such as the string assemblage (Figure 7.2) by a 2½-year-old. A quick overview shows how Feuerstein's theory is distinct from other dominant theories of how we learn.

***Distinction: Mediation vs. Earlier Theories.*** Compare Feuerstein's mediated learning with behaviorist, constructivist, and early sociocultural views.

**Behaviorist.** The behaviorist view of stimulus/reward as the basis for learning denies the role of internal motivation: Being motivated by a reward might make a child learn the sound of the letter "a" but will have no impact on the child's other behaviors, much less the child's belief about himself as a learner.

Figure 7.2.
Intricately tied
strings show
this interaction:
The teacher
who selects
the material,
the child who
explores it, and
the product
suggested and
constrained by
the material.

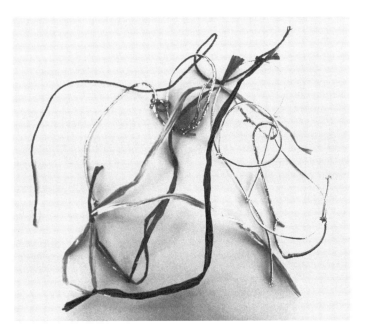

**Constructivist.** The constructivist view that experience shapes intelligence denies the role of another human; thus, constructivist theory, as developed by Piaget, proposes that development occurs naturally and on schedule without human interaction: Children will learn "it" at the appropriate biological time; there is no need to teach "it" until children are "ready." "Readiness," as the key factor in learning, denies a role for an adult.

**Sociocultural.** Vygotsky's sociocultural theory recognizes adults' central role in children's development and learning. But Feuerstein goes farther than Vygotsky by saying that the adult is not merely central but *essential*: "The readiness of the individual, and the capacity to benefit from exposure to stimuli . . . *is strongly dependent on the nature of the . . . [mediation—adult intervention] to which the individual is exposed*" (Feuerstein et al., 2006, p. 26, emphasis added).

Here we have the central message of this book: Teachers' intention and reflection are strongly determining factors in whether, what, when, and how children learn.

*Why the Distinctions Matter.* If we believe in something, we accept it as true without personal observation or experience. If we adhere to a theory, we accept a comprehensive statement that embraces known facts, although the theory may be revised as new facts are admitted or be discarded if the facts are disproven. The belief in a flat world was accepted without observation or experience; the theory of relativity may change as we learn more about deep space. It is one thing to espouse a belief about how children learn or about effective teaching; it is different to accept a theory about learning and teaching. However, both beliefs and theories shape teachers' actions.

We read in prior chapters about actions:

- Chapters 1, 2, and 5—subtle differences in words that describe behavior
- Chapter 2—nuanced ways of observing and micro-actions in human facial expression
- Chapter 3—precise meanings in different sequences of sound
- Chapter 4—how beliefs affect teaching behaviors
- Chapter 5—the impact of the words we choose to phrase requests or instructions, and the power of mindfulness
- Chapter 6—the hand's role in learning and in constructing and conveying meaning

In contrast to these ideas, which are mainly actions the body performs, holding beliefs and espousing theories are mental acts. Reflection is the key to changing beliefs and adopting theories; change will depend on what connections we make among belief, theory, and action. In other words, teachers must watch themselves teach and listen for beliefs or theories that constrain what they think about children's learning. I have no illusions that this is easy; it requires great motivation, the will to monitor yourself in action, and the courage to change your behavior midstream. Such changes are exemplified in peak performers.

✦ Exercise 1: One strategy to try to change a belief.

- Carefully consider what you believe.
- For purposes of this exercise suspend your belief.
- Accept instead the belief that by engaging children cognitively you can change their behavior.
- Apply that belief to "Jane," the child who acts out the most, to "Donald," who is "on the autism spectrum," to "Walter," who is unmotivated, and to other "problem" children.
- Think of a specific cognitive intervention to engage each child, with the goal of changing one single behavior (e.g., the imprecise movement of always spilling milk).

*Note:* You are changing *one specific behavior* at a time; it may not happen with one intervention but may require several. You may need to try different interventions. Your ingenuity will be challenged, your goal may be frustrated. But with time, patience, experimentation, self-observation, self-correction, and perseverance, you will change the behavior.

- Try out your ideas.
- Reflect on whether a trial worked and why or why not.
- If your trials did not work, think of other ideas and try again.
- When something works, consider how your actions reflect your beliefs and theory.

Read Greenspan's book *The Challenging Child* (1995) and keep trying.

✦ Exercise 2: Put a cognitive approach to work.

- Study the examples of teachers' cognitive approaches in the scenarios later in this chapter.
- Practice a cognitive approach.
- If you are unsure of what to do, write to me (ann@annlewin-benham.com). I'll listen and try to discuss your case with you.

## Universal Cognitive Functions That Change Behavior

Feuerstein says that two main goals of teaching are to provide (1) *content* so in time the learner gains access to a universe of knowledge that may not be available in the environment or to which the learner has not had sufficient direct exposure, and (2) *mediation* to enable the development of operational, conceptual, logical, and emotional aspects of learning (Feuerstein et al., 2006, p. 330). Teachers themselves can determine their goals for changing children's beliefs and/or behaviors.

Shortly, I will describe scenarios in which teachers engage young children cognitively in responding to emotionally challenging situations. Consider as you read the scenarios that young children "need skills to recognize and explain certain emotional conditions" (Feuerstein et al., 2006, p. 329), both conditions they experience within themselves (what they feel) and conditions without (what they see, hear, or otherwise perceive). Behavior is both cognitive and emotional. But, especially in young children, emotions can overwhelm cognition.

The cognitive elements of behavior involve a child's asking such questions as:

- *What* have I done?
- *Where* have I done it?
- *When* did I do it?
- *How* did I do it?

The emotional elements of behavior involve a child's asking such questions as:

- *Why* did I do it?
- *What did I believe* the result would be?

The cognitive elements provide structure because they refer to the time and place in which the "what" happened. The emotional elements provide motivation, which Feuerstein calls "energetic," because motivation energizes action. In other words, actions are driven by emotions (pp. 328–329).

Children who learn to use cognition to structure emotional experiences will expand their repertoire of emotional responses. For example, children who, for many different reasons, may not have the vocabulary to explain "why" may be able to say what, where, when, or how—all cognitive responses. As teachers elicit cognitive responses, they engage children's attention. Underlying the development of "social/affective cognition are many skills and awareness"; all are linked to "the more basic development of cognitive functions" (p. 329).

What does this mean? Consider: To perceive another's emotional reaction is not a passive process. To perceive involves constructing a reality that has "coherence, consistency, and transferability" (p. 330). Such construction is an example of higher order cognition that involves the consolidation of a number of other lower-order cognitive operations. Lower-order does not mean less important; to the contrary, lower-order operations are essential to higher-order thinking. Children will stumble when confronted with higher-order thinking tasks if they have not first mastered basic—or lower-order—thinking skills. While this idea seems obvious, in practice it is often ignored: Curricula that are driven by the clock and the calendar force children to use higher-order thinking without having mastered basic skills. I cannot make this point too strongly; it is captured in the adage: "One must crawl before one walks."

## Summary

Here we have read about changing beliefs or theories and the difference between evoking children's cognition and evoking children's emotions. We have read that cognition and emotion are integral to all learning. And we have read about psychological processes that occur when young children's cognition is harnessed to redress emotional responses. As you read the following scenarios, watch how cognition and emotion interact.

## SCENARIOS

Each of the following scenarios shows a teacher enabling a child to change her or his behavior by using lower-order cognitive skills. The skills are sharing, focusing, attending, tracking, classifying, ordering information, and forming conclusions.

As you read the scenarios, keep in mind Stanley Greenspan's (1995) caution:

> Children who can't get along well with other children or with adults, who can't negotiate one-on-one relationships or group relationships, have a fundamental challenge to meet before they can accomplish other developmental tasks. This is because in the early years not only intimacy and self-esteem but also most learning—insights, intuition, principles—comes from what we learn from relationships. . . . The sense of quantity or time, as well as the meaning of words, is very much tied to the child's relationships and the emotions and experiences that are a part of them. All abstract, intellectual concepts that children will master at later ages are based on concepts they learn in their early relationships. If children haven't the fundamental ability to relate, much of their learning is in danger of being undermined and sabotaged. (p. 17)

### Scenario 1, 18 Months Old: Focusing and Social Interaction

Tommy spotted a new truck on a high shelf. Spying his teacher, he eagerly toddled to her, confident that she could reach the truck for him. The teacher was sitting on a pad engaged with four children who were not yet walking. Tommy came up behind her, out of her line of sight. With highly intentional and increasingly agitated hand signs and gestures, Tommy "told" the teacher what he wanted. Vaguely aware of the child behind her but preoccupied with the babies, the teacher gave Tommy no recognition. Frustrated that she did not turn around, Tommy tugged gently at her ponytail. Startled, annoyed, and feeling overburdened with the babies, the teacher responded: "Tommy, please keep your hands to yourself!" Feeling thwarted and rebuffed, Tommy burst into tears.

*Alternative Reaction: Cognitive Engagement.* Vaguely aware of the child behind her, the teacher made sure the babies were safe, then shifted her position so she could see Tommy. He was gesturing with all his might at something she could not see. "Tommy," she said, reaching around, drawing him into the group of babies, and giving him a big hug, "you're trying to tell me something. Point at what you want," and the teacher pointed to explain the meaning of the word *point.* Tommy whirled around and pointed in the direction of the truck. Glancing quickly where Tommy's finger pointed, the teacher remembered the new truck. She engaged Tommy's eyes with hers and, when he was focused on her eyes, said in a firm, clear voice using as few words as possible: "Tommy, look at my eyes when you talk to me. Then I can help you."

*What Happened?* In the first example, the teacher matched Tommy's agitation with her own, thereby increasing Tommy's emotional distress. In the second example, the teacher tempered Tommy's agitation with affection and attention. Calmly, in positive, to-the-point declarations, she showed Tommy how to get her attention. When children internalize a calm response, it calms their agitation. The teacher's eye contact and pointing caused Tommy to perceive, register, imitate, and thereby experience how to get her attention. Gradually, children widen their repertoire "of similar—and contextually related—responses" (Feuerstein et al., 2006, p. 330). The teacher's calm emotion was interlaced with cognitive actions as she:

- Showed Tommy how to point, a social interaction
- Demonstrated how to get someone's attention by looking directly in their eyes, a social interaction for focusing and theory of mind

In these ways, the teacher helped Tommy learn techniques for two universal cognitive skills that are essential in *all* learning—pointing and making eye contact.

## Scenario 2, 24 to 36 Months Old: Classifying and Vocabulary Expansion

A teacher was taking five 2½-year-olds to the park. Before leaving, the teacher told the children to take a bag to collect things to bring back for the nature table. As they left, each child pulled a plastic bag from the bag holder. It was fall, so there was a bounty of natural material:

- Leaves crisp from lying on the ground, soft from just falling, different colors and sizes
- Leaves uniquely formed—simple, compound, opposite, alternate, awl-shaped, scale-like, needles

- Leaves distinctly shaped—linear, heart-shaped, oval, elliptical, deltoid, star-shaped
- Leaves with varied apexes—acute, obtuse, bristle-pointed, rounded
- Leaves with varied margins—dentate, toothed, wavy, lobed

There were also seeds from many trees:

- Acorns from oak
- Pine cones large and small—8" from the longleaf, 4" from the loblolly, 2" from the pinyon
- Pods from redbuds
- Burrs—prickly from buckeyes, spiny from sweet gums
- Samaras differently shaped from maples, elms, and ash, the seed pods children call whirly-gigs or helicopters
- Drupes—nut-like from basswoods, seed-like from cherries, plum-shaped from hackberries

There were twigs with alternating, opposite, and whorled branches; mosses, lichen, birds' nests and feathers; and evidence of other animals. Nature provides a great plenty.

On arriving, the teacher said, "Let's see what we can find." The children put leaves, seeds, feathers, and twigs in their bags for a few minutes. Then, two ran off, chasing each other in a grassy area; two others found pebbles that they threw at each other; one cried because a burr had hurt her hand.

"Time to go," the teacher called, "get your bags." When two children fought over whose bag was whose, the teacher said it did not matter, to take any bag. After school, the teacher inspected the contents, found a few leaf fragments, dried and crumpled, a few burrs and acorns, and some pebbles. Not seeing anything for the nature table, she threw everything away.

*Alternative Reaction: Cognitive Engagement.* The teacher gathered five children whom she had observed several times using the collections on the nature table and brought them to the table. "Tell me," she asked, "what do you see here?" Speaking in the partial sentences and half-formed words typical of 2-year-olds, the children used gestures, body language, and facial expressions to indicate that they liked to feel the smoothness of the shells; to look at the crystals of quartz and amethyst; to play with the leaves, piling them, arranging them on the mirror the teacher sometimes laid on the table, crumbling them in their hands, separating the long vein if it was prominent, or removing the many small leaves from some twigs. "Would you like to visit the park to find things for the nature table?" the teacher asked, and took the children's air of excitement as their assent.

The teacher had downloaded a color copy of "Trees of Texas" (texastreeid. tamu.edu/), which has clear drawings of over 36 leaf forms and 24 different seeds. Knowing that children this age are noun-hungry, she and the children looked at the pictures as she named each form. The array of illustrations and the plethora of words mesmerized the children. (*Note:* Why limit children's new words to names of dinosaurs when there are thousands of names to describe life-forms and objects in the natural and man-made worlds and thousands more words for their attributes?) The naming lasted over 30 minutes. A few days later, the teacher visited the park. To her delight, she found a plethora of leaves, seeds, and twigs, some the very species she and the children had named. She took samples of all. The next day, the teacher and the five children laid out the samples, pored over the pictures, and matched several samples to pictures. The children returned to the matching activity for the next two days.

The following week, the teacher again gathered the five. The prior night, she had found smallish paper bags with handles. With the children watching, she wrote each child's name in dark marker on a bag, then had each child draw on the blank side of his or her own bag. "Would you like to visit the park to find more leaf, seed, and twig specimens?" she asked. Yes! Their excitement was palpable. "I'll bring the identification pages. You might be able to identify the specimens you find."

On reaching the park, the teacher brought the children to the open area: "Let's have a good run before we start to hunt." The children raced off. When two of them drifted back, the teacher brought all five together. They sat on the grass and as a group examined the identification pages, naming several objects with obvious or strange characteristics. Then, with somber tone and concerned expression, the teacher asked, "How are we going to handle our specimens?" The question led to a serious conversation about delicate and fragile leaves, seeds, and other natural forms; ideas they had discussed in the classroom; about what happens if delicate leaves or seeds are not carefully handled; and how to protect fragile specimens. The teacher showed them plastic sheets she had brought just in case. The children were relieved that there was a way to keep specimens safe.

"Now!" said the teacher, her eyes sparkling and with an air of great expectation, "See what you can find. Remember: Think about how to keep your specimens safe."

The children collected for over 40 minutes, sometimes running back to the teacher to match their finding to the identification sheets, sometimes remembering a name, other times simply putting the specimens into their bags. They exercised great care, bringing fragile leaves to the teacher for safekeeping in plastic, evidence that they considered the specimens precious. Back at school, teacher and children agreed on a safe place to keep the bags. Next week, they would unpack the bags and classify the specimens.

*What Happened?* In the first example, the teacher did not:

- Observe the children to select those who might be interested in collecting natural specimens
- Engage the children in examining or talking about natural specimens prior to the experience
- Find supplemental material to enlarge the children's knowledge
- Visit the park in advance to gather specimens to discuss with the children, thus familiarizing them with what they might find
- Interest the children in examining specimens with the goals of (1) observing distinguishing characteristics by which botanists classify plants and (2) expanding the children's vocabulary

- Allow a couple of weeks for experiences with natural objects as well as time for the children's excitement to mount
- Prepare bags that children could identify as "theirs"
- Encourage the children to dispel pent-up energy before hunting for specimens
- Have a conversation about how to protect fragile specimens
- Treat what the children collected with respect
- Build on the experience with a future activity in classification

We would not be surprised to learn that in the second teacher's class, activities with natural specimens continued for months. The children:

- Made trips to the library and looked online to find names of specimens they had collected that were not on the identification sheets (classifying)
- Had many conversations about how to sort their specimens—by overall size, color, or shape? by leaf shape? by leaf margin? The varied twigs and seeds were even harder to classify (discriminating)
- Examined leaves under a microscope and on the light table (attending)
- Made several trips to the park to gather more specimens or to the library to find resource material on leaves (researching)
- Created ways to save leaves and protect them (ordering information)
- Copied leaves freehand or traced around them (tracking)
- Enlarged leaves on an overhead projector and traced the huge forms (transforming)
- Decorated their enlargements with natural objects (attending):
  - ➤ Bits of crushed leaves
  - ➤ Glued-on bits of paper in leaf-like colors
  - ➤ Paint
  - ➤ Watercolor
  - ➤ Markers

The excitement of enlarging images aroused other children's interest, and by year's end the classroom was alive with activities with natural objects.

***What Else Happened?*** The activities developed children's capacities for careful observation, conversation, and research. Projects emerged that required classification skills, increasing hand skills, and collaboration. All relied on teacher preparation and a mindset open to following children's interests in unscripted, unpredictable directions. Such activities tap into another of Gardner's intelligences—the naturalist. In her book *Darwin's Ghosts* (2012), Rebecca Stott traces the stories of outstanding naturalists' quests to learn about life forms. Naturalists include Aristotle and da Vinci. The book is a resource for stories that connect children to age-old quests to understand the planet's life forces. Activities with natural materials and connections to notable naturalists can spur children's lifelong interests that may blossom into meaningful avocations or satisfying careers.

## Scenario 3, 3 Years Old: Enlarging Content and Attending

Nan and Janice sat side by side, using a new container of pencils the teacher had set on a table, along with small squares, about 4" × 4", of light-colored fadeless art papers. The materials were attractive; the two girls had been drawn to them immediately and now were deeply engaged. The teacher felt that she had hit the mark in providing an activity that produced such intense focus in using writing implements.

Suddenly, there was a ruckus. The teacher did not see what happened, but heard Nan crying loudly. She noticed that Nan had no pencil, assumed that Janice had taken Nan's pencil, and said firmly, "Janice, please give the blue pencil back to Nan." When Janice did not, the teacher held out her hand and said more firmly and slightly louder, "Janice, give me the blue pencil." Janice did so, burst into tears, and through tears said, "I want the blue one." The teacher gathered the pencils and papers and addressed both girls: "If we cannot share, I'll have to put the materials away."

*Alternative Reaction: Cognitive Engagement.* The teacher did not see what happened, so she decided to encourage the children to tell her. In a calm, firm voice and squatting beside Nan so she could look at her eye-to-eye, the teacher said, "Nan, please tell me what you want." Her sobs subsided enough for Nan to stammer: "A 'geen' . . . one, I want . . . a 'geen' pencil."

The teacher took a green pencil from the container and handed it to Nan, who, to the teacher's surprise, cried harder. Gently wiping Nan's tear-stained face with a tissue, the teacher quietly said, "Nan," then, after pausing to engage Nan's eyes, said, "This *is* a green pencil." But Nan pointed to Janice, who was using the blue pencil, and her tears increased as she stammered, "The . . . geen . . . one."

The teacher realized that Nan did not know the word *blue*, or had not learned to distinguish between blue and green. Deliberately taking a blue pencil from the container, the teacher declared: "Nan. Look! This . . . ," picking up two pencils, one green, the other blue, and tapping the green pencil next to Nan's hand in order to focus Nan's attention, ". . . is green and . . . ," tapping the blue pencil, ". . . this is blue. Show me which you want." Nan pointed to the blue pencil. The teacher gave it to her and said, "This is blue; say 'blue,'" and did the same with the green pencil. Nan's tears vanished, and both girls went on with their drawing.

*What Happened?* In the first example, the teacher acted on an assumption, attempted to resolve the altercation with no discussion with the children, and when her attempt failed, removed the materials. Perhaps she thought that would be a quick way to quiet both girls. Perhaps she is uncomfortable when children cry and does whatever she thinks will stop the crying. Perhaps she thinks that being denied the materials will teach children to share. We don't know what the teacher believes about crying or sharing, so we can only guess. Perhaps she had an entirely different thought in mind. Perhaps she had no other behaviors in her repertoire of teaching techniques.

In the second example, the teacher is aware that because she did not see what happened, she cannot make an accurate or fair judgment. So the teacher *asks* Nan, while she is sobbing, what she wants—a question requiring a cognitive response. Nan, realizing that her feelings are being recognized, controls her sobs enough to stammer out an answer. But because Nan continues to cry, the teacher realizes that Nan lacks content information.

The teacher knows she must do something to cause Nan to attend to the content. So using visual and auditory sensory stimulation to alert Nan's attention, the teacher taps the pencils in a place where Nan cannot fail to see ad hear them. Then, with Nan's attention focused, the teacher supplies the words for each color and reinforces the association by asking Nan to say "green" and "blue" with her. Nan attends to the teacher's actions, cooperatively says the words, recognizes the blue pencil as the one she wants, and quiets. Both children continue with their drawing, again intently focused.

Later that morning, the teacher asks Nan, "How did you feel when Janice had a blue pencil and you did not?" "Angry!" Nan answered, frowning. "And," the teacher asks, "how did you feel when you had a blue pencil again?" "Happy," Nan answered smiling, "I feel happy." By age 2 to 3, children can "form ideas about their wants, their needs, and their emotions" (Greenspan, 1995, p. 19) and can express ideas about emotions in words. "Do you remember what changed your feelings from angry to happy?" the teacher asked. "I got the blue pencil," Nan responded. "Remember," the teacher said, giving Nan a hug, "use words to tell someone what you want."

### What Else Happened?

1. The teacher solved the immediate problem by:
   * Providing Nan with missing content—the difference between green and blue
   * Teaching Nan the names of the two colors—content
   * Using sensory stimuli to engage the cognitive skills of attending to differences and discriminating subtlety

Attending and discriminating make children's perceptions more accurate.

2. Later the teacher drew on Nan's emotional skill by asking Nan to reflect on her feelings and to describe, name, and compare them. Because the teacher did this at a later time, she did not interrupt Nan's focus on her drawing. The interaction led Nan to form conclusions.
3. The teacher reinforced the association between Nan's emotion (anger) and her behavior (using words) as the way to quell her anger.
4. The teacher made Nan aware that she could communicate her needs without crying—cognitive control of an emotional experience. With repetition, Nan can master this cognitive skill and extend it to handle other similar emotional situations so that her cognition will prevent her from breaking down in tears.

## Scenario 4, 3½ Years Old: Hand/Eye Tracking and Motivation

Matthew had a hard time settling down. He was drawn to pencils but found Montessori metal insets frustrating and could not trace letters or names, as many other children did. He had rejected out-of-hand the simple mazes in the shapes of bears or ladybugs with cutesy eyes or smiles, typical of game books produced for young children. When he used pencils to draw freehand, he broke the points, and when he used the pencil sharpener, he ground the pencils down. His teacher was as frustrated as Matthew, and had trouble finding activities that interested him, but steered him away from using pencils after he failed at the available pencil tasks. Matthew remained a wanderer, rarely becoming involved in anything for more than a few minutes, and prone to frustration.

*Alternative Reaction: Cognitive Engagement.* Talking about Matthew in the teacher's lounge, a colleague suggested that Matthew's teacher try harder mazes and suggested the website krazydad.com/mazes/. This site has 25 maze books, with 20 mazes in each, and answer sheets. The mazes are graded from easy to very challenging. None are cutesy. They can be downloaded at no cost. They are harder than most activity books geared for preschoolers. Feeling that she had nothing to lose, the teacher downloaded four.

Matthew completed the four mazes quickly. Over the next month, Matthew worked his way through several easy maze books and also did mazes from the animal collection, more challenging than the mazes rated "easy." Matthew eagerly looked for new mazes every day, settled down instantly, and was occupied throughout the entire work time. He also calmed down and stopped breaking or grinding down pencils. Ten weeks later, he asked to try the metal insets.

*What Happened?* In Example 1, Matthew was not challenged and because he was bored and frustrated, he worked carelessly, damaging pencils, not intentionally but through frustration or inattention. Even though his teacher knew Matthew did not intend to do damage, she was frustrated. Matthew "read" her frustration, which increased his anxiety.

In Example 2, the teacher decided to ignore what a 3-year-old typically is expected to do. To her delight (and Matthew's), she found a good solution. She allowed Matthew to spend as much time as he wanted doing mazes. The other children admired Matthew's prowess. Matthew glowed in his friends' praise. He acquired a strong hand with a pencil and became known throughout the school as "the maze-cracker."

Some children require more challenging work than they find in typical ECE classrooms. The cognitive skills Matthew acquired were precision and accuracy in visual tracking and fine-motor coordination in the use of pencils. Cognitively, Matthew developed a long, focused attention span. Emotionally, Matthew became calm and settled as he perceived his success and saw that he had a skill others valued.

## Scenario 5, 4 to 6 Years Old:
## Organizing Information and Collaborating

Baltie, like many boys around age 4, loved cars. There was no TV in his home, but his parents chose movies and on Saturday mornings allowed him to watch one movie. He fell in love with the 1968 British musical *Chitty Chitty Bang Bang,* based on the book by Ian Fleming (1964). Verbal and imaginative, Baltie's contribution to morning meeting, day in and day out, was a lengthy recounting of the adventures of Caractacus Potts, Chitty's owner. The teacher groaned inwardly because Baltie connected his telling with seemingly endless "ands" and other children began to squirm. After enduring Baltie's stories for several days, the teacher took Baltie aside before morning meeting and told him to talk about something other than Mr. Potts. Baltie was deflated. Even when his teacher told him that once every other week he could tell a Mr. Potts story, he chose not to and refused to contribute at morning meeting. After all, 4-year-olds don't understand what a week is, much less "once every other." Nor do 4-year-olds want to postpone gratification. Unaffected by the squirming, Baltie had enjoyed the class' attention.

*Alternative Reaction: Cognitive Engagement.* After enduring Baltie's stories for several days, the teacher had an idea. If she could involve other children in Baltie's stories, it might spark group story-making. The teacher knew that young children may not separate fantasy and reality, appreciated young children's attraction to make-believe characters, and saw that Baltie believed Mr. Potts was real.

That day, the teacher took Baltie aside and asked if he had ever met Mr. Potts. Oh, yes! Mr. Potts visited Baltie every night and, "actually," as Baltie told his teacher, "we have adventures together." At Baltie's request, his father "told him a Mr. Potts story"; Baltie told his father the details of the adventure and his father wove Baltie's ideas into a narrative, the outline becoming established through nightly repetition: Mr. Potts always arrived in Chitty Chitty Bang Bang after Baltie's family was asleep. From his window, Baltie saw Chitty's bright lights or heard Chitty's OOGWAH horn, roused his dog, and they were off! But they always returned before anyone woke up, even if the sky was becoming light (see Figure 7.3).

Baltie's teacher had an inkling—if Baltie was amenable, the class could watch the movie and every day a small group of children who were interested could supply details for a Mr. Potts adventure. Baltie could be the narrator or, if he did not want to, the teacher would narrate and Baltie could lead his classmates in supplying the details. Baltie was euphoric, and five of his classmates were eager to join the Mr. Potts story-making group.

Each child brought details from his private fantasy world: One was enthralled by the story of the Nautilus (Jules Verne's *20,000 Leagues Under the Sea* [1869/2008]) and contributed those details. Another lived in a high-crime neighborhood, and Mr. Potts, with Chitty, became the heroes who rescued the boy from bullets and other scary things. Another loved Batman, and occasionally Batman rode alongside Caractacus Potts on a superhero adventure. Another brought in aspects of Peter Pan's adventures. And the fifth boy wove in Pinocchio's roguish doings. (*Note:* Advise parents to read these classic books to their children: Jules Verne's

Figure 7.3. Chitty Chitty Bang Bang has kindled children's imagination and inspired many an adventure.

*20,000 Leagues,* Ian Fleming's *Chitty Chitty Bang Bang,* J. M. Barrie's *The Adventures of Peter Pan* (1911/1991), and Carlo Collodi's *Pinocchio* (1883/1995). In the references, Jules Verne's book is a children's version; the others are unedited originals.)

Excitement spread from the story-makers to other groups of children. The block-builders built places where Chitty ventured. Painters made entire backdrops. Drawers created detailed characters. Children who were facile with clay made a host of cars to accompany Chitty. Several who frequented the housekeeping area cooked elaborate dishes that they managed to bring to Mr. Potts no matter where in the world he might be. Three children who loved rhythm instruments made musical accompaniments when, at the end of the year, the groups collaborated on a play, *Adventures of Mr. Potts and Chitty.* Some class thespians acted out fights between Peter and the lost boys and villains; others brought to life Geppetto's angry warnings at Pinocchio's wayward doings. All elaborated details of Mr. Potts's amazing car.

*What Happened?* In Example 1, the teacher's fear of a child's monopolizing group time shut down the child and truncated an experience rich with potential to mesh children's love of fantasy with diverse skills.

In Example 2, the teacher figured out how to turn one child's passion into an activity for many. Baltie became a leader who sparked other children's imagination and drew their interests in storybook characters into elaborate and lengthy story-making projects. The story-makers' enthusiasm spread to many areas of classroom work and in time involved every child. All the children wanted to hear each day's evolving story, so the teacher began recording the children and added their voices to the room's media area. In the process, all children built vocabulary, learned to organize information, and integrated the information with a multitude of work in diverse media—focusing, ordering information, and forming conclusions.

*What Else Happened?* The children developed wide-ranging cognitive behaviors—imagination; increasing hand skills; listening, speaking, and other early literacy skills; and the logical thinking processes of explaining and concluding. They also learned social skills of collaboration and appreciation for class members' different interests and abilities. Children were motivated to make high-quality productions. The experience was not scripted; therefore, there was a role for expression in all of Gardner's multiple intelligences, including humor. Above all, the children's ideas were honored. As a result, cognitive skills blossomed in many different areas, and the children felt fulfilled emotionally, laughing and enjoying their own and their friends' competence. In fact, the class became the learning community that we are told is important in the 21st century.

## CONCLUSION

In this chapter, we learned that ideas about the permanence of personality have changed, and as a result we now know that personality (also called temperament) is changeable. We have seen the essential role of teachers in mediating the changes. And we have seen scenarios in which teachers' intention and reflection (or lack thereof) cause children's emotional anguish to lessen—whether it springs from a child's state (as with Nan) or seems to be a permanent trait (as with Matthew).

We have seen children learn how to make their emotions serve them well and use their emotions as the foundation for increasingly complex tasks that rely equally on the emotional/motivational/social aspects of personality and on attentional, analytical, and language skills that are the bedrock of universal cognitive functions. Finally, we have seen how teachers succeed at helping children change dysfunctional behavior to emotionally controlled performance. We have watched children, with emotions under control, enjoy satisfying interpersonal relationships and focus on activities that increase cognitive capacities.

# CHAPTER 8

# Structuring an Intentional/Reflective Classroom

The whole is greater than the sum of its parts.

—Aristotle

**TECHNIQUE 8**
Structure motivating lessons:
Cause children to strengthen both cognitive and socio-emotional skills.

We have seen seven techniques that are essential in intentional/reflective teaching. In this last narrative chapter, we watch teachers use these techniques: Scenarios show intention/reflection as they impact other vital aspects of teaching:

- Managing time in an open-flow day
- Using conversation
- Giving lessons to small groups or individuals
- Arranging a classroom
- Selecting children for groups
- Determining lesson content

## SELF-REGULATED CHILDREN

In this scenario, notice how Jackie manages time, holds conversation, and selects children for small groups. This intentional teacher prefers working with a mixed-age group of 3- to 6-year-olds. Her children are highly self-regulated because, Jackie says, she organizes time to allow long conversations and to spend most of the day in individual and small-group work. "Schedules," Jackie says, "jerk children from subject to subject, to things children are not interested in. When they are interested, they get really involved."

### Beliefs and Practices

Jackie's class has 23 children—equal numbers of 3-year-olds, 4-year-olds, and 5-year-olds—who stay together for 3 years. Annually, the oldest leave for 1st grade and are replaced by new 3-year-olds. The school is in a Hispanic working-class neighborhood in a city of 400,000 and is housed in a community center. A nearby park has a refurbished playground, green spaces, playing fields, and a community garden. The children have special hiding places, including a huge oak with branches near the ground.

**What Jackie Believes.** Jackie believes in the innate capacities of all children and has deep feelings of empathy. These qualities enable her to forge close relationships with students' families. In the neighborhood, the word is: "Get into Jackie's class."

Whether with parents or peers, Jackie never conveys an attitude that "they" cannot learn, behave, achieve, or meet high standards. She never waters down the work but fully expects her students to excel because she believes they can. For 10 years Jackie has watched economically disadvantaged children outperform those who are economically advantaged.

Jackie believes that children learn at different paces and that one-size-fits-all curricula cannot provide the skills students need when they need them. She believes *her* students succeed because of the long time blocks for individualized instruction, one-on-one or in small groups. Jackie pinpoints the cognitive or emotional skills children lack and devises ways to build those skills in one-on-one lessons.

✦ Exercise 1: Analyze your beliefs.

- Review the above section.
- List Jackie's beliefs.
- Compare your beliefs with Jackie's.
- Determine where your beliefs and Jackie's concur or differ.

**Early Morning.** Children arrive between 7:30 and 8:30. A community program provides breakfast, lunch, and two snacks. Most children leave by 5:30. Parents work as paid aides, one from 7:30 to 9:00, a second from 3:30 to 5:30. Jackie works from 8:00 to 4:00, her assistant from 9:00 to 5:00. At breakfast children choose when to eat, with whom, and where to sit. They set out and clean up their places. Before the 9:00 full-class meeting, children choose to work alone or in small groups on activities they select or projects under way. The children in Figure 8.1 and their teacher are poring through books to find a bird that resembles what they have in mind for a project. During this time Jackie gives lessons to individuals or small groups—new materials, sandpaper letters, or other didactic materials—or works with children on ongoing projects. At 9:00, Jackie sits on the line, a signal for children to join her. Visitors comment on the children's independence: They select their own work, concentrate, collaborate easily, return materials when finished, and make transitions smoothly. Their actions reflect Jackie's belief in their capacities.

**Morning Meeting.** Transition to morning meeting takes about 4 minutes without Jackie's intervention. All exchange "good mornings," smiles, or hugs with the person next to them. Meeting length varies because conversations differ; flexibility

Figure 8.1. Children pursue their own interests before the morning meeting.

is possible because the schedule is not time-bound. At meeting's end, Jackie and the children slowly take three deep breaths, pausing between each. She asks the children to close their eyes; it is a mindful time to clear their thoughts so they can focus on what they want to do next. Afterward, they say in turn what they will do, leave the group, and begin.

✦ Exercise 2: Examine your early morning routine.

- Review early morning (above).
- List how activities reflect Jackie's beliefs.
- Consider what beliefs your early-morning activities reflect.

*Open Flow.* Whom Jackie works with depends on:

- What transpired in the full-class conversation
- Ongoing projects
- Lessons Jackie has in mind for particular children

The day continues with children flowing from one activity to another. Some children stay with the same activity all day or for many days. Jackie works with the least focused children. She believes focus is the key to learning and stems from children's interests.

The need to entice children with different interests is the impetus for Jackie's equipping the classroom with diverse materials and organizing them so children can see and reach them easily. Jackie reserves challenging or new materials to stimulate specific interests. She prepares the environment to foster independence so that children handle materials respectfully and maintain order.

Children eat morning snack when and with whom they choose, setting out, serving, and cleaning up themselves. Independent work continues until lunch. If music teachers or other specialists are scheduled, children may choose whether to join or continue working. Parents report that children sing songs they learned at school. Jackie notes that children who do not participate in music are just as likely to learn the songs. "Why?" Jackie explains: "We have eyelids, not ear-lids."

Children use the bathroom and water fountain whenever they want. Jackie announces lunchtime 10 minutes before to remind children to do the hand-washing they practiced. Lunch tasks are divided so, by month's end, children have rotated setting places, distributing food, and cleaning up. Teachers eat with the children. Lunch is relaxed and sociable, another time for conversation.

✦ Exercise 3: Analyze the amount of flow in your morning work time.

- Describe your morning flow.
- Are there activities that interrupt children's work?
- Consider what activities you could eliminate to lessen interruptions.

After lunch, younger children nap and older children return to work. Children who want to may go to the playground or park. Most go, but some continue working. After all are awake, there is storytime, currently *The Adventures of Pinocchio*. Its themes echo in children's conversation and play.

The end of the day continues in the same calm manner. The parent in charge has been trained in the structure and use of materials and thus maintains order.

✦ Exercise 4: Consider the best uses for time after nap.

- Consider your class' after-nap activities.
- List the activities that extend children's focus and/or build cognitive skills.

**Conversation.** Jackie is skilled at holding conversations. Visitors note the children's maturity. They:

- Listen to one another respectfully
- Stay on topic
- Do not interrupt
- Do not side talk, annoy others, or crawl off

The following conversation shows Jackie's expertise. After the greeting (described above), Jackie asks: "Who has something they want the class to know?"

Juan relates that his father is home sick. Izzie explains that her goldfish died, they put it in the toilet, and her brothers, mother, and father asked sweet baby Jesus to take it home. Three-year-old Miguel has been waving his hand excitedly: "We see . . . we see a digger . . . that *beeeeg* digger thing."

Jackie sees Miguel's intensity and senses it might spark a project: "Miguel, show us with your hands how big the digger is."

Miguel stands, puts one hand on the floor, the other toward the ceiling: "Thi-i-i-i-i-i-s big. A-wa-a-a-a-y down here, a-wa-a-a-a-y up here."

Five-year-old Moses breaks in gravely: "I know, I know. It's called a backhoe."

Miguel, emphatically: "No! Is a digger thing!"

Lupe, knowingly: "I saw it too. It's that yellow thing."

Isaac, age 4, excitedly: "Wait! Wait! Wait!" He runs to the bookshelves, all eyes watching as he searches and triumphantly returns carrying a hardcover book on earth-moving equipment with a plethora of oversized, detailed color photographs.

Jackie: "Would you like to research what Miguel saw?"

A chorus of emphatic "YESSES!" from six children, 3 to 5½.

Jackie notes the six whom she will gather to pursue the digger and continues addressing other children: "Who else has something they want everyone to know?" Responses fly back and forth. Conversation continues, the children addressing one another, for 25 minutes.

✦ Exercise 5: Examine the potential in conversations.

- Take notes during your next three conversations.
- Study your notes.
- Have children said anything that might lead to an engaging project?
- Continue taking and reviewing notes until you find a remark that might spark a project.
- If you find nothing, have more conversations.

## STRUCTURING OPEN FLOW INTENTIONALLY

Managing open-ended time depends on how teachers arrange the classroom, select and display materials, choose children to work with, and decide what lessons to give. These highly intentional processes are based on listening to and observing children. Selecting lesson content that taps children's deep interests *and* simultaneously build skills is a reflective process. Flow results from how time is structured, as shown in the diagram in Figure 8.2.

### Classroom Arrangement and Materials

Arrangement means that each area's purpose, contents, and order are readily evident. The intention is for children to choose their activities themselves and manage activities independently. The teacher selects materials because the materials:

- Contain important content, enumerated below
- Have readily observable, distinctive characteristics
- Can be used for varied purposes—with blocks, puppets, housekeeping, trains, etc.

**Figure 8.2. In an open-flow day the schedule is flexible, conversations can be completed, and teachers have long blocks of time for lessons to individuals and small groups.**

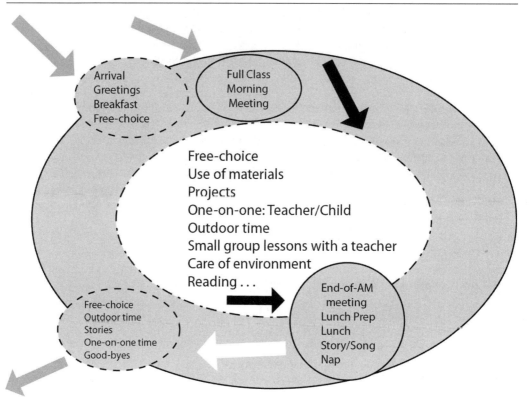

KEY:
**Black arrows:** Time and activities are similar
**Medium arrows:** Time and activities vary

**White arrow:** Time and activities are flexible
**Solid ellipse and circle:** Daily happening
**Dotted ellipses:** Differs for each child

- Are pleasing aesthetically—well-finished wood, attractive colors, realistic detail
- Are inherently challenging—such as the Montessori trinomial cube, a sorting box with hard-to-distinguish shapes that represent a mathematical formula

Items are mainly wood and other natural materials.

***Selection and Display of Materials.*** Materials are selected to convey varied content that appeals to Gardner's multiple intelligences:

1. Color, shape, size, texture (visual)
2. Puzzles, tangrams, Feuerstein's *Orientation in Space* instrument (spatial) (Feuerstein & Lewin-Benham, 2012, pp. 53–55)
3. Number and related arithmetic principles and procedures (mathematical)

4. Cymbals, triangle, tambourines, shakers, and a music-listening area with headphones (musical)
5. Cause-and-effect relationships—weights and balances, science experiments (logical)
6. Care of plants and animals (naturalist)
7. Feelings and moods—dolls, puppets, stories that express sorrow, joy, or other emotions (interpersonal, intrapersonal)
8. The body's parts and functions (linguistic, kinesthetic)
9. Basic skills for daily living—brushing teeth, fastening clothes, etc. (linguistic, kinesthetic)
10. Symbolic play—using blocks as cars, fabric as blankets, pots or dishes as if they contained food (linguistic, kinesthetic, interpersonal)
11. Motor skills—using scissors and markers, riding trikes, playing on slides and swings (kinesthetic) (categories adapted from Feuerstein, Feuerstein, & Falik, 2004, pp. 21–25).

Materials are displayed logically, with items conveying particular concepts grouped together. Arrangements are uncluttered. Presentation is aesthetic: Simple, attractive containers do not compete with materials. Study images of Reggio schools and look at classrooms on the website of the North American Reggio Emilia Alliance (www.reggioalliance.org/narea). These classrooms differ from the typical because of the varied soft colors, natural materials, and elimination of all commercial graphics, whether on walls, materials, or floor coverings.

✦ Exercise 1: Reflect on the intentionality of the materials in your classroom.

- Use items one through eleven above as a checklist
- "Read" your classroom.
- Are your materials intentional?
- Reflect on why or why not.

*Choosing Children for Work.* Teachers choose children for one-on-one work who require undivided attention. These are children who:

- Are difficult and disrupt the class, bite, hit, or rarely focus
- Slip through the cracks, are retiring, quiet
- Need to learn special techniques—new letters, counting, scissors, or any of an infinite number of other skills

In forming groups, teachers consider the influence of children on one another. One child may:

- Have mastered a technique that others want to learn
- Be adept at interpreting others' actions and therefore help peers with the task at hand
- Be a leader whose derring-do encourages others to try
- Possess the skill to solve a problem beyond classmates' ken

Forming groups thoughtfully depends on astute observation, what teachers:

- Hear children say
- See when they observe
- Have experienced in their interactions with children

In choosing children for groups, teachers consider disposition, interpersonal skills, and linguistic, cognitive, behavioral, or other abilities. Teachers choose a mix of children who will "contaminate" (Filippini, 1992) one another with their strengths. Small-group work fosters complex undertakings, creative endeavor, and solution of complicated problems—all powerful motivators.

✦ **Exercise 2: Think about why you choose the particular children you include in small groups.**

- Consider particular content you intend to teach.
- Use the above criteria to determine which children you are selecting and why for small group or individual work.

*Selecting Lessons.* Teachers devise lessons to build children's content knowledge, cognitive thinking capacities, or socio-emotional behaviors. Content knowledge can be anything that catches a child's interest. Basic content, necessary for successful cognitive functioning, was enumerated in the 11 items on pages 152–153.

Cognitive capacities include wide-ranging thinking skills with which to manipulate content and build relationships between different objects or events. A short list of *essential* cognitive skills includes the abilities to:

1. Attend to stimuli or focus without attention wavering
2. Observe: "Last year when I was 3, I was as tall as James." "Katie's mommy came early."
3. Assess: "The water's too hot to wash my hands."
4. Compare: "Donny has more in his cubby than I do."
5. Differentiate: "That red triangle is facing the other way."
6. Connect to past experiences: "When we collected leaves, they were wet 'cause it rained."
7. Project future ideas: "If the sun shines, the icicles will melt."
8. Sequence information logically: "Johnny should stand between; he's taller than Nancy and shorter than Tom."
9. Form concepts: "My favorite color is blue." Counting: "There is this many: One, two, three, four, six, seven . . ."
10. Put information in context: "That's the American flag at the post office."
11. Synthesize information: "Every day we have breakfast, talk on the line, do our work, then have lunch."
12. Manipulate quantities: "If she takes one of mine, she'll have more than I do."
13. Manipulate spatial relations: up/down, right/left
14. Manipulate temporal relations: then/now, before/after

15. Recognize the absurd: "The giraffe is wearing a hat!"
16. Correct one's mistakes: "I meant one, two, three, four, five . . ."
17. Make symbolic representations: "Here's your sandwich" (handing a plate with a piece of paper on it).

This list contains a very few of the simpler essential cognitive acts the brain can perform.

✦ Exercise 3: Consider what cognitive acts your lessons stimulate.

- Analyze the next three lessons you give.
- Note the cognitive acts you want the lessons to elicit.
- Consider whether the lessons elicited the cognitive acts.
- If not, redesign the lessons or make up other lessons and reteach.

***Socio-emotional Behavior.*** This means how we act with others, how we think about ourselves, whether we are motivated, and what we believe. Following are examples with the approximate age first seen:

1. Imitating—a primary way humans learn (starting in infancy)
2. Sharing—pointing (infants and toddlers)
3. Laughing together (around 4 months)
4. Taking another's perspective (3 to 4 years)
5. Identifying emotions in oneself and others (2 to 3 years)
6. Initiating interactions with adults or other children (birth)
7. Engaging in symbolic play reflecting actual or imagined situations (12 months)
8. Expressing empathy in actions or words (6 months)
9. Collaborating and cooperating (2 years)

The lists in this chapter provide a sense of what intentional teachers consider in setting up their classroom, selecting children for groups, and planning lessons.

✦ Exercise 4: When you comment on what children have done, use words that describe cognitive actions.

- In your next week's lessons, use the above criteria to observe children.
- Make children conscious of their actions by naming their behaviors: "Alice, you imitated Jamie's hand movement exactly." "Derrick, you expressed great empathy when LaShandra's arm became caught in her sweater."

## Summary

An open-flow day is one indication of how a teacher's beliefs influence everything in the classroom—space, its arrangement, the organization of materials, time, and how children change activities. Children's self-regulation results from teachers' beliefs about how children learn cognitively and socio-emotionally.

## CONVERSATIONS AND CONTENT

Here I recount a first conversation with children new at conversations. Then we watch a young teacher, dissatisfied with her calendar lesson, struggle with a new technique. We question the meaning of content. Finally, we watch mature teachers who intersperse conversation in all their activities.

### A First Conversation

When we began to hold conversations at the Model Early Learning Center, the teachers were terrified, unsure of what to talk about, how to launch conversations, what to say after their opening line. They knew conversations were not scripted, that responding would be like walking a high wire with no safety net. If anyone had told them that, in time, their conversations would last an hour, they would have thought it impossible.

The teachers learned by trial and error, above all by being critical of themselves and asking colleagues for help. I recount my own experience here, hopeful that it can help teachers new to conversation.

*Setting Ground Rules.* Currently, I work in schools where I demonstrate techniques I write about. I usually begin by demonstrating the art of conversation. A teacher gathers a full class, has the children sit on the floor in a circle, and introduces me as Ann; then I begin. In advance, I have explained that any teachers are welcome to observe. Sometimes many attend; sometimes I work in single classrooms.

Before I start and with children present, I briefly tell adults that this is a serious conversation. I ask adults not to:

- Talk among themselves
- Interrupt
- Laugh, no matter how amusing a child's remarks

They are welcome to take photographs or notes. I explain that later we will reflect using their observations, questions, and comments.

*Opening.* I greet the children: "Good morning, my name is Ann. We're going to have a conversation. If you know what a conversation is, raise your hand." I have heard unusual answers. One 4-year-old gave a dictionary-perfect definition. Another said, "It's when I go to my gramma's." One 3-year-old said (not metaphorically) a conversation was "a door." Children have made off-topic comments and given run-on answers connected by many "ands." When children's answers make sense, I nod my head or say, "Yes." When a child's answer makes no sense, I say nothing. I continue until every child with a raised hand has spoken.

*Managing Behavior.* I do not call on children whose hand is not raised. Most children catch on fast. If children call out, say "Me! Me!" or make noises to get my attention, I repeat: "I will call on anyone whose hand is raised." No matter what another child does, the child on whom I call receives my full attention: I face only that child and listen intently so everyone sees that I am attending only to the speaker. If a child is unruly, I call on an observer (preferably the child's teacher) and describe precisely what to do:

- Please sit next to (motioning because I do not know names) so she calms down.
- Please hold (motioning) on your lap and keep him from hitting.
- Please remove (motioning) and sit on the side until she can sit still.
- Please take (motioning) outside until his tantrum stops.

During conversations children have thrown major tantrums, wiggled, punched, karate-chopped, chattered incessantly, and crawled off. Other than addressing the teacher (as above), I do not interrupt the conversation or mention behavior. Usually children attend. Why? They are interested in what their friends have to say. It is different than when a teacher speaks. When there is respectful listening, children capture one another's attention. Because children want to speak, most bring their behavior into line themselves.

***The Second Question.*** When the process has yielded a reasonable definition of conversation, I summarize the definition using the children's words. Next I ask: "What would you like to have a conversation *about*?" I follow the same procedure: calling only on children who raise their hand and giving the speaker total attention. My role is facilitator. I do not provide information but orchestrate so the conversation:

- Sticks to a topic the majority has chosen
- Includes what many speakers want to say
- Involves listening with attention and respect

My process, demeanor, tone of voice, and expression are intentional, serious, and alert. My role is to manage the process, follow children's interests, and listen carefully for good remarks that can lead to the next conversation on another day. If a child's remarks are off-topic, I say, "Please tell me later. This conversation is not about trips to Grandma's." If a child runs on and on, I interrupt and say, "Please hold some of your good ideas until later."

✦ Exercise 1: Have a conversation with children about having a conversation.

1. Ask: What do you do when you have a conversation?
2. Develop rules (with older children) for holding conversations.

## A Formulaic Lesson

Sondra, the 4-year-olds' teacher, sat in the corner for morning meeting, 22 children in a pie-shaped wedge facing her. Sondra was teaching the calendar. First she pointed to the large word (November), then to the day (Tuesday), then to the date

(12). As she pointed to and read each, the children called after her in rote. Using a large calendar, Sondra called five children, one at a time, to her side to point to the word *November*, then another five, one by one, to point to the word *Tuesday*. None could connect name or number to symbol, even after Sondra had shown several. The remaining 12 children were called, one by one, to point to successive days and count the numbers to today. None succeeded at this task either. After 10 minutes every child was moving to relieve boredom, some obstreperously. Sondra droned on, interrupting frequently to try to restore order. As the lesson proceeded, children became more interested in watching classmates' misbehavior than in attending.

## Changing

Sondra and her calendar lesson are similar to many teachers' experiences. The question is not how Sondra can be more intentional in teaching the calendar, but how an intentional teacher can stop using lessons that do not work. The answer lies in how a classroom's space and time are structured.

Frustrated with herself and the children, Sondra confided in another teacher, who confessed the same problems. They tentatively raised the issue in the teachers' lounge. As in "The Emperor's New Clothes," no one would admit the problem. Yet, most had the same issues: squirming children and little actually learned. With no solutions, Sondra looked online, in books, and at an ECE conference. Her principal hired a consultant on conversation. What struck Sondra as most important was to record conversations, read her notes, and select a child's remark as the basis for the next conversation.

## An Intentional Lesson

Here Sondra presents a calendar lesson to a small group. First Sondra studied her recordings of children's conversations, intending to find topics that interested them. Three children were excited by the approaching Thanksgiving holiday.

Jennie: "We goin' to my gramma house. At Thanksgiving."
Gerald: "When you go? Tomorrow?"
Alise: "Gerald, you so dumb. Thanksgiving at Christmas."
Gerald, emphatic: "It not! Thanksgiving now!"
Jennie: "I don' know, but we goin'."

Two days later, Sondra gathered Jennie, Gerald, and Alise, read them their conversation, then asked, "Would you like to know when Thanksgiving is?" Three heads bobbed enthusiastically and a conversation ensued.

Sondra: "How can we find out when Thanksgiving is?"
Jennie: "We can aks my gramma."
Alise: "I can aks my mommy."
Gerald, excited then trailing off: "What that thing? . . ."
Alise: "What 'thing' you mean, boy?"
Gerald, looking expectantly at Sondra: "You know what I means, Ms. Sondra?"
Sondra: "Can you show me?"

Gerald rushes off to the communication center. On the workbench is a small tent-shaped calendar, one page per month. Sondra had put it there last year when summer vacation approached. Unaware that the calendar had caught Gerald's attention, Sondra's pleasure is genuine: "Gerald! What have you . . .?"

Gerald, excited, interrupting: "This that thing . . ."

Jennie, knowingly: "That a calendar."

Gerald: "Yeah! That calader."

Sondra, excited: "Yes! Gerald! We can figure out from the calendar when Thanksgiving is!"

The children were attentive as Sondra tore off the months that had passed, rhythmically saying the name, emphasizing the stressed syllable, and pausing between each: "June (tearing it off), pause . . . Oc-TO-ber (tearing it off) . . . ," and a lengthy pause: "Now comes the month with Thanksgiving: "No-VEM-ber. Say it with me."

In unison, children and teacher repeat "No-VEM-ber."

Sondra: "NoVEMber is the month for Thanksgiving." Pausing dramatically: "Now let's find the day."

She brought a typical 8" × 11" calendar, a page for each month, a square for each day. "On this calendar we can easily see each day." She first showed the children today, November 12. Then: "Thanksgiving this year is on November 27; let's start today and say the number for each day until Thanksgiving. November 12, November 13 . . ." The children chimed in, not always saying the teens correctly.

When Sondra read November 23, the children recognized the 1, 2, 3 pattern and counted along with her: "No**vem**ber twenty-**three**, No**vem**ber twenty-**four**, . . . No**vem**ber twenty-**SEVEN**." The children broke into applause.

"Do you want to mark November 27?" Sondra asked.

"I'll get it," called Jennie, as she rushed to bring a marker and mark the correct box.

Sondra suspected interest would still be high when, in a day or two, she would gather the children again and ask: "How many days is it from *today* to Thanksgiving?"

## Lesson Content

Calendars contain abstract concepts: months, days, numerical sequences, lengths of calendric divisions, irregularities. It took centuries to develop a calendar to accurately reflect relationships among sun, earth, moon, day, night, months, weeks. Yet, starting in preschool, we begin rote calendar lessons that are boring: Children see no use for calendars because most have little firsthand experience with time divisions or intrinsic interest in them. Moreover, few can read, recognize numbers, or make one-to-one correspondence—three of the prerequisite cognitive processes necessary for using calendars. Calendar lessons require children to read words by sight without sounding out and to count without manipulating objects. Research has proven that learning words by the "look-say" method is folly and that children need to manipulate objects to understand quantity, sequence, and other arithmetic concepts (Mix, Huttenlocher, & Levine, 2002; Singapore Math: en.wikipedia.org/wiki/Singapore_math).

When children are not interested, the brain stem—responsible for keeping the mind alert—shuts down and children become bored or drowsy. Some act out in an attempt to keep themselves alert. Shutting down, acting bored, or acting out are children's ways of saying that their mental processes are being stymied.

When did calendar lessons become enshrined as a daily regimen of preschool? And why? Is it not better to allow calendar concepts to form gradually as children spontaneously ask questions about *when*? Is it not better to introduce calendars in 2nd or 3rd grade when children begin to find uses for calendars, can read or sound out words, and recognize numbers? Could we replace *all* formulaic lessons with the kind of active listening and conversation we saw Sondra learn?

Using small-group lessons based on children's interests is essential in an open-flow day. For open flow to succeed, children must be able to work independently, but they will do so only when interested. Space—both a classroom's layout and the materials in the classroom—facilitates children's independence and stimulates interest. We look at space next.

✦ Exercise 2: Analyze the kinds of teaching in Sondra's lessons.

- Reread the two "Sondra" scenarios.
- For each, list behaviors that define:
  ➤ Traditional teaching
  ➤ Intentional teaching
  ➤ Reflective teaching

### Summary

Here we watched two teachers. Scenarios showed:

- A day in an open-flow classroom
- How open flow helps children's self-regulation and cognition grow because activities engage their interest and stretch their capacities
- Techniques for using conversation
- How conversations reveal teachers' intention and reflection

## FOSTERING BETTER BEHAVIOR AND INCREASED COGNITION

How can you increase children's cognitive and behavioral skills? Where do you start if your intention is to break away from prescheduled time and instead make time open-ended? Some Reggio-inspired schools start by changing their environment, then turn children loose in the lovely-looking classroom, but maintain their teaching behaviors and lessons. However, the space will remain beautiful and function *only* if children learn what materials are available and the ground rules for using them.

### Establishing Ground Rules

Lillian's class has 25 children, older 3s and younger 4s from multiethnic, middle-income homes in a large city. The fact that most parents work is reflected in the school's hours: 7:30 A.M. to 6:00 P.M. Most children are present from 8:00 to 5:30. Lillian organizes the day so that from 7:30 to 8:00 and 5:00 to 6:00 part-time staff read chapter books or poetry. From 8:00 to 8:30 children have breakfast. The open flow worked as Jackie's did. At day's end children can choose to work on their own rather than listen to the story with the group. The bulk of the day is open-flow, with conversations throughout.

Lillian recalled when she was changing from a scripted curriculum to open flow: "I was really confused about management, how to get children to choose, to clean up, to know what to do next. They might start okay, but everything broke down. It seemed a mess."

Lillian remembered a unit on the Montessori method in her college ECE courses. She recalled that Montessori children work independently for long periods, and that classes have many materials. She feared that long work time and lots of material would generate chaos, but found two interesting things: Maria Montessori understood the importance of movement and ensured that teachers allowed movement. Montessori understood that motionless does not mean good, and in fact is counter to nature, an insight supported by current research in neuroscience (Ratey, 2002). Montessori urged teachers to observe children carefully, to distinguish purposeful movement, and not to interrupt children who move purposefully. She urged teachers to engage children whose movements were random and settle them—one at a time or in a small group—into activity that would hold their attention.

Montessori (1948) describes a child whose random movement disrupted others and how she isolated the child at a small table where everyone could see him

> in an armchair in front of the class and giving him all the objects he wanted. This isolation always succeeded in calming the child. He saw from his position the whole band of his companions, and their way of behaving was an object lesson more efficacious than any teachers' words could have been. Little by little he realized the advantages of being in others' company, and began to want to do as they did. . . . The isolated child was made the object of special care as if he were helpless or sick. . . . I went first of all straight to him, caressing him as if he were a baby; afterwards I turned to the others, interesting myself as if they were men. . . . The "conversion" of isolated individuals was always decided and thorough. They became proud of being able to work and of behaving properly; generally they displayed tender affection for their teacher and me. (p. 91)

Just as Montessori urged teachers to "avoid rigorously the arresting of spontaneous movements" (p. 79), she was emphatic that "useless or dangerous actions" (p. 79) should be prevented. She was equally emphatic that the goal of all intervention should be to help children become independent. To *do for* a child, Montessori says, is the work of servants. To *teach how* is the work of educators (p. 87).

> The liberty of the child ought to have as its limit the collective interest of the community. . . . [We must] prevent the child from doing anything which may offend or hurt others and check behavior which is unbecoming or impolite. But . . . every action which has a useful purpose in view, whatever it may be and in whatever form it shows itself, ought not only to be permitted, but it ought to be kept under observation: *that* [observation] is the essential point. (p. 79, emphasis added)

## Listening to Children

After rereading Montessori, Lillian rethought her reaction: She would interrupt any and all movement that might disrupt others. So for now she would ignore children who were engaged, who were observing others, or who were wandering. Children behaving raucously she would ask her assistant to isolate, to "tend" to, and to make an example of their inability to manage freedom within bounds. She would concentrate on helping children learn how to become independent.

*A Better Snack.* Lillian began with snack. Children could eat when or where they wanted, but often spilled and left a mess. Lillian structured simple activities to help children learn how to carry, to pour without spilling, to clean up. By nature detail-oriented and sensitive to aesthetics, Lillian bought unique items from a secondhand store: a glass pitcher with an elegantly shaped handle, an etched table crumber, a miniature painted tin bucket for the floor sponge, an old-fashioned, lace-edged cotton cloth to wipe the table. She prepared a special place near the sink for each item.

Then Lillian introduced the items to the 3-year-olds, who were messier than the 4s. Lillian was delighted: The children enjoyed precision in carrying, pouring, and wiping up; needed no reminder to use the cloth on the table or the sponge on the floor; and found it a privilege to be the first to use the beautiful new things, greatly enjoying both the challenge of being independent and their new success. The 4-year-olds wanted the same privilege. Soon all children were serving more carefully and cleaning up themselves.

*Taking the Trains in Hand.* Excited by the success of the new snack procedures, Lillian looked critically at her classroom with a small band of boys in mind, concerned that their random behavior, if not channeled into purposeful activity, could become boisterous. The train area, she decided, was not interesting. The secondhand store had a huge selection of miniature objects—old railroad sets, abandoned games, sets of people, tiny trucks—that might enliven the trains. Why not take the boys to choose appealing items? First she brought them to look at the train area and asked, "Why do you think no one uses the trains?" Their answers surprised her.

Casey: "They're messy. And some are broken."

Daniel: "There's no place for the trains to go, no cities, no bridges, no highways."

Darryl, gesturing: "They're for little kids. We played with these when we were over there," indicating the wing for infants and toddlers.

Lillian was astounded. No wonder no one touched the trains. Next morning, Lillian gathered the three boys: "How could we make the train area appealing, so it isn't messy, boring, or babyish?"

Darryl, recollecting: "We could get some of those things like they have at Christmas when . . . you know, lots of those little trains that run on tracks through all the mountains and places."

Daniel, excitedly: "Yeah! And some people, like the cops, and firemen and ambulances so if there's a wreck or the trains fall off a bridge, they can save the people."

Casey, shaking his head from side to side and trailing off: "We need to get this place straightened up. All the trains is in this basket where you can't find anything and, ummmm . . ."

Again, Lillian was astounded. The children knew what had to be done to make the area work. Back to the secondhand store! Would the manager allow the children to make choices? Could he discount anything? Could she pay the bill slowly?

The manager shut his eyes tightly. Lillian's heart fell. "Just a minute," he said, and emerged with a large cardboard box: "I was going to throw this out. Take it to school, there may be some stuff you can use. You don't owe me nothing."

The minute Lillian arrived next morning, Casey, Darryl, and Daniel rushed to her: Casey had an old box, shallow, narrow, and made from nicely finished wood. The boys wanted to rearrange the trains. Lillian thanked them for so cleverly solving one of the problems. The boys spent the next two mornings configuring and re-configuring the trains in the box, in the process playing with them. Wisely, Lillian did not present the cardboard box until the boys' interest in arranging trains had waned. It took a full week for the boys to unpack, sort, and select from the trove in the cardboard box. In the process they found objects for the trains, blocks, puppet theater, and housekeeping areas.

Lillian had stumbled onto an approach to arrest wandering children by arous-ing their interest: She would ask other wanderers to analyze areas of the classroom. More important, Lillian reflected: "I learned I can trust children's judgment; they have experiences way outside the classroom that can direct their energy here."

✦ Exercise 1: Consider what areas of your class to critique with particular children.

- Look at your classroom critically to find an area that is not working.
- Select a small group—each child chosen for specific reasons—to help you analyze the area.
- Elicit children's suggestions.
- Listen, take notes.
- Later, recall with the children what they have said.
- Discuss with the children how to implement their ideas.

## Maintaining Order

Carol, Lillian's colleague, the teacher of a different 3-/4-year-old class, watched Lillian's efforts. "I've got wanderers too, the 4-year-old boys. No matter what I show them, it's 2 minutes and they're off." Lillian was amazed because Carol's room was rich in interesting things. Carol was a collector. Her assortment of con-tainers and the many unusual things throughout her room were enticing to adults and children. "My class can't keep order. It takes me forever to straighten up," Carol lamented.

*A Problem.* Lillian observed. Yes. At morning's end the room was a mess. The teachers conferred and finally decided: Carol would take all her attractive, interest-catching materials out of the classroom. They agreed her room would look barren, but their plan was to tell the children why and somehow—they weren't yet sure how—involve children in the solution.

During the work period on the day after the "denuding," many children found Carol: "Miss Carol! Where is the . . . ?" Each child named some favorite material. Unprepared for this reaction, Carol said, "We'll talk about it at end-of-morning meeting." A plan was forming in her mind.

Carol did not begin with her usual question: "Who would like to tell everyone what you did this morning?" but instead: "Did anyone notice anything different today?" The children were experienced at conversation and raised their hands for a turn. Annette noticed the shells were gone. Janine, Nancy, and Patty noticed *all* the beads were gone, not just the glittery ones. "And," added Patty, "the wire is gone too." "The castle blocks are missing," moaned Andrew. He spent hours building castles, each with its own narrative. "And I couldn't find any of those special pens," complained Charles, who lately had been using a magic marker with silver ink to cover page after page with elaborate figures. "No rocks in the geology area," said Roger, a rock hound, solemnly. On went the observations until every child had reported something missing.

Slowly, somberly, Carol announced: "I removed everything," and paused to let the fact sink in. A clamor of voices—no hands raised—asked, "Why?" stunned because they knew their classroom had a reputation for its special things. It was a resource for the entire school; other teachers or children frequently sought something extraordinary, which Carol or one of the children usually could find. Wanting to make her point by continuing the misery, Carol said they would talk about it tomorrow. Actually, she needed time to consult with Lillian and figure out what to do next.

*A Solution.* The plan, which took many weeks to implement, was that Carol would reintroduce items gradually. As each item was brought back, a small group of children would discuss its nature, where it belonged, rules for handling it, how to store it, how many children could use it at once, and who would be responsible for putting it away. The full class would listen to the proposed rules and develop rules for the use of each material. The project, which the children named "Rules About Our Materials," lasted most of the year. It evolved from rules about each material to rules about materials in general and what the children named "Special Rules." One Special Rule was that wire had to be stored lying down so it would not poke you. Another Special Rule was that markers had to be sorted by color so you could find what you wanted more easily.

Carol's room stayed neat for the rest of the year. The children leaving for kindergarten volunteered to return to help new children learn the rules. In subsequent years, Carol added her collections gradually, introducing each material with a conversation, not about the nature of the material or what to make with it, but about rules for using it. Over the years, the rules morphed, according to different children's ideas and experiences, but Carol never again had a problem maintaining order, and children developed rules for other procedures, not just care of materials.

✦ Exercise 2: Engage children in devising a process for maintaining order.

- Consider what your room looks like at the end of the morning. Is it orderly because an adult cleans up or because children maintain order? If it is disorderly, who cleans up?
- Involve the children in considering the disorder.
- Elicit children's ideas about how to maintain order.

## Summary

Jackie, Lillian, and Carol are experienced teachers. Sondra, a younger teacher, wants to grow. This chapter shows that, experienced or inexperienced, teachers can always grow, be reflective, and become more intentional. Change may be driven by teachers' reflections or may result from:

- A higher than usual number of challenging children
- A teacher's personal circumstances, having nothing to do with school
- A new administrator who institutes a regimen that impacts teachers
- Government programs that impose new requirements

Changes from without are unpredictable. The best way to meet change, whatever drives it, is with belief in your own competence, trust in your beliefs, and collaboration with your colleagues.

## CONCLUSION

Here we saw self-regulated children, open-flow days, meaning-full conversations, and teachers changing their practices. These conditions are possible when teachers believe in themselves as competent educators and have the autonomy to structure their teaching. Doctors are not told what medicines to prescribe, lawyers what trial tactics to use, CPAs what tax strategies to apply. Teaching is as much a profession as medicine, law, and accounting. Yet everyone tells teachers what to teach.

The questions for teachers are:

1. Do you believe your children's cognitive and behavioral skills are not growing as well as they could?
2. Do you believe you could better enable your children's cognitive and behavioral skills to grow if you adopted a new theory and different practices?
3. Do you know what practices you want to adopt?

If you answer yes to all these questions, get on with it! If you answer no, reflect on what you need to know or do to answer yes. Or, if you believe in what you are already doing, stick with it. The caveat is to be honest in answering the questions. If you are unsure how to answer, the next chapter, a self-assessment, may help.

# CHAPTER 9

# Am I Teaching
# Intentionally and Reflectively?

To begin, begin.

—William Wordsworth

In the final analysis, intention and reflection are about how we behave—our actions—those that are visible and invisible. Visible actions are what others can see us do. Invisible actions are what we think. If it does not make sense to you that "thinking" is an "action," recall that neuroscientists tell us *all* thought is based on action, that the same brain networks used to control movement are active when we think.

This self-assessment tool is for teachers:

- To use intentionally and reflectively to examine their own actions—both what they do and what they think
- To look critically at actions that, over time, have become habitual, that is, actions done automatically, without thinking

Through scenarios and exercises, I have tried to help readers (1) see anew the impact of habitual thinking/doing on children and (2) break down habits in order to become better at helping children grow cognitively and socio-emotionally.

I have organized this chapter by the techniques in Chapters 1 through 8. For each technique, I provide questions for you to answer and I list behaviors that you can observe in yourself and your children. Some questions need to be answered in the classroom as you work with children.

*Note:* I use the words *child* and *children* interchangeably. Whether you are teaching one child or a group, questions apply equally.

*Important Note:* If your answers are mainly positive, you probably are teaching intentionally and reflectively. If your answers are mixed, reread the scenarios and use this self-assessment to pinpoint actions that will make your teaching more intentional and reflective.

## TECHNIQUE 1
## OBSERVE YOURSELF TEACHING: DIFFERENTIATE THESE BEHAVIORS—
## INTERRUPT, INTERFERE, INTERVENE, INTEND, REFLECT, MEAN, TRANSCEND

### 1. Questions Re: Interrupting, Interfering, and Intervening

1. Do you interrupt, interfere, or intervene with children who are working? Consider:
   - What were the children doing before you interrupted/interfered/ intervened?
   - Why did you decide to interrupt/interfere/intervene?
   - What did you want/expect the child to do as a result of your interruption/interference/intervention?
   - Was the child's reaction what you anticipated?

   To change this behavior, when you next approach a child, do you:

   - Jot down what the child is doing?
   - Jot down what motivated you to interrupt, interfere, or intervene?
   - Jot down what the child did as a result?
   - Note whether the child's actions were what you anticipated?

   Repeat this activity several times. Your behavior will have changed if you:

   - Observe what children are doing before you interrupt, interfere, or intervene.
   - Consider beforehand possible outcomes of your interrupting/interfering/ intervening. For example, ask yourself: Is my behavior likely to have a negative effect by:
     - ➤ Breaking children's concentration?
     - ➤ Stopping a cycle of activity before the child completes it?
     - ➤ Cutting off the possibility of children's solving a problem for themselves?
     - ➤ Disrupting collaboration among children?
     - ➤ Substituting my goal for the children's?

   Note any other negative consequence(s) you observe.

2. What distinctions can you make among the acts of interrupting, interfering, and intervening? Consider: After you interrupted/interfered/intervened, did children:
   - Continue their work?
   - Deepen their concentration?
   - Adopt—either immediately or at another time—whatever you showed or told them?

- Implement a suggestion you made, for examples:
  - ➤ Find a book or other resource?
  - ➤ Enlist the help of a child not part of the activity?
  - ➤ Fetch a tool or material?
- Solve a problem that was stymieing them?
- Display appreciation by smiling at you, saying thank you, or in some other way acknowledging you?
- Actively engage you in the work they were doing?
- Behave in some other positive way? Describe.

Children's positive behavior suggests that you were intervening rather than interrupting or interfering.

Children's negative behavior suggests that you interrupted or interfered. Examples follow. Did children:

- Leave their work?
- Display negative behavior toward one another, for example:
  - ➤ Snatch something another child was working on?
  - ➤ Hit or use another physical act to show displeasure?
  - ➤ Say something negative?
- React negatively toward the work, for example:
  - ➤ Make negative remarks such as, "This work is stupid"?
  - ➤ Scrunch up a paper?
  - ➤ Throw the work aside, knock it down, or make some other destructive act?
- Act negatively toward you, for example:
  - ➤ Hit, kick, or use another negative physical act?
  - ➤ Say "No!," whine, or otherwise verbalize displeasure?

If you cannot distinguish between interrupting, interfering, and intervening, reread the scenarios in Chapter 1, try the exercises suggested, then repeat this self-assessment. Or, discuss your reactions with a colleague. Or, email me (ann@ annlewin-benham.com) and I'll try to respond.

## 2. Questions Re: Intention and Reflection

1. When you have intended to do something and are reflecting on the outcome, is your recollection nonexistent or vague? Consider, do you:
   - Write or make a mental note of what you intend to do but have little or no recall of the outcome?
   - Feel concerned that you rarely recall what you intended to do?
   - Have little or no awareness of whether your actions are intentional?
   - Remember which children were involved, what lesson you gave them, and their reactions?
   - Remember children/lesson/reactions (yours and the children's) for everything you do in a day?

2. When you have intended to do something and are reflecting on the outcome, is your recollection imprecise? Consider:
   - Do you wish your recall was exact, more detailed, or specific?
   - Are you aware that your actions are intentional but do not recall exactly what you intended?

   *Note:* If your recollections of what you intended are not exact—and few people's are—devise a system to aid your memory. Most people find written notes most helpful. Notes can be made both in advance and on-the-fly, as many intentions arise in response to what is happening at the moment.

3. If you recall your intentions, do you use your recollections:
   - Not at all?
   - Once in a while?
   - Regularly and often?
   - Always?
4. If you recall your intentions sometimes or always, consider:
   - What motivated or sparked the intention?
   - How did you carry out the intention?
   - How did your intentional action make you feel?
     ➤ Surprised
     ➤ Disappointed
     ➤ Delighted
     ➤ Amused
     ➤ Frustrated
     ➤ Awkward
     ➤ Angry
     ➤ Indifferent
     ➤ Other (Describe)
   - Do the effects of your actions motivate you to be intentional:
     ➤ All the time?
     ➤ More than you are now?
     ➤ Less than you are now?
     ➤ Never?
   - If the effects of your intervention are indifferent or negative, consider what disappointed you:
     ➤ The children's behavior or reactions?
     ➤ Your actions?
     ➤ Your feelings about yourself as a teacher?
   - If the effects are positive, continue what you are doing and in several months repeat the self-assessment. Consider:
     ➤ Have you, your practices, and/or children's cognitive and socio-emotional behavior changed?
     ➤ How they have changed?
     ➤ Have your intention and reflection influenced the change(s)?

### 3. Questions Re: Mean

To "mean" refers to your actions in regard to the content of your lessons. For example, if you are teaching 3½-year-olds to recognize a cube, will you focus on the corners? The squares on the sides? The number of sides? Will you ask the child to compare this cube with others? Will you ask the child to consider how the cube can be used? Will you make the experience transcendent by asking what the cube reminds the child of? Any of the above aspects constitute the "meaning" of a cube.

Consider: Before giving lessons, do you use any of the following intentional behaviors to convey to children the meaning of the content in the lesson?

1. Select content with specific meaning in mind
2. Convey content using contrast or attributes
3. Plan how to use tactile, visual, auditory, gestural, vocal, or other modes of presentation
4. Rack your brain, talk with colleagues, or check the web for other ways to convey meaning if none of the above work

### 4. Questions Re: Transcend

1. Do you end lessons or meetings by asking children to relate the content to what they know or can imagine?
2. Do you use different questions to stimulate children to use transcendence?
3. Do you keep a list of your questions?
4. Do you enlarge your list of questions?

## TECHNIQUE 2
## COMMUNICATE PRECISELY: MASTER NUANCES IN USING THE BODY, EYES, FACE, HANDS, AND VOICE

Nuances are subtleties and micro-actions are the slightest of movements. We are unaware of how much we communicate when our smallest movements are nuanced. Use these exercises and questions to determine whether your expressions are nuanced and to become aware of the micro-actions you make.

### 1. Looking at Yourself in a Mirror

1. Imagine something that evokes strong feelings—fear, anguish, terror, joy, love, annoyance. For example, situations that cause your heart to race:
   - There is an armed intruder in your room
   - A loved one has been lost in a plane crash
   - Your daughter has just become pregnant
   - You are in love with a new person
   - Your friends raved that your chocolate pie was the best ever
   - You have just been told that you are being fired

Or recall some actual experience of your own that evoked strong emotion.

Or think of actions of your spouse, parents, children, or others in your life that irk you, those behaviors that the person repeats continually regardless of how you plead, scold, or remind him or her to stop or change.

For any situation you choose, watch the mirror closely to spot reactions in your face and/or eyes. Do you notice *obvious* expressions and movements?

2. Repeat the exercise (perhaps using a different situation) and now note *your smallest movements*. Freeze frame them in your mind; impress the expressions and movements in your memory. Practice using them to communicate positive or negative emotions.

*Practice:* What are the *slightest* possible expressions and movements you can use to communicate the emotion you are feeling?

## 2. Looking at Yourself with a Partner

Display the expressions and movements you have practiced to a friend. Ask your friend:

- Can you identify my emotion?

If your friend identifies your emotion correctly, ask:

- Precisely what did I do that informed you?

If your friend misses, ask:

- Why did you make that answer?

Consider:

- Was your mouth sad but your eyes neutral?
- Were your hands tense but your posture relaxed?
- Were your eyes glaring but your shoulders slumped?

## 3. Looking at Yourself with a Camera

Unless you are great at making "selfies," ask a friend to help. Take a photo anytime your body, eyes, or face registers an emotion. Study the photos: Can you identify the nuanced expressions that reveal the emotion?

*Tip:* All reactions with body, eyes, and face are controlled by muscles. As with swimming, tennis, or riding a bike, mastering new muscular movements takes practice. The purpose of mastering body, eye, and face movements is so that you can use them intentionally when you communicate with children.

## 4. Using Your Voice Effectively

Record your voice and listen. Do you use any of these effects: vary tone and pitch, pause, change pace, or chant? Save the recording. On different days record your voice as you practice one of the above effects. Practice until each effect becomes natural. Record again, compare to the first recording, and note any changes. Keep practicing and recording until you effortlessly combine different effects.

*Note:* If my suggestions for evoking emotion do not work, try other ways to observe yourself when you communicate. The purpose is not the evoking of emotion, but your observing your behaviors so that you can re-create them, at first with effort and eventually with ease, to make your communication more effective.

## TECHNIQUE 3
## USE LANGUAGE EXUBERANTLY: BUILD ON CHILDREN'S LOVE OF LANGUAGE BY PLAYING WITH WORDS AND HANDS TO EXPRESS MEANING

In Chapter 3, I suggest 2 dozen or so exercises and games to play with children to make them aware of sounds in words and to sharpen their ability to distinguish and reproduce sounds. Some games engage teachers in playing with language; others build children's awareness of word meaning and capacity with pronunciation. Your enjoyment of words and play with sounds will instill a love of language in children at a young age and will lay a good foundation for literacy.

Here are questions about whether you are intentional in bringing language play into your life and into the classroom.

### 1. Intentionally Using Word Games

1. Study the games in Chapter 3 and categorize them: Which sharpen teachers' word awareness? Which sharpen children's? Which build children's knowledge of word sounds? Of word meanings? Make categories and list the games in each.
2. Within each category, consider which games you are most likely to play and list the games in that order. Put games that appeal to you most or the ones you would find easiest to play at the top of the list.
3. Decide which category you want to use first—for teachers? for children with sound? for children with meaning?
4. Read and reread the first game on your list until you understand what to do.
5. Rehearse the game alone, either in your head or aloud.
6. Review the tips in Chapter 3. The most important are tips about frequency of repetition and length of play.
7. If you chose a game for teachers, play the game until you master it. If the first game you chose is a game to play with children, continue with this game until children play it readily. Introduce another game only when you have exhausted possibilities with the first one or if children's interest has waned.
8. Ask children to name each game after playing it. Involve all children in choosing the name. Make note of the name(s). As the repertoire of games builds, children can ask for favorite games by name.
9. Consider whether you gradually are building up a repertoire of games:

- You play yourself?
- You play with children?
- You have taught parents to play?

*Note:* Set your own pace. There is no right or wrong game order, length of time, or number of times to play one game before going on to another.

## 2. Reflectively Using Word Play

Once game play is under way, reflect on its use:

1. How often are you playing?
2. What are the children's reactions?
3. Are you enjoying yourself?
4. Are the children enjoying themselves?
5. Do you hear echoes of word play when children are engaged in other activities?
6. Do parents report that they hear children using word play at home?
7. Do parents play the game(s)?

Your "yes" answers indicate that your intentional/reflective use of word play is successful.

## 3. Intentionally Using Hands

1. Watch a colleague:
   - Note every use of the hand to communicate.
   - What was the teacher trying to communicate?
     - ➤ Did the way she or he used the hand strengthen the communication?
     - ➤ How did hand use strengthen or not strengthen the communication?
     - ➤ Suggest ways hand use might have strengthened the communication.
     - ➤ Make a record of whatever effective hand use you noticed.
2. Watch yourself:
   - Become conscious of how you use your hand(s) to communicate.
   - Make notes on how you use your hand(s). Consider what you do with:
     - ➤ Fingers
     - ➤ Wrists
     - ➤ Full arm
   - Note the effect(s) on children of your hand use.
3. Experiment:
   - Restrain hand use.
   - Note any effects not using your hand(s) has on your communication.
   - Exaggerate hand use.
   - Note effects of exaggerated hand use.
   - Communicate the same idea (1) with hand(s) and (2) without hand(s). Which is more effective? Why?

TECHNIQUE 4
EXAMINE YOUR BELIEFS HONESTLY: SEARCH FOR MINDLESS HABITS AND
REPLACE THEM WITH DETERMINED ACTIONS

Changing your beliefs is likely to be the most difficult challenge you face in becoming an intentional and reflective teacher. Recall the statement: "We don't know
who discovered water, but we know it wasn't the fish." Because beliefs are incul-
cated from birth, it is difficult to trace their origin, much less change them. We are
all, as another pundit said, "creatures of habit." This technique is about changing
habits.

### 1. Using This Book to Analyze Your Beliefs

1. Reflect on your reactions to the information in Chapter 4 and to various
   scenarios. Reread if you need to refresh your memory.
2. Begin with information (from Chapter 4) or a scenario (from any chapter)
   where you strongly *agreed* with statements, behaviors, or beliefs. Pick apart the
   details to pinpoint precisely what you agreed with.
3. Can you determine what your own beliefs are that cause you to agree? Start a
   list of those beliefs.
4. Now choose information (Chapter 4) or a scenario (any chapter) with which
   you strongly *disagreed*. Pick apart the details to pinpoint precisely what you
   disagreed with.
5. Can you determine what your own beliefs are that cause you to disagree?
   Add them to the list you are making of your beliefs. *Tip:* In your head, have
   a dialogue or argument with me or with the teacher in the scenario you
   chose.
6. Extend the analysis of your beliefs: On your list, separate information or
   scenarios you agree with from those you disagree with.
7. Once you have made your list, read your beliefs and put them into categories.
   For example, which beliefs are about:
   • Discipline?
   • Keeping a classroom orderly?
   • Children's crying?
   • Sharing?

Make as many categories as you see; there is no right or wrong list or number.
   *Note:* Keep adding to your lists as you become increasingly attuned to what
you do and do not believe.

### 2. Using Media to Analyze Your Beliefs

1. Choose two newspapers, one reputedly liberal, the other conservative. Begin
   with whichever bias you prefer.
2. Read the editorial pages in six different issues (that is, on six different days).
   *Note:* There is no time schedule—do this at your convenience.

3. Make a record of date, topic, and writer for each article or political cartoon that you read. Record the writer's bias. Record your reactions. Pinpoint what you believe caused your reaction. Consider:
   • What is the relation between your reactions and your beliefs?
4. Repeat step 3 several times, choosing other biases.
5. When you have finished 10 or 12 issues (five or six of each of the two papers), compile what you wrote about your own beliefs.
6. Compare your lists of beliefs—from your responses to this book and your responses to the newspapers.
7. Combine your beliefs into one list.
8. Use the list of your beliefs to analyze your classroom behavior.

*Note:* You do not have to confine the examination of beliefs to this book and newspapers. Anything to which you react strongly offers material with which you can examine your beliefs—a movie, a TV show, others' comments. Whenever you find something that reveals a belief you hold, add the belief to your list.

9. When you have completed a list of a dozen or so beliefs and disbeliefs, ask yourself:
   • Are my beliefs consistent?
   • Do my beliefs influence my behavior as a teacher?
   • What is the evidence for how my beliefs influence my teaching?
   • Would it improve my teaching if I changed any of my beliefs?
   • Which belief(s) would you change? (Be specific.)
   • How might the changes impact your teaching?
   • How might your children benefit if you changed any of your beliefs?

*Note:* Be very specific about which belief(s) you would change and how it might benefit your children.

## TECHNIQUE 5
## CHOOSE WORDS STRATEGICALLY: UNDERSTAND THE IMPACT OF WORDS ON CHILDREN

Words can calm anger or incite riot; words can fuel dictatorships or instigate revolution. Teachers' choice of words influences whether children pay attention and how they react. Specific words and/or how they are said can evoke positive responses or can shut down all desire to cooperate. In the latter instance, word choice or use triggers an emotional response that blocks cognition.

### 1. Choosing Words That Evoke Children's Cooperation

1. For 1 week write down every instance in which you ask or tell a child to do something.
2. For each instance write how the child responded.
3. Record whether the child fulfilled your request.

4. Describe *how* the child fulfilled your request:
    - In response to your request?
    - With your help?
    - With the help of another child?
    - By you, the teacher, without the child?
    - By another person in the class, adult or child(ren)?
    - Other? (Describe.)
    - Was the request not fulfilled at all?

    Expand the list of responses from further observations.
5. Review both the words you use to make your requests and the children's responses.
6. Categorize responses by whether and how the request was fulfilled. Use your own categories or those listed in 4 above, including your additions to the list.
7. Analyze your categories: Is there a relation between the words you use to make requests and whether the requests are fulfilled?
8. If your analysis shows that children do not fulfill requests made with certain words, can you choose different words?
9. Begin this exercise again and make the request with different words. Record, reflect, categorize, and analyze to determine whether different words cause children to respond differently.

*Tip:* In beginning this exercise, you may find it easier to observe and analyze one single request (for example, Put your work away) until you master the process of analyzing the impact of word choices on children's behavior.

## 2. Listening Intentionally with Active, Focused Attention

1. For 1 week watch yourself while you listen.
2. Write down every time your mind wanders.
3. Note what you were doing.
4. Write the thoughts your mind wandered to.
5. Review what you wrote:
    - Are there patterns to when your mind wanders?
    - Are there patterns to what you think about?
6. If you find a pattern, can you change your listening behavior by:
    - Being aware that your attention wanders?
    - Reminding yourself to pay attention?
    - Consciously forcing your mind back to the matter at hand?
    - Refocusing your mind by one or more of these movements:
        ➤ Taking a deep breath?
        ➤ Arching your back and relaxing it?
        ➤ Extending and stretching your fingers, then relaxing them?
        ➤ Identifying a problem that grabs your attention and either solving it or silencing it when you are with children?

### 3. Considering the Mindfulness in Your Teaching

Children's minds are likely to wander more than adults' for many reasons—for example:

- They do not know the meaning of words they hear.
- Concepts or context are unfamiliar.
- The topic is boring.
- They are required to be passive and listen rather than active and participating.
- Movement is not made part of listening.

To keep children's attention active and engaged:

1. Review the exercises in Chapter 5, section on Techniques in Mindful Communication.
2. Try each mindful technique for 1 week under the same circumstances—morning meeting, or one-on-one work with an unfocused child, or work with a small group of children who are among the least attentive.
3. Note:
   - What are children's responses to each technique?
   - What techniques are effective?
   - What is your evidence that a technique is effective?
4. After trying all techniques, compare your notes:
   - Which technique(s) is (are) most effective?
5. Continue use of effective techniques.
6. Use Chapter 5 as a start to create techniques of your own.

*Note:* The goal is not to use techniques because they are in this book, but to use the book to stretch your mind so that you develop techniques that work for you to focus attention—yours and the children's—and to listen intentionally and reflectively.

## TECHNIQUE 6
## MANIPULATE MATERIALS PURPOSEFULLY: PROVIDE DIVERSE MATERIALS TO STIMULATE INCREASINGLY SKILLFUL EYE/HAND COORDINATION FROM BIRTH ON

Hand skills may be the most important, least appreciated skill that young children can develop. Hand skills are important because:

- They require coordination between two complex areas of the brain—the eyes and the hands—that underlie most other cognitive activity.
- They provide virtually unlimited opportunities to channel children's need to move into productive endeavors.

- Children are intrinsically motivated to use the kinds of tools and materials that develop hand skills.
- Children are motivated to produce things that are complex and/or aesthetic.

### 1. Using Materials as a Measure of Your Intention to Develop Hand Skills

1. Determine whether you are providing adequate tools. Do you have:
   - Scissors?
   - Hole punches?
   - Rulers and other measuring devices?
   - Staplers, rubber bands, clips, and other fasteners?
   - Wire cutters?
   - Clay cutters and shapers?
   - Markers for use with varied papers?
   - Diverse brushes for use with varied media?
   - And more?
2. Consider: Do you have "papers in many colors, thicknesses, finishes, and degrees of transparency, from cardstock and cellophane to rag, tinsel, and tissue" (Lewin-Benham, 2011, p. 194)?
3. Determine whether materials vary:
   - Tempera, watercolor, and other kinds of colors mixed by children?
   - Markers, pencils, and other writing implements in varied colors, thickness, and hardness?
   - Clay, wire, and the tools to shape them?
   - "Rope, string, raffia, streamers, and fabric strips to weave or use in other ways" (Lewin-Benham, 2011, p. 195)?
4. Consider: Are you providing enough natural and man-made materials to attract children with different interests?
5. Assess the likelihood of children's learning to use tools and materials competently. Are materials:
   - Organized to be accessible—visible and within reach?
   - Displayed attractively?
   - Introduced to children one-on-one or in small groups to ensure that children acquire the ability to handle materials independently and with increasing skill?

*Note:* If you answer "no" to any of questions 1–5, consider the items in the question as new ways to stimulate hand/eye connections.

6. Is what children produce:
   - Formulaic, with all children's work looking similar?
   - Imitative, with all work made from a limited number of materials?
   - Unimaginative and lacking in originality and complexity?
   - Simplistic, easy to put together, and/or offering children little or no challenge?

*Note:* Answering "yes" to any items in question 6 indicates that you need to stimulate more complex hand/eye connections.

## 2. Using Children's Productions as Indications of Hand Skills

Are children:

- Drawing competently?
- Making complex constructions?
- Using natural materials creatively?
- Solving problems by making things in two and three dimensions?

## 3. Using Children's Attitude as Indications of Hand Skills

Are children:

- Proud of their work?
- Appreciative of their friends' efforts?
- Collaborative with one another's endeavors?
- Asking to use materials and tools?
- Cooperative about learning to use new materials and tools?

## 4. Providing Diverse Materials for Children of All Ages

Intention in providing material is evidenced by the materials provided for children from infancy on. Consider:

- Do infants have materials that stimulate them:
  - ➤ Visually?
  - ➤ Tactilely?
  - ➤ In auditory ways?
  - ➤ In gustatory ways?
  - ➤ In olfactory ways?
  - ➤ To move their head, eyes, hands, arms, legs, fingers, and toes?
- Do toddlers have materials that encourage them to move:
  - ➤ In increasingly challenging ways?
  - ➤ With coordination of all parts of the body?
  - ➤ By using their hands to manipulate different materials:
    - – In time to music?
    - – Rhythmically without music?
- Do older children have:
  - ➤ Increasing access to more and more materials?
  - ➤ Opportunities to use the materials listed in items 1–4 under "Materials as Indicators of Intention in Developing Hand Skills" above?
  - ➤ Experiences that require them to use their hands on playgrounds, in parks, and in other outdoor environments?

*Note:* If you answer "no" to many questions in this and the two previous sections, reread Chapter 6.

## TECHNIQUE 7
## ENGAGE CHILDREN'S COGNITION: USE COGNITION TO MEDIATE DISRUPTIVE OR DISTRACTING EMOTIONS

Controlling their emotions may be children's greatest challenge. Teachers' role in supporting socio-emotional growth is vitally important. The first step is for teachers to watch their own responses to determine whether they are cognitive or emotional. Emotional responses can intensify children's emotions because of the human tendency to imitate.

### 1. Subjectivity and Objectivity: Recognizing Your Own Reactions

1. When approaching a child in distress, assess your own feelings. Are you:
   • Disturbed when children cry?
   • Concerned that you might not be able to stop the tears?
   • Afraid one child's emotions will infect others?
   • Angry that Timmy is, once again, disturbing the calm in your class?
   • At wits' end because Maria never settles down?
   • Frustrated at the children's constant squabbles over sharing?
   • Annoyed at the mess the children make of your orderly room?

*Note:* These reactions are normal. But children read teachers' emotions, mimic them, and thereby escalate their own emotions.

2. Do you try one or more of these techniques for de-escalating your emotions before approaching the child:
   • Take a deep breath—or two or three?
   • Count to five—or ten?
   • Do a full body stretch and release?
   • Think of something funny?
   • Recall a similar incident when your intervention was successful?
   • Repeat to yourself: I can help (Timmy) quiet his emotions?
   • Determine to give (Timmy) a big bear hug before saying anything?
   • Know that if nothing works, you are bigger than (Timmy), can pick him up, and can carry him someplace where he will not be embarrassed by his friends seeing his discomfort?

*Tip:* Try these techniques to increase your confidence that you can handle the situation.

### 2. Recognizing Cognitive Opportunity

1. Before you intervene, do you size up the situation? Is the child crying because:

- She has wet her pants?
- He has gotten paint on his clothes?
- Another child has pushed/hit/shoved her or him?
- Another child has taken his or her toy/paintbrush/whatever?
- She or he is overtired or hungry?
- She or he is carrying a negative emotion from home?
- She or he is frustrated because of the inability to perform some act—remove the top of a bottle, turn on the water, open the door, whatever?
- She or he has a limited repertoire of responses to anger, frustration, and other negative feelings?

2. Do you calmly, firmly, unemotionally engage the child's cognition by saying, for example:
   - "I'll help you find clean pants. Do you know where your box of clothes is?" And, after the child says yes or nods, offer your hand, saying: "Let's go there"?

3. Do you explain: "This paint will wash out. Show me where your clean clothes are"?
   - Do you go with the child, asking: "Can you put your blouse/shirt on yourself?"
   - If the child says yes, do you give her or him the blouse/shirt?
   - Do you ask: "Do you want to come with me while I wash off the paint?"

4. Is your goal for children to return to an activity as soon as they are calm?

5. In altercations (Robert shoved Peter) do you say to Peter: "Tell me what happened"?
   - Do you listen unemotionally and ask, "Can you continue playing now?"
   - If Peter is still distraught, do you say: "*Show* me what you were (building, drawing, doing)"?
   - If Peter is still distraught, do you say: "*Tell* me what you were doing"?
   - If Peter continues to be distraught, do you ask: "Do you want to come with me or return to what you were doing?"
   - Do you keep the focus on Peter, thereby denying Robert the satisfaction of getting attention for his antisocial act?

6. If Robert is a child who often hurts others and if ignoring his behavior has not tempered it, as soon as Peter settles in, do you say to Robert: "Please come with me"?
   - Do you tell Robert: "Until you stop (hitting, pushing, whatever) I will keep you with me"?
   - Do you restrain Robert from contact with other children by keeping him at your side or on your lap?
   - If Robert is resistant, do you tell him: "I cannot let you go if you continue to hurt other children"?
   - Do you explain: "If you hurt children, I will isolate you from them"? (See the technique of the "table at the front of the room," Chapter 8)
   - When Robert calms down, do you ask him, "Are you ready to be with other children without hurting them?"

7. Sara has grabbed Alice's paintbrush and Alice is screaming. Do you calmly and unemotionally go to Alice and say, "Tell me what happened"?

- Do you repeat your statement until Alice manages, in some way, to respond?
- Do you then say, "Come!," take Alice to the jar with brushes, and have her choose another?
- Do you ask: "Would you like to continue painting?"
- Do you keep the focus on Alice and what she was doing, not on the incident?
- Is your goal to re-engage Alice cognitively, not to reinforce her crying?

*Note:* These are all cognitive interventions. The goal is to restore children's cognitive focus, to take their minds off the emotional altercation, and to avoid dealing with negative emotions while in the heat of the moment.

8. Do you use conversations in full-class meeting to ask, "What do you do when someone takes something you are using (or hits you or other negative behavior)?" Do you:
   - Listen to all children?
   - Over time, engage the children in developing ways to respond in such situations? (See how Carol in Chapter 8 involved the children in creating rules to care for things.)
   - Elicit children's knowledge about social and antisocial behavior?
   - Respect children's insights and suggestions by using those likely to foster cognitive responses?
   - Report to the class, in later conversations, about children's insights/suggestions that calmed other children?

## TECHNIQUE 8
## STRUCTURE MOTIVATING LESSONS: CAUSE CHILDREN TO STRENGTHEN BOTH COGNITIVE AND SOCIO-EMOTIONAL SKILLS

Giving lessons to individuals or small groups of children requires long blocks of time that are uninterrupted by clocks, specialist teachers, or schedules. Technique 7 was about eliciting cognitive responses and attending to negative socio-emotional behavior. Technique 8 is about management—how to organize an open-flow day so that you have time to focus on small groups and individuals, and time to hold lengthy conversations with the entire class in which all children can speak and be heard.

### 1. Orchestrating Conversations with Intention and Reflection

1. Do you have regular meeting times at the beginning and/or end of the morning?
2. Do you have conversations in which you pose a question and orchestrate a discussion?
3. Have you taught conversation skills:
   - Raising a hand for a turn to speak?
   - Listening without interrupting?

- Sticking to a topic?
- Speaking succinctly to a point that has been made?
- Addressing the last speaker or other children, not only the teacher?
- Synthesizing conclusions?
- Not misbehaving?

4. Are conversations of interest to children because:
   - They are about something you have heard children themselves say?
   - You quote children's prior remarks to refocus them on what interested them?
   - Children, not adults, do most of the talking?
   - You use techniques that keep children on topic?
   - You use conversation to address problems in socio-emotional areas by:
     - ➤ Seeking children's opinions and solutions?
     - ➤ Encouraging children's debate?
     - ➤ Not rushing to conclusions?
     - ➤ Continuing the conversation for however long (a week, a month) it takes to reach conclusions?
     - ➤ Not labeling children's contributions as "good" or "bad" ideas but encouraging children to make their own judgments?

   *Tip:* Good questions are: What do you think of that? Would that work? Why do you think (quote what the child has said)?

5. Do you implement rules children have generated for holding conversations?
6. Do you implement procedures children have generated to solve nonbehavioral classroom problems (such as maintaining materials in orderly condition, bathroom procedures, lunch procedures)?
7. Have you precluded misbehavior by:
   - Not recognizing children who speak out of turn?
   - Not recognizing children who misbehave?
   - Agreeing in advance how other adults will handle misbehavior so that your focus remains on listening and orchestrating the conversation?

## 2. Organizing Time and Space with Intention and Reflection

1. Is there enough in the classroom to sustain children's interest for long periods?
2. Is the classroom organized so that children can function independently in choosing materials and returning them when finished?
3. Have you eliminated interruptions for toileting and snacks by establishing procedures that enable children to perform these tasks independently?
4. Are you and your co-teacher or assistant conversant and in agreement on the order of the day and thus supportive of each other's activities?
5. Do you think outside the box in choosing activities for children who are the most unfocused or antisocial or whose behavior breaks down the order in a classroom?
   - Recall Chapter 7: Nan's emotional reaction when Janice took her pencil. The point: Cognition can trump emotion.

- Recall Chapter 7: Matthew and the mazes. The point: Some children need materials that are more challenging than those in the classroom.
- Recall Chapter 7: Baltie and Mr. Potts. The points:
  - ➤ Superheroes can be part of significant activity.
  - ➤ Ideas that originate with children can powerfully motivate other children.
- In open flow, do your activities:
  - ➤ Spread to many small groups?
  - ➤ Diverge to involve many different skills?
- Do you use cognitive techniques to focus children's attention if they:
  - ➤ Ignore some materials?
  - ➤ Leave a mess at snack time?
  - ➤ Fail to put materials away when finished?

*Note:* Recall Lillian, Chapter 8, whose day is organized so that she has enough time for repeated work with small groups of children and for continuing as long as needed (over several days or longer) to resolve problems.

## CONCLUSION

Teaching is not for the fainthearted, and teaching young children has challenges that teachers in ECE classrooms know better than any other group in our culture—better than teachers of other age groups, better than teacher trainers, better than parents, better than authors. Your work requires:

- Energy, humor, imagination, patience, insight, and empathy
- Being open to change and being flexible
- Willingness to work without a script
- Being responsive and present in every moment
- Courage to use adult authority

There is no coffee break when you work with children from 0 to 6. You are fortunate if there is a bathroom break.

As evidence seeps slowly into the culture's consciousness about brain development in the early years, pressure on ECE teachers increases. Specifically, we face new demands to make children "perform" and are given new requirements to provide evidence that children are performing to a "standard." Tomorrow there may be a call to have 12-month-olds "ready" for the 13-month-old group. Yet, ECE teachers know that the path of early development is more like the paths of hens in a barnyard than the lines of draftsmen's rulers, that the timetable for when any child will reach some particular milestone is unpredictable. There are no schedules for children's learning to control behavior and to tame emotions. But these facts do not comfort parents, who are worried about their own competence, or calm administrators, who are nervous about how their schools will be judged. So ECE teachers are alone—unless they have one another with whom to discuss concerns, share ideas, and try new approaches.

I hope you can use this book as your own private diary, as a nonjudgmental, uncritical "other" with which to share your innermost thoughts about your teaching. I have crammed many "mights" and "coulds" into its pages. If you find one—just a single idea—that helps your insight about children, that provides an "aha" moment about your teaching, that in some way affirms what you are doing, or that helps you change something you want to change, I will consider the book a success.

Please know, as you reflect on this book, that you have my undying appreciation for your work with young children. As a culture, we should be on bended knees in thanks to ECE teachers. We should feel awe for your staying power in the face of pressures that seemingly have no end, and we should offer praise for your intrepid courage. In this spirit I have dedicated this book to you. And to Sheppy, my grandson, who, at this writing, is 14 years old and who, thanks to some wonderful teachers in school and out, delights in his own uniqueness. And to Moo, my beloved mother, intentional, reflective, and full of humor. May Shep continue to evolve, and may you continue to persevere with the knowledge that the work you are doing is our culture's most important—wiring the brains, molding the character, and inspiring the minds of the next generation.

# References

Allman, J. (2007). Moral intuition: Its neural substrates and normative significance. *Journal of Physiology, 101*, 179–202.

Barrie, J. M. (1991). *The adventures of Peter Pan*. New York, NY: Viking. (Original work published 1911)

Bell, M. K. (2014). "We spoke the right things." *Teaching Tolerance, 48*, 56–58.

Brown, R. (1973). *A first language: The early stages*. Cambridge, MA: Harvard University Press.

Browning, R. (1888). *The Pied Piper of Hamelin*. London, UK: Frederick Warne.

Burr, C. (2002). *The emperor of scent: A story of perfume, obsession, and the last mystery of the senses*. New York, NY: Random House.

Ciardi, J. (1963). *John J. Plenty and Fiddler Dan*. New York, NY: Lippincott.

Collodi, C. (1995). *The adventures of Pinocchio*. Mineola, NY: Dover. (Original work published 1883)

Csikszentmihalyi, M. (1990). *Flow: The psychology of optimal experience*. New York, NY: HarperCollins.

Cullum, A. (1971). *The geranium on the window sill just died but teacher you went right on talking*. New York, NY: Harlin Quist.

Cullum, A. (1976). *You think just because you're big you're right*. New York, NY: Harlin Quist.

Damasio, A. (1994). *Descartes' error*. New York, NY: HarperCollins

Darwin, C. (1838). *Expression M*. Darwin Online. Available at darwin-online.org.uk/content/frameset?viewtype=side&itemID=CUL-DAR125.-&pageseq=1

Dee, T., & Jacob, B. (2009). The impact of No Child Left Behind on student achievement. National Bureau of Economic Research. Available at www.nber.org/papers/w15531http://www.nber.org/papers/w15531

Dweck, C. S. (2008). Can personality be changed? The role of beliefs in personality and change. *Current Directions in Psychological Science, 17*(6), 391–394.

Eliot, T. S. (1982). The song of the Jellicles. *Old Possum's book of practical cats*. New York, NY: Harcourt Brace. (Original work published 1939)

Erichsen, J. T., & Woodhouse, M. J. (2014). Human and animal vision. Available at www.springerreference.com/docs/html/chapterdbid/318221.html

Feuerstein, R., Falik, L., Feuerstein, R. S., & Rand, Y. (2006). *The Feuerstein instrumental enrichment program: Creating and enhancing cognitive modifiability*. Jerusalem, Israel: ICELP Publications.

Feuerstein, R., & Lewin-Benham, A. (2012). *What learning looks like: Mediated learning in theory and practice, K–6*. New York, NY: Teachers College Press.

Feuerstein, R. S., Feuerstein, R., & Falik, L. (2004). *User's guide to the theory and practice of the Feuerstein instrumental enrichment program—BASIC*. Jerusalem, Israel: ICELP Publications.

Filippini, T. (1992). Lecture. International Summer Symposium, Reggio Emilia, Italy.

Fleming, I. (1964). *Chitty Chitty Bang Bang: The magical car*. London, UK: Macmillan.

Fontanili, M. (2007). *Play +: Arredi per l'infanzia*. Reggio Emilia, Italy: Scuole e Nidi d'Infanzia Istituzione del Comune di Reggio Emilia.

Gardner, H. (1983). *Frames of mind: The theory of multiple intelligences*. New York, NY: Basic Books.

Gardner, H. (1991). *The unschooled mind: How children think and how schools should teach*. New York, NY: Basic Books.

Gardner, H. (1993). *Multiple intelligences: The theory in practice, a reader*. New York, NY: Basic Books.

Gardner, H. (1999). *The disciplined mind: What all students should understand*. New York, NY: Simon & Schuster.

Gardner, H. (2004). *Changing minds: The art and science of changing our own and other people's minds*. Boston, MA: Harvard Business School Press.

Gardner, H. (2014). The nine types of intelligence. In *Overview of the multiple intelligences theory*. Association for Supervision and Curriculum Development and Thomas Armstrong.com. Available at skyview.vansd.org/lschmidt/Projects/The%20Nine%20Types%20of%20 Intelligence.htm

Gelman, R., & Au, T. (1996). Perceptual and cognitive development. In E. Carterette & M. Friedman (Eds.), *Handbook of perception and cognition* (2nd ed., Vol. XIII, pp. 3–34). San Diego, CA: Academic Press.

Goleman, D. (2005). *Emotional intelligence: Why it can matter more than IQ*. New York, NY: Bantam Books.

Greenspan, S., with Salmon, J. (1995). *The challenging child: Understanding, raising, and enjoying the five "difficult" types of children*. New York, NY: Addison-Wesley.

Greenspan, S. I., & Shanker, S. G. (2004). *The first idea: How language and intelligence evolved from our primate ancestors to modern humans*. Cambridge, MA: Da Capo Press.

Groff, P. G. (1977). The new anti-phonics is same old look-say. *The Elementary School Journal, 77*(4), 323–332. Available at www.jstor.org/stable/1001094

Gunderson, E. A., Gripshover, C. R., Dweck, C. S., Goldin-Meadow, S., & Levin, S. C. (2013). Parent praise to 1- to 3-year-olds predicts children's motivational frameworks 5 years later. *Child Development, 84*, 1526–1541.

Hawkins, D. (1974). *The informed vision: Essays on learning and human nature*. New York, NY: Agathon Press.

Huttenlocher, J., Haight, W., Bryk, A., Seltzer, M., & Lyons, T. (1991). Early vocabulary growth: Relation to language input and gender. *Developmental Psychology, 27*(2), 236–248.

Kagan, J. (1986). *The power and limitations of parents*. Austin, TX: University of Texas Hogg Foundation for Mental Health.

Kagan, J. (1998). *Galen's prophecy: Temperament in human nature*. Boulder, CO: Westview Press.

Kahneman, D. (2011). *Thinking, fast and slow*. New York, NY: Farrar, Straus & Giroux.

Keats, J. (1884). Sleep and poetry. Available at www.bartleby.com/cgi-bin/texis/webinator/ sitesearch?FILTER=colKeats-Jo&query=They+shall+be+accounted&x=10&y=11

Keltner, D., & Ekman, P. (2003). Introduction: Expression of emotion. In R. J. Davidson, K. R. Scherer, & H. H. Goldsmith (Eds.), *Handbook of affective sciences* (pp. 411–414). New York, NY: Oxford University Press.

Lacey, S., Stilla, R., & Sathian, K. (2012). Metaphorically feeling: Comprehending textural metaphors activates somatosensory cortex. Available at www.ncbi.nlm.nih.gov/pmc/ articles/PMC3318916/

Lewin-Benham, A. (2010). *Infants and toddlers at work: Using Reggio-inspired materials to support brain development*. New York, NY: Teachers College Press.

Lewin-Benham, A. (2011). *Twelve best practices for early childhood education: Integrating Reggio and other inspired approaches.* New York, NY: Teachers College Press.

Longfellow, H. W. (2003). *The song of Hiawatha, Introduction* (M. Early, Illustrator). Brooklyn, NY: Handprint Books. (Original work published 1855)

McNeil, M. (2014, February 4). Sluggish pace for Race to Top spending. *Education Week.* Available at www.edweek.org/ew/articles/2012/04/17/28rtt_ep.h31.html

Milne, A. A. (1950). Disobedience. In *When We Were Very Young.* New York, NY: Dutton. (Original work published 1924)

Mischel, W., & Shoda, Y. (1995). A cognitive–affective system theory of personality: Reconceptualizing situations, dispositions, dynamics, and invariance in personality structure. *Psychological Review, 102*(2), 246–268. Available at psych.colorado.edu/~carey/Courses/PSYC5112/Readings/psnSituation_Mischel02.pdf

Mithen, S. (2006). *The singing Neanderthals: The origins of music, language, mind, and body.* Cambridge, MA: Harvard University Press.

Mix, K. S., Huttenlocher, J., & Levine, S. C. (2002). *Quantitative development in infancy and early childhood.* New York, NY: Oxford University Press.

Montessori, M. (1948). *The discovery of the child* (M. A. Johnstone, Trans.). Madras, India: Kalakshetra Publications.

Montessori, M. (1963). *The absorbent mind.* Madras, India: The Theosophical Publishing House.

Parker, A. (2003). *In the blink of an eye: How vision sparked the big bang of evolution.* New York, NY: Perseus.

Petitto, L. (1992). Modularity and constraints in early lexical acquisition: Evidence from children's early language and gesture. In M. R. Gunnar & M. Maratsos (Eds.), *Modularity and constraints in language and cognition: The Minnesota Symposium on Child Psychology* (Vol. 25, pp. 25–58). Hillsdale, NJ: Erlbaum.

Pinch, A., & Armstrong, M. (Eds.). (1982). *Tolstoy on education: Tolstoy's educational writings 1861–1862* (A. Pinch, Trans.). London, UK: Athlone Press.

Pinker, S. (1994). *The language instinct: How the mind creates language.* New York, NY: HarperCollins.

Ratey, J. (2002). *A user's guide to the brain: Perception, attention, and the four theaters of the brain.* New York, NY: Vintage Books.

Reggio Children. (2004). *Children, arts, artists: The expressive languages of children, the artistic language of Alberto Burri.* Reggio Emilia, Italy: Author.

Rock-Payne, K. (2013). Sherman Washburn: Renaissance man. Available at www.academia.edu/5415978/Sherwood_Washburn_Renaissance_Man

Sacks, O. (1989). *Seeing voices: A journey into the world of the deaf.* New York, NY: Vintage Books.

Sacks, O. (2008). *Musicophilia: Tales of music and the brain.* New York, NY: Vintage Books.

Sacks, P. (1999). *Standardized minds: The high price of America's testing culture and what we can do to change it.* Cambridge, MA: Perseus.

Sandburg, C. (1916). "Fog." *Chicago poems.* New York, NY: Henry Holt.

Schnurer, E. (2013, August). Just how wrong is conventional wisdom about government fraud? *The Atlantic.* Available at www.theatlantic.com/politics/archive/2013/08/just-how-wrong-is-conventional-wisdom-about-government-fraud/278690/

Schwarz, A. (2013a). ADHD experts re-evaluate study's zeal for drugs. *The New York Times.* Available at www.nytimes.com/2013/12/30/health/adhd-experts-re-evaluate-studys-zeal-for-drugs.html?pagewanted=1

Schwarz, A. (2013b). The selling of attention deficit disorder. *The New York Times.* Available at www.nytimes.com/2013/12/15/health/the-selling-of-attention-deficit-disorder.html?_r=0

Spelke, E. (2002). Principles of object perception. *Cognitive Science, 14*, 29–56.

Spelke, E., & Kinzler, K. (2007). Core knowledge. *Developmental Science, 10*(1), 89–96.

Stevenson, R. L. (1944). The land of counterpane. *A child's garden of verses.* New York, NY: Heritage Press. (Original work published 1885)

Storkel, H. L., & Maekawa, J. (2005). A comparison of homonym and novel word learning: The role of phonotactic probability and word frequency. Available at www.ncbi.nlm.nih.gov/pmc/articles/PMC1389618/

Stott, R. (2012). *Darwin's ghosts: The secret history of evolution.* New York, NY: Spiegel & Grau.

Sturloni, S., & Vecchi, V. (2000). *Everything has a shadow, except ants.* Reggio Emilia, Italy: Reggio Children.

Tanner, L. N. (1997). *Dewey's laboratory school: Lessons for today.* New York, NY: Teachers College Press.

Tomasello, M., Carpenter, M., & Liszkowski, U. (2007). A new look at infant pointing. *Child Development, 78*(3), 705–722. Available at wwwstaff.eva.mpg.de/~tomas/pdf/Liszkowski_ChildDevlp_07.pdf

Twain, M. (1936). *The adventures of Tom Sawyer.* New York, NY: Heritage Press. (Original work published 1876)

Verne, J. (2008). *20,000 leagues under the sea.* New York, NY: Baronet Books. (Original work published 1869)

Vygotsky, L. (1986). *Thought and language* (A. Kozulin, Trans. & Ed.). Cambridge, MA: The MIT Press. (Original work published 1934).

Wells, H. G. (1904). The country of the blind. Available at www.online-literature.com/wellshg/3/

Wilson, F. R, (1998). *The hand: How its use shapes the brain, language, and human culture.* New York, NY: Pantheon.

Wilson, K. G., with Dufrene, T. (2008). *Mindfulness for two: An acceptance and commitment therapy approach to mindfulness in psychotherapy.* Oakland, CA: New Harbinger.

# Index

# About the Author

When not writing, lecturing, or professionally engaged, *Ann Lewin-Benham* gardens, travels with her husband, Robert, or reads. For most of her life Ann founded and ran schools. In the mid-1970s she founded and for 20 years ran a large hands-on children's museum in Washington, DC, an early one in a genre that today is found worldwide. Educators know Ann best for founding and directing the Model Early Learning Center (MELC), also in Washington, DC. There she forged a close relationship with the Italian pioneers of the Reggio schools, ultimately adapted Reggio practices at the MELC, and continues to study and write about the Reggio philosophy and practices.

After 18 years in Memphis, in 2013 Ann and Robert moved to Southern California. A life-long East Coaster, Ann now lives on the "other" ocean. The Schnauzer Lucy likes the new life and has not yet crawled under the fence to the canyon where coyotes and other dangers lurk. Severe drought conditions led to Ann's new pastime—xeriscaping—as she replaced grass and learned a whole new plant vocabulary.

## About the Illustrator

*M. Shepard Lewin (Sheppy)*, Ann's grandson, just turned 14. His favorite pastimes are reading, photography, and making things, an interest shared with his father. Most recently he and a friend have been working on an ATV (All-Terrain Vehicle) with first-person view capabilities. In good weather he likes to kayak, sail, and bike. His interest in drawing is inherited from his architect grandfather Alan Meyers and his artist mother Linn Meyers. Shep is an 8th-grader at Georgetown Day School in Washington, DC.